Ministering to Today's Adults

Understanding Teaching

Beloved Physician

Leadership for Church Education

The Family First

So You Want to Be a Leader!

Between Christian Parent and Child

Competent to Lead

24 Ways to Improve Your Teaching

The Gospel and the Gay

*You Can Be an Effective Sunday
    School Superintendent*

Lessons in Leadership from the Bible

*Building Leaders for Church
    Education*

Thus Spake Qoheleth

*Christian Education—Its History and
    Philosophy* (coauthor)

Unwrap Your Spiritual Gifts

*Toward a Harmony of Faith and
    Learning*

Building a Christian Family
    (coauthor)

Personal Growth Bible Studies:
    Matthew 1–14
    Matthew 15–28
    Acts
    1 and 2 Timothy and Titus
    Romans 1–12
    Romans 13–Galatians

Church Education Handbook

*The Christian Educator's Handbook
    on Teaching* (coeditor)

Feeding and Leading

Key Words for the Christian Life

*The Christian Educator's Handbook
    on Adult Education* (coeditor)

*Communication and Conflict
    Management in Churches and
    Christian Organizations* (coauthor)

Volunteers for Today's Church
    (coauthor)

Accent of Truth Bible Study Series:
    Defending Christian Liberty
    Growing in Grace and Godliness
    Knowing the Heart of God
    Learning to Be the Church
    Living in the Light of Promise
    Loving the World through Jesus
    Rejoicing in Faith and Freedom
    Sharpening Our Eyes of Faith

*The Christian Educator's Handbook
    on Spiritual Formation* (coeditor)

Your Family (coauthor)

Called to Teach

*Christian Team Leadership in
    Ministry*

*The Christian Educator's Handbook
    on Family Life Education* (coeditor)

SWINDOLL
LEADERSHIP
LIBRARY

Ministering to Today's Adults

KENN GANGEL

CHARLES R. SWINDOLL, GENERAL EDITOR
ROY B. ZUCK, MANAGING EDITOR

WORD PUBLISHING
NASHVILLE
A Thomas Nelson Company

MINISTERING TO TODAY'S ADULTS
Swindoll Leadership Library

Published in association with Dallas Theological Seminary (DTS):

General Editor: Charles Swindoll
Managing Editor: Roy B. Zuck

The theological opinions expressed by the author are not necessarily the
official position of Dallas Theological Seminary.

Library of Congress Cataloging-in-Publication Data

Gangel, Kenneth O.
Ministering to today's adults / by Kenneth O. Gangel.
p.   cm.—(Swindoll leadership library)
Includes bibliographical references.

ISBN 0-8499-1361-6

1. Church work.   I. Title.   II. Series.

BV4400.G37   1999   98-39063
253–dc21   CIP

Printed in the United States of America
99 00 01 02 03 04 05 06 BVG 9 8 7 6 5 4 3 2 1

To the memory of my dear friend, Dr. David L. Edwards, whom Jesus called home while I was preparing this manuscript. David was a premier adult educator, my trusted and valued associate dean at Dallas Theological Seminary, and a close friend for almost a quarter of a century.

Contents

❧❧❧

LIST OF DIAGRAMS

LIST OF TABLES

Foreword

Augustine said, "He is not an effective teacher who is not first a listener within." These words are a fitting description of the life and ministry of Dr. Kenneth Gangel. For decades my good friend and colleague, Dr. Gangel, has been an effective teacher, due in large measure to his deep commitment to listening from within.

First, he has listened to the voice of culture. Refusing to sit and do research with his head in the sand, Gangel has provided the church with volumes of material on Christian education that remain freshly in touch with modern society. Textbooks full of scholarly theory do little good if they fail to answer questions real people are asking. Gangel's work is practical.

Second, Gangel has listened to himself. What you have in your hands is not a theoretical mixed bag of ideas and methods quickly distilled into a catchall book on adult education. I am so grateful to Gangel for his willingness to resist the temptation to please everyone, and I applaud his determination to write from his own heartfelt convictions and personal experience. As a result, he writes with an irenic authority that is calm and reassuring to anyone needing workable guidelines for a philosophy of ministry among adults. Gangel's work, therefore, is authentic.

Third, Gangel has listened to his God. Starting with the Scriptures as his guide, Kenn prepares us for a journey of adult education that draws us into an understanding of how God speaks, teaches, molds, and leads His children. You don't read too far before you realize that this powerful and highly esteemed scholar-educator is also a pastor-shepherd. He never forgets that he is writing to us about *Christian* education. And the unique contribution Kenn's years of serving the local church brings to this series is impossible to measure. You inevitably come away sharing his conviction that the only true impact you can have is when you are surrendered to the power of the Holy Spirit. Gangel's work then is spiritual.

Ministering to Today's Adults is all these things—practical, authentic, and spiritual—and these are the reasons I commend this book to you. Read. Reflect. Respond. And most of all, listen and learn from one who models what he writes.

—CHARLES R. SWINDOLL
General Editor

Preface

❧ ❧

*F*or *almost forty years* I have taught a course in adult ministries at both the graduate and undergraduate levels. For this book I transformed my class notes into chapters in order to convey the information to the wider evangelical fellowship.

Over the past decade or so, the number of adults in our society has increased substantially. Blessed peace and better health have given us millions of older people, who earlier in this century could not have expected to live much over fifty. At the same time, the baby-boom population has entered middle adulthood with very different ideas about family, church, and life.

I have attempted in this book to help readers understand adults in general as well as grasping their needs in various age- and experience-related categories. The book unfolds in four parts beginning with Foundations for Adult Ministries. Part 2 describes and explains ministry to adults in various age brackets, from college students to seniors. Part 3 centers on family-life education, the backbone of any significant adult ministries program. Five of the chapters in this section are adapted from *Your Family,* a book I coauthored with my wife, Betty, some years ago. Part 4 identifies how to design a program of adult ministries that can really work in the twenty-first century.

After Jim Wilhoit and I pulled together twenty-four authors for *The Christian Educator's Handbook on Adult Education* in 1993, I never expected to undertake another book on the subject. However, this one is different. That work offered a scholarly approach by evangelical experts, providing an overview of virtually every aspect of adult education. In this book, however, I have written for lay leaders, churches, and Christian organizations, and I have made a deliberate attempt to avoid a scholarly tone. Nevertheless, readers of this book may want to consult the *Handbook* for a more detailed treatment of important subjects.

Several acknowledgments are essential. My wife, Betty, read each chapter and offered helpful comments. She also coauthored five of the chapters, as I noted earlier. My secretary, Kathy Howard, has typed and retyped the text with patience and skill. Without these two dedicated women, the book would have been impossible. My appreciation, too, to Dr. Roy B. Zuck, managing editor of the series, for his many helpful comments and corrections.

PART 1

Foundations for Adult Ministries

1

❦

Adults Are Different!

Like many newlyweds, Debbie and Jim attended church only sporadically. In earlier years they had rarely missed a Sunday, spending their childhoods in Sunday school and their teen years in various youth activities—which is where they met. Most people who knew them understood they were believers, and their concerned parents assumed their lethargic attitude toward church could be blamed on newly found independence. Not a bad diagnosis.

After marrying in their early twenties, Jim and Debbie moved about 150 miles away, where they both took jobs in a city of approximately 50,000. Together they worked nearly one hundred hours a week, ate out most of the time, and scrambled to fit in trips to the mall, occasional golf, and twice-weekly workouts at the health club. By Saturday evenings they were pretty well worn out, and though they made the effort once in a while, heading for church on Sunday mornings did not seem appealing.

Their theology had not changed, nor did they inwardly abandon the idea that God should be directing their lives and that they should respond to Him in public worship as well as private prayer. But the preaching did not seem relevant, and they had yet to visit their first adult Sunday-school class. They did not know it, but they had moved into a situation which few evangelical churches really understand, that is, how adults learn differently.

A LEARNING MODEL

As you read through this book, you will find several models of adult ministry, and we begin by emphasizing one key word of that ministry—need. If this were a secular book, we would move immediately from need to philosophy and up the scale to program. But the dominating factor in the approach in this book comes in the form of "theological foundations." We will come back to need and talk about how to assess it and the difference between prescribed needs and felt needs. But here we want to emphasize that *Christian education always builds on solid theological foundations.*

DIAGRAM 1—THEOLOGICAL FOUNDATIONS

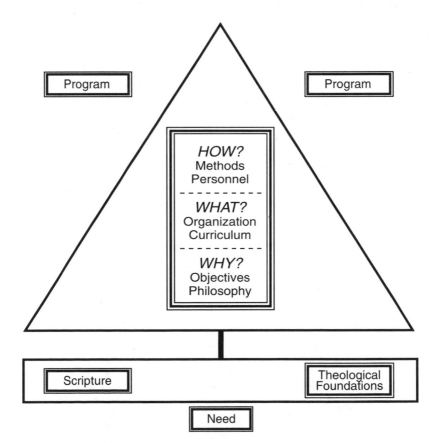

Some may ask, "Why not just start with theological foundations and come to need later?" The answer to this excellent question lies in the model's point of departure. Thirty years ago in adult education we began with Scripture and then considered its impact on need. But breaking through to modern adults requires an analysis of their needs and struggles, which we then pass through the Bible, finding biblical answers to contemporary problems. Many adults in our churches may or may not be interested in Bible study. But they all understand need. What our model (diagram 1, page 4) tells us is that we must look at needs through the gridwork of theological foundations, a concern we will revisit in chapter 3.

In this chapter the six components above the Scriptures present three kinds of questions: why, what, and how. Remember to read this model up rather than down.

Why Questions

Why questions lead us to a philosophy of adult education from which flow our objectives for adult learning. As stated, we first examine the needs of adults in light of biblical information about adults. At times we struggle with the time it takes to consider *why* questions. It seems so much easier to dash ahead to the *how*. People naturally want *how* answers to *how* questions: How can I get people to come to church? How can I get them to study their Bibles at home? How can I make my class more interesting?

Of course, these are valid questions, but not the ones we should ask initially. When we ask *how* questions before *why* questions, we distort our philosophy of ministry. The model instructs us to ask why we have adopted a certain philosophy of ministry with adults (instead of some other) and why we have written our objectives as they appear. Some churches may want to ask why they have not thought through a philosophy of ministry or why their objectives have no priorities. In any case these are still *why* questions.

What Questions

Both *what* and *why* questions precede the *how* questions. What structure do we need in order to carry out an effective program of adult ministry?

What published curriculum should we use that agrees with our theology and philosophy of ministry? What is the scope and sequence of curriculum? What involvement will the pastor or pastoral staff have in all this? What connection will our adult-ministry program have with the overall ministry of our church?

How Questions

In answering *how* questions we should identify people who will carry out this ministry and ways in which they will do it. When we put these six steps together, in order—philosophy, objectives, curriculum, organization, personnel, and methods—we can design a meaningful program. This model could be used in any phase of education, but it becomes strategic for adult education because of the need component in the foundation. Of course, children and young people have needs as well, but this book focuses on adult learners' needs.

My daughter, Julie, following in the tradition of her mother, teaches kindergarten. Her students do not understand learning needs; they never think about such matters. They wait impatiently for recess; they get excited about show-and-tell; they wonder why rest time seems so long or what's in their lunch bags; but they do not think about learning needs. In kindergarten that is exclusively the teacher's job.

We would hope, however, that as they grow and move on through high school, they will develop considerably more concern for need. For example, students take honors courses to establish their academic status so they can gain acceptance to a college of their choice. Or perhaps students take relatively easy courses to protect their eligibility for the football team. In either case we see a student-recognized need.

Adults, on the other hand, are normally need-focused, and when they are not, it becomes the task of ministry leaders to help them gain that focus. Adults may not think about needs or talk about them much, but self-recognized learning needs are crucial. From the top of our pyramid model, we should be able to look down at the six components and ask, "Does our program of adult ministry meet the needs of our adults?" And, of course, God's Word dominates the model.

BASIC GUIDELINES FOR ADULT LEARNING

One of the premier leaders in adult education in the twentieth century was Malcolm Knowles. In his extensive writings he suggests four propositions that serve as "guidelines" for reaching and teaching adults. These are not developed from Scripture because Knowles was a secular educator. But the extensive amount of research on adult education in the second half of the twentieth century tends to substantiate these general "guidelines." These are not axioms or laws; they are flexible signposts along the road of adult ministry.

Voluntary Involvement

Knowles's first guideline is that *adults must enter willingly into educational experiences.* In other words Debbie and Jim must do their own learning. Changing from dependence to independence may be one reason this young couple does not go to church; but it can be turned around as a motivating factor for their involvement. When daughter Julie goes to school on Monday morning, she does not ask her kindergartners, "What would you like to learn today? What do you think we should study this week?" Kindergarten children are not capable of answering those questions; but adults should be.

However, modern adult-learning settings have often either stifled learning independence or have never allowed it to develop. College and even seminary students struggle when asked to take responsibility for their own learning experiences. How much easier to inquire, "How long should the term paper be? What will be on the final exam? How many books must I include in the bibliography?"

Teachers who assign papers of a specific length, who require rigid memorization for examinations, and who specify everything in the learning process only increase the duration of student dependency. In this respect teaching is a lot like parenting in that students move from total dependence to relative independence, as the diagram on the following page shows.

DIAGRAM 2—INDEPENDENT LEARNING

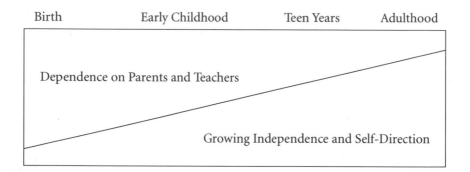

| Birth | Early Childhood | Teen Years | Adulthood |

Dependence on Parents and Teachers

Growing Independence and Self-Direction

We hope that college and seminary students develop learning independence, and many do. Yet their lives and lifestyles are often far removed from the real world. Many of the questions seminary students ask are not those asked by a UPS driver, a stockbroker, or an insurance agent. When we deal with adult education in today's churches we need to adopt the perspective of laypersons, not the more advanced theological outlook of Bible college and/or seminary graduates.

Developed Experiences

Knowles's second guideline, based on his research, states that *adults bring a large and varied amount of experience to the learning situation.* In some cases it is simply a matter of age—one tends to accumulate experiences the longer he or she lives. But adults also have a greater capacity to organize their experiences; that is, to see their lives in reasonably defined segments, little boxes of happenings. We could wish they were able to integrate biblically all those happenings into a holistic Christian lifestyle. And one of the major goals of adult ministry is to assist people in finding that integrative key.

When adults gather for learning, they bring many experiences with them. One woman may bring experience of forty years as a wife, thirty-five years as a mother, and ten years as a grandmother. A businessman comes with common business sense cultivated since he started his own hardware store seven years ago. A young woman teaches third-graders in a Christian school, and a middle-aged manager oversees the town's largest custodial services company.

The traditional system of education teaches us to block all this out and start with everyone on even ground on Sunday mornings. I have heard adult Sunday-school teachers say, "Let's forget everything that happened during the past week and concentrate on our Scripture passage for today." Who can do that? The fast-paced mental activity of adults in a cyberspace world bombards them with constant reminders of who they are and what they do.

And why would we want to dislocate Scripture from experience? The fact that all life is sacred, that there are no "secular" duties for the people of God, forms one of the foundation stones of Christian theism. We dare not be locked into the idea that the students sit quietly while the teacher dumps his informational data on the class.

Do eight-year-olds have experiences? Of course. They have climbed a few trees, played on the community soccer team, skateboarded all over the neighborhood, and probably learned to work a computer quite well. But compared to the life events of a twenty-eight-year-old, these things are inconsequential because the *amount, variety,* and *organization* of one's experiences create the climate for learning.

Reality Relatedness

Knowles's research on education also indicates that *adults approach learning with a different kind of readiness than children and youth.* We have already seen that adults have a different self-concept and a wide variety of experiences. Those differences now demonstrate themselves in readiness to learn. Adults bring a much greater self-direction and willingness to "option" on issues. Motivation for adult education therefore relates inseparably to what we might call "ownership": Adults must clearly understand that learning experiences relate to life; we don't just contrive them to keep congregational machinery functioning.

Another concept fits here, namely, developmental tasks. Developmentalism says that adults learn various aspects of a subject, behavior, or skill before they move on to the next one. Learning tennis, mastering a foreign language, or using a computer—virtually everything we teach adults in churches or elsewhere can be seen as a developmental task. Developmental design brings *scope* and *sequence* clearly into the adult curriculum. *Scope* asks how much material we should cover in a given learning experience (a Sunday morning, a weekend seminar, a thirteen-week quarter, a one-week conference), and *sequence* addresses the order in which we teach course content. Every college graduate can remember at least one course in which he or she wondered at the global size of the scope or the seemingly irrational pattern of sequence.

Life Application

Adults enter learning experiences in a problem-centered frame of mind and commonly show a concern for immediacy. They tend to see their lives as a series of challenges and problems that must be dealt with, not a body of content they must memorize for a test. Paul wrote that Titus ought to teach others to "live self-controlled, upright and godly lives in this present age" (Titus 2:12). Adults (particularly younger and middle adults) seem more present-oriented than any other age-group. The educational implication emphasizes immediate practicality and specific problem-solving in the educational task.

Immediacy causes adults to think (even when they don't say it), "I'm a very busy person. If you can't show me something I can use in my life now, I really don't have time for this class."

Why do we require algebra in the ninth grade? What adult uses algebraic formulae in daily life? The traditional argument for offering algebra lies in the scary thought that geometry is coming up next year. We tell students they have to know algebra in order to learn geometry. The early years of school are based on the idea that one learns something now because something else is coming later.

But not so with adults. They want to understand that everything has a life application; what comes out of life fits back into life.

ADULT-LEARNING PRINCIPLES

Six principles of adult learning stand beside the four guidelines we have just reviewed.

Adults Learn by Their Own Initiative

Have you ever been in a class whose content was so overwhelming and whose structure so shaky you were forced to do your own learning? I recall one such experience in which a brilliant professor taught with great warmth but none of us had the foggiest idea what he was talking about. We had to take the initiative, gathering in small groups outside of class to put some design on the information he provided. I would love to believe he drove us to that activity because of his familiarity with adult-education theory and a concern to have us take the responsibility for learning, but I doubt that was the case. Adult education requires a genuine unleashing of the internal desire to learn, and that desire provides the proper basis of motivation.

Adults want to know the importance of learning. In an information age, knowledge bombards us from everywhere. When adults sit in a Sunday school class (and even a church service) they question, "What is taught here that I can use? Is my time wisely spent in this educational experience?"

We become so accustomed to junk mail and television commercials that we find it easy to turn off genuinely valuable information sources. Sometimes we have to teach adults how to learn since formal schooling has conditioned them to a dependent posture.

Adults Learn through Understanding Ideas and Concepts

Adults prefer to interact with ideas and concepts rather than memorize lists of numbers or names. That's why you will find numerous diagrams and models throughout this book; they enhance learning. In our culture, lists seem to hold an unshakable place—but a pictorial design can stimulate conceptual thinking foundational to adult study.

Adults Learn through Creative Participation and Personalization

Involvement in the process promotes learning. Creative participation describes how the student relates to the class, the group, and the content. Personalization describes intake, how adults apply the information gained.

Adults Learn by Assimilating Positive Traits of a Role Model

On this point adults are not greatly different from children and young people. In the process of human maturation we learn from parents, teachers, pastors, youth directors, and friends. Mentoring has become a common procedure in some local churches; it helps developing leaders because it is both biblical and practical. We'll discuss this further later on.

Adults Learn by Practicing What They Learn

The writer of the epistle to the Hebrews wrote, "We have much to say about this, but it is hard to explain because you are slow to learn. In fact, though by this time you ought to be teachers, you need someone to teach you the elementary truths of God's word all over again. You need milk, not solid food! Anyone who lives on milk, being still an infant, is not acquainted with the teaching about righteousness. But solid food is for the mature, who by constant use have trained themselves to distinguish good from evil" (Heb. 5:11–14).

The initial readers of this Bible book, who should have been teachers, needed someone to teach them again even "the elementary truths of God's word" (5:12). How does one move from infancy to maturity, from "milk" (5:13) to "solid food" (5:14)? The writer did not hesitate to tell us that mature people "have trained themselves to distinguish good from evil" by constant use of solid food. Herein lies one of our major problems. People come to church, sit and listen politely, and head out the door to go back to the real world. We can only interrupt this unfortunate cycle if we take the focus off content assimilation and place it on life application.

How do we make that work? How do we implement the information of this chapter into a program of adult ministry? One way is to view all learning activities from the student's perspective and work within what may be called "a learning cycle." The following diagram shows that the approach is grounded in need and moves on to exploration. Effective exploration yields the fruit of discovery, which could push our adult learners to appropriate biblical truth and fit it into their lives. When they actually begin to do that, they have assumed responsibility for their own learning and for living out what God's Word says.

DIAGRAM 3—THE LEARNING CYCLE

Learning and living the Scriptures—what a noble goal. But we will rarely see it realized unless we understand and act on a basic truth: Adults learn differently!

2

⮮⮮⮯

From Preschool to Grad School

As the twentieth century turns into the twenty first, we know more about adult learning than ever before. The understanding of how adults process information and use it (often called "andragogy") has drawn enormous attention in the last three decades as the adult population keeps increasing. As noted in chapter 1, the key idea here is to avoid teaching adults the way we teach children. Young people represent a middle group which can exhibit some characteristics of both the others, but teachers of adults must be aware of the learning process best fitted to that age-group.

In the past we commonly called all teaching "pedagogy," from *paidos,* "child." Now many educators emphasize the difference between the two approaches. Knowles explains it this way: "The body of theory and practice on which we have self-directed learning has been labeled 'andragogy,' from the Greek word *aneµ* (meaning adult)—thus being defined as the art and science of helping adults (maturing human beings) learn."[1]

These two models do not represent bad/good or child/adult dichotomies, but rather a continuum of assumptions for particular learners in particular situations. If a pedagogical assumption seems realistic for a certain setting, then pedagogical strategies are appropriate. For example, if a learner enters a totally strange content area, he or she will be dependent on a teacher until enough content has been acquired to enable self-directed inquiry to begin.

TEACHING ADULTS —TEACHING CHILDREN

Think for a moment about Stan and Susan. They have been faithful in church since they first came to Christ at summer camp as children. Now over forty, with two teenagers and a six-year-old "caboose," they sit in their Sunday school class week after week as they have for years, only now with considerably less participation. Three problems present themselves to any class visitor familiar with adult learning. First, their teacher seems to know nothing about facilitating self-directed learning; second, Stan and Susan have never heard anything about the difference between the way they learned as children and the way they could learn now. Third, even if awareness of the problem surfaces, their teacher needs training to handle class time with the best approaches for adult education. Consider the following problems related to pedagogy.

Pedagogy Encourages Passivity

Pedagogy keeps the spectator approach alive in church. People may admire a teacher, listen carefully, even on occasion take notes. But most adult-learning experiences in churches are not designed for application to life.

Pedagogy Fails to Use the Rich Resource of Experience

Imagine a class with approximately thirty people between the ages of thirty-five and fifty. If we assume a median age of forty-two, that would bring 1,260 years of experience to class every week, walking in, sitting down, and shutting up, while one person with perhaps fifty or sixty years of experience talks to the people with 1,260 years of experience.

Pedagogy Places the Responsibility of Learning on the Teacher

We go astray in adult education because dependence can ultimately destroy the motivation and participation of adult learners. To be sure, many adults want the responsibility to remain on the teacher. And too many teachers of adults, for a variety of reasons, happily retain their roles of prominent influence and have no intention of shifting into a self-directed learning gear.

Some years ago I was scheduled to preach at a church in Illinois and showed up just before 9:30 A.M., the beginning time for Sunday school. I intended to chat with the pastor in his office and that's just what we were doing when (at about 9:35) the Sunday school superintendent rushed in and asked if I could teach a class whose teacher had not arrived. I agreed and my total preparation time consisted of the two or three minutes it took to leave the pastor's office and head upstairs to the classroom.

I always carry outlines in my Bible and I would usually just work through one of those. But on the way up the stairs I thought, "I wonder if this group is accustomed to participating in their class? I think I'll attempt to initiate involvement right from the start."

I began with two or three questions. "What have you folks been studying lately in your class? Is it in the Old Testament or the New? Can anyone tell me what last week's lesson covered?" The years have dimmed the memory a bit, but I think I asked seven questions before receiving a response. But their silence shouted an answer—they were saying, "This is a Sunday school: you talk, we listen. Haven't you ever been to Sunday school before?" That group of adults had been conditioned to passivity and had no intention of taking responsibility for their own learning in any way.

COMPARING HOW CHILDREN AND ADULTS LEARN

Let's suppose the church where Stan and Susan attend wanted to hold a seminar for its adult teachers to bring them up to speed on adult-learning procedures. What kinds of things would they need to know? The following grid (page 18), more easy to understand than apply, seems a good way to start. This chart, adapted from Knowles, describes different assumptions about learning and different process elements of learning for children and adults. Twelve concepts form a gridwork, a bridge that can take us across the gorge from teaching children to teaching adults. We will look at some of them separately, and some in groups.[2]

TABLE 1—ASSUMPTIONS AND PROCESS ELEMENTS

ASSUMPTIONS		
	Pedagogical	**Andragogical**
Concept of the learner	Dependent personality	Increasingly self-directing
The learner's experience	To be used as a foundation for further learning	To be used as a resource for learning by self and others.
Readiness to learn	Uniform by age-level and curriculum	Develops from life tasks and problems
Orientation to learning	Subject-centered	Task- or problem-centered
Motivation	By external rewards and punishment	By internal incentives and curiosity

PROCESS ELEMENTS		
Elements	**Pedagogical**	**Andragogical**
Climate	Tense, low trust, formal, cold, aloof, authority-oriented, competitive, judgmental	Relaxed, trusting, mutually respectful, informal, warm, collaborative, supportive
Planning	Primarily by teacher	Mutually by learners and facilitator
Diagnosis of needs	Primarily by teacher	By mutual assessment
Setting of objectives	Primarily by teacher	By mutual negotiation
Designing learning plans	Teacher plans content Course syllabus Logical sequence	Learning contracts Learning projects Sequenced by readiness
Learning activities	Transmittal techniques Assigned readings	Inquiry projects Independent study Experiential techniques
Evaluation	By teacher Norm-referenced (on a curve) With grades	By learner-collected evidence validated by peers, facilitators, experts Criterion-referenced

Self-Concept

The first essential of education reminds us that the learner brings some kind of self-concept to the learning experience. He may consider himself too old to learn; she may think she has no reason to invest in serious Bible study. In children that self-concept shows up as a dependent personality committed to whatever the teacher has designed. In adults, however, we hope the approach to learning becomes increasingly self-directed. That can only come about in two ways: by teachers utilizing more participation techniques and by learners intentionally taking responsibility for their own outcomes.

Experience

We keep coming back to this component. Certainly children and young people have experience but, as we have noted, it is minimal and unintegrated. Children have not put their lives together in such a way that they can relate new experience to what they have learned before (apperception). Adults, by contrast, add new learning to old ones and provide a rich resource for learning—both their own learning and that of the entire study group.

Readiness to Learn

Those who teach children know that for their students the issue of readiness is both active and unchanneled. A third-grader coming into class may be eager to participate, but he or she may be unfocused in content and goals. Adults usually come with readiness molded by their social roles. They rarely divorce themselves from complex cultural, domestic, and economic concerns. Along with those social roles they bring accumulated experiences to whatever will be learned; because we have fixed ideas that determine lifestyles, new ideas have to stick like Velcro.

This distinction also applies to the difference between college students and middle-aged adults. College students don't really have fixed social roles, and in many cases they have few ideas about what they will do after graduation. Stan and Susan, on the other hand, have a home, a family, and jobs, all of which contribute massively to their readiness for learning.

Orientation to Learning

With children, everything is subject-oriented—language arts, social studies, arithmetic, geography. Amazingly, seminary studies are strikingly similar—Greek, Hebrew, theology, church history. But adult-learning theory reminds us that adults move from a subject-centered to a task- or problem-centered frame of mind. If you measured your church education program on this particular point, how would it score? Is it unfair to suggest that many adult-learning experiences coagulate around subjects and themes? "Come and study Ezekiel." "Come and review the history of our denomination." But since adults enter learning situations in a problem-centered frame of mind, they want to learn something that will make a difference in their lives now. Of course, studying Ezekiel and denominational history *can* be life-relevant, but that is the challenge for teachers teaching those subjects.

Motivation

Here again we face a major difference between the two approaches. We commonly offer children external rewards for achievement—pencils, stars, certificates. Actually research shows that adults will work more enthusiastically toward some public recognition such as a certificate or a plaque, but that can never be the primary motivational scheme. We have not really crossed the line into serious learning until class members independently pursue learning goals they have identified, and then find their motivation in the achievement of those goals.

Climate

Every experienced teacher wants to create some kind of atmosphere in the classroom. Although Knowles's description may sound too negative, we would certainly agree with his words "authority-oriented" and "competitive." Obviously those words could describe many adult classes in church and could probably fit on many college and university campuses. But in a relaxed and trusting adult learning situation, we would hope to find mutual respect among class members and between the class and teacher. Then the climate could be honestly described as "informal, warm, collaborative, and supportive."

How might Stan and Susan respond to a learning situation that displayed these characteristics? If they fit the research summarized in table 1 (page 18) they would not only learn more but could very well become eager to do so. It may take awhile to get them back, but once they get into the flow of this kind of learning, they could be spark plugs to attracting others their age.

Planning from Needs and Setting Objectives

We take these together because they appear so much alike in the two educational approaches. In childhood education planning, diagnosis of needs, and setting objectives are all handled primarily by the teacher. With adults, we want to develop intentional mutuality for facilitating, assessing, and negotiating their own learning.

Here we also find the important distinction between dogmatism and openness on the part of the teacher. More often adults listen like children, not noting the disparity between a teacher's opinion and what that teacher can genuinely support from Scripture. I find it useful, therefore, to tell students when I argue something biblically and when I just offer an interpretive viewpoint. We have an infallible Bible; we do not have infallible interpreters of the Bible.

Learning Plans and Activities

In childhood education the dominant design reflects what we might call "transmittal techniques." We would hope that teachers of adults would make the switch to experiential techniques which pull those mature students into the center of the learning process.

Evaluation

Adults and teachers constantly tell children they should learn things today because they will need them in the future. That is very true, and it is appropriate in childhood education. But for adults immediate application is crucial. Of course, many adults still buy into the "learn-it-now, use-it-later" pattern. We have conditioned them well into the system of pedagogy.

In childhood education evaluation is carried out almost exclusively by teacher-designed instruments and almost always with grades attached. Without faulting that system we must notice that evaluation in adult education occurs best by one's peers and teachers. One can see a learning contract fitting well here. A Sunday school teacher sits down with a superintendent or Christian education pastor and works out a plan for teaching enhancement which covers the next calendar year. At points during that year and at the end of the year they evaluate the teacher's progress based on the objectives they set at the beginning.

DEVELOPING AN ADULT EDUCATION PATTERN

As we think about the developmental growth of people, we could very well distinguish between natural growth rate (usually measured by age) and a culturally patterned rate of growth by which students fit into some kind of grade. The first is naturally designed by God and the second superimposed by any given culture (obviously different in varying cultures). As seen in the first chapter, the flow moves from dependence to independence. That dependence decreases during childhood and youth and drops significantly around age seventeen or eighteen when students go off to college or perhaps enter a career. The problem comes when the superimposed cultural line dips below the natural line too soon. The point is that childhood learning techniques (pedagogy) work quite appropriately on a diminishing scale through most of the teen years.

In fact, parents often make two parallel mistakes in raising their children. One is to keep them dependent too long, and the other is to release them to independence too early. How sad to see a sixteen-year-old who can't make any decisions unless she consults her mom or dad. Even more frightening, however, is a six- or-seven-year-old who makes decisions he shouldn't be making and who controls the family from his nonauthoritative perch. As G. K. Chesterton reportedly said after a visit to America, "It is amazing how the parents obey their children."

The key word here is *process*. We should move the line of independence in concert with the line of natural growth, with no precipitous drops or jumps except the change at about eighteen to twenty when students actually leave home. Take another look at Table 1 with Stan and Susan in mind. Think about their ages in relationship to the pedagogy/andragogy process. What kind of learning experiences would help them most? If they attended your church, what kind of teacher would you want in charge of that class?

TEACHABLE MOMENTS

How commonly we use this poignant phrase in parenting. No formally construed learning experience can match the vitality of real life. Positive experiences such as a trip to the state fair or the sight of a child's first pet provide wonderful opportunities to teach basic values in the family. The same holds true for negative experiences such as the death of that pet or a minor automobile accident. Wise parents stand constantly ready to grab every teachable moment because they know such times offer the classroom of life.

However, we often forget the same opportunities apply with adults, even though we know the importance of reality factors in their learning. Teachable moments do not require *crisis* as we have come to know that word. Junction points at which decisions must be made should provide adequate opportunity for learning. Many such experiences are developmental tasks, which will be discussed frequently throughout this book. Indeed, many of these items will appear again as we study the various age segments of the adult population. Here we focus only on the significance of the teachable moment, the opportunity afforded family members, peers, friends, teachers, and ourselves to grow in knowledge and wisdom.

Starting a Career

With or without college, starting a career presents a worthwhile learning experience. How has God gifted me? What does He want me to do with my life? Will what I choose now become my lifelong career? Do I really enjoy this kind of work? Dozens of other questions crowd in to promote learning at this crucial point in life.

Choosing to Marry or Remain Single

For many adults, deciding whether to marry is a decade-long experience. For some, it may continue for several decades. To be sure, the choice is not perpetually with us morning and night, but as young adults meet potential life partners and as relationships develop, teachable moments occur repeatedly around this question.

Becoming Parents

Deciding whether to become parents presents a teachable moment as well. The expectation of bringing new life into the world and investing eighteen years per child in the parenting process brings every adult face to face with the necessity of serious learning.

Facing Financial Responsibility

In today's world one can no longer place this duty at a husband's doorstep. Single parenting has become a way of life, and adults of both genders face the tasks of maintaining income and fiscal responsibility. In the case of single mothers, this may be one of the most dramatic teachable moments in life, a true crisis experience.

We could add liberally to the list above—selecting new friends, living with teenagers, adjusting to aging—and a host more. The key is not lengthening the list but understanding how such experiences offer us teachable moments for ourselves and for those God has called us to lead in the church.

What can the educational leaders in a congregation do to help adults understand their life needs and relate them to opportunities for learning in the congregation? More to the point, what can *your* church do?

3

❧ ❧

Is It Biblical?

Over the last forty years, when I begin to talk about teaching adults differently, the response has been mostly encouraging. That happens, I believe, because so many churches are dissatisfied with the interest and learning levels of their adult Bible study groups. The idea of adults as self-starters, responsible for their own learning, can sound quite exciting.

But one can always find the naysayers, people who are not the least bit interested in trying something they've never heard about before. Some may say the kind of radical revisions this book calls for are too much work. Others ponder the practicality, wondering how seasoned adults will respond to the andragogical approach. But the ultimate litmus test, the fair and honest question that must be addressed, comes before us in this chapter: Is it biblical?[1]

We start with a simple and basic premise—*the Bible is an adult book written by adults for adults.* Of course it has wonderful passages for young people and children. Of course we want them to read it and understand it. But we cannot escape the simple fact that the lion's share of Bible teaching aims squarely at adults—one could probably make a good case for 95 percent. So we want to look at one chapter in the New Testament that shows adult education at work on the island of Crete. No, we dare not read modern research patterns into the New Testament. But we can see what the passage tells us about the way we might approach learning and particularly about the ways early congregations dealt with adults in learning situations. Surely it is highly unlikely that what we find in Titus 2 applied only to the congregation on Crete. The principles seem to be quite reflective of other New Testament passages, particularly most of the Pauline Epistles.

A one-chapter approach offers merely an example; one could choose many ways to get at the biblical theology of adult education. We could look at the way Jesus taught His disciples or the way Paul handled members of his missionary team. Roy B. Zuck has explored both of these areas. Readers of this book are referred to his fine works on the teaching styles of Jesus and Paul.[2] Or we could study God's covenant model throughout the Old and New Testaments, a solid picture for both family and congregation. A third way would synthesize numerous New Testament passages that deal with teaching. All three are a bit more complex and considerably more scholarly. Our approach here will take six basic elements of the learning process (see "The Educational Cycle" in chapter 4) and superimpose them like a grid on this one New Testament chapter without trying to force the text into an unnatural grid.

NEEDS IN ADULT EDUCATION

The Greek text of Titus 2 includes eleven words for instruction and the English text, thirteen. The first and last verses emphasize teaching, and the entire chapter deals with different groupings of adults. Against the background of Titus 1—in which Paul affirmed this young pastor's call and described the difficulties in that local congregation—Paul called on Titus to "teach what is in accord with sound doctrine" (Titus 2:1).

Older Men

Five groups are addressed in this chapter, and the first represents a typical New Testament starting point. Paul wrote, "Teach the older men to be temperate, worthy of respect, self-controlled, and sound in faith, in love and in endurance" (Titus 2:2). This verse speaks neither about evangelism nor worship. It deals specifically with education. For older men, both then and now, we see the Bible calling for solid doctrine to produce healthy Christians. Maturity certainly reflects self-control, dignity, and being worthy of respect—something we find as early as the selection of the seven servants in Acts 6. The word "sound" in Titus 2:2 can be translated "healthy." Spiritually healthy teaching makes spiritually healthy Christians, and every church ought to be interested in that.

Many evangelicals today strongly emphasize the need for "healthy churches." Sadly, much of the literature equates health with size and numerical growth rather than spiritual maturity. Neither Paul nor any other Bible writer made that mistake. Congregations become healthy as their members, particularly adults, "grow in the grace and knowledge of our Lord and Savior Jesus Christ" (2 Pet. 3:18).

Older Women

Mature women must be able to teach younger women in the context of the church. In short, they are to reach outside their own homes, avoid the pitfalls of gossip and alcohol addiction, and gear up to train younger women (Titus 2:3–5). If this passage is as clear as it seems, why do so few churches have any organized plan in which older women with experience and background teach younger women what they need to know? Certainly it need not be difficult for serious congregations to design some system by which they can follow the admonition of these verses.

Younger Women

Older women can help younger women mature in seven areas. Young Christian women in this context (those who are married) must be self-controlled, pure, kind, submissive, and must function that way while they are loving their husbands, loving their children, and serving God at home.

Verses 4–5 do not say women should not choose careers; the passage simply states that husbands, children, and homes should not be sacrificed. Career women, like Lydia and Priscilla (Acts 16:14; 18:2–3), are in fact some of the New Testament's brightest heroines. They stand, however, against the background of how women function at home. New Testament scholars remind us that first-century Christianity was judged especially by the impact it had on women. Titus was not to teach the young women because of the temptations that situation could present. Older women were to do the teaching.

So the adult education program of that first church on Crete focused on developing homes by developing godly women. Hiebert writes, "If Christian wives ignored these demands and flouted the role their culture demanded of good wives, the Gospel would be maligned, criticized, and discredited by non-Christians. Christianity would be judged especially by the impact that it had on the women. It, therefore, was the duty of the woman to protect God's revelation from profanation by living discreet and wholesome lives. For Christians, no lifestyle is justified that hinders 'the Word of God,' the message of God's salvation in Christ."[3]

Young Men

Of all the things Paul might have said regarding the ministry to this group, he told Pastor Titus to "encourage the young men to be self-controlled" (Titus 2:6). As noted earlier, one of the greatest impacts on the Roman world was the way the church conducted its family life; that behavior stood in contrast to the looseness of pagan Rome. Healthier domestic relationships, much more than church services, attracted people to the gospel. As young women stood out by their chastity and devotion to their families, Christian young men were marked by self-control. Young men still tend to be somewhat unrestrained and impetuous, so the Spirit of God focused on a specific learning need in their behavioral development.

Have you ever seen a young man out of control? I recall attending a deacon's meeting years ago. One deacon became very unhappy with something the group had just approved. He sprang to his feet, knocked over a chair, hastily gathered up whatever materials he had, stomped out of the room, and slammed the door. He was a man out of control. Worse, he was a church officer out of control. Congregations that fail to take seriously the biblical requirements for church officers found in 1 Timothy 3:1–13 will usually end up with the leaders they deserve, but not the leaders God wants them to have. Doubtless, self-control was not the entire curriculum, but it certainly represented the core.

Slaves

Slavery is desperately wrong and evil; the general tone of Scripture makes that very clear. But as the gospel spread around the Mediterranean world, thousands of the sixty million slaves in the Roman Empire trusted Christ. The Cretan adult-education program for slaves, therefore, seems designed to meet the needs of slaves, including their seriously seeking to please their masters, avoiding contradiction or argument, practicing genuine honesty, and developing attractive, godly lives (Titus 2:9–10).

Colossians 3:22–25 is informative here, and both Titus and Colossians must be set against the background of Philemon, which expresses Paul's personal preference for voluntarily giving freedom to slaves. To put it another way, slaves who had become Christians were responsible to function biblically in their present roles. But slaveholders like Philemon were asked to take the next step and defy the current culture by treating slaves like brothers and sisters. "Slaves, obey your earthly masters in everything; and do it, not only when their eye is on you and to win their favor, but with sincerity of heart and reverence for the Lord. Whatever you do, work at it with all your heart, as working for the Lord, not for men, since you know that you will receive an inheritance from the Lord as a reward. It is the Lord Christ you are serving. Anyone who does wrong will be repaid for his wrong, and there is no favoritism. Masters, provide your slaves with what is right and fair, because you know that you also have a Master in heaven" (Col. 3:22–4:1).

Five groups on Crete. Hardly a full menu for adult education in that church or in ours. Yet, though not an exhaustive list, these categories provide an example of how we can look at adults in any congregation by need-based categories. The variations from this passage to the twenty-first-century church are vast, but that does not make it any less useful for us to see how one pastor (Titus) did it many years ago.

OBJECTIVES FOR ADULT EDUCATION

Tucked away amid the practical admonitions of Titus 2, we find an interesting paragraph on the foundations for godly living. It offers both negative and positive instruction with respect to objectives for the adult-education program at Crete. Of course, good educational objectives should be brief, clear, specific, and worded in terms of student achievement. One would hardly expect the peerless educator Paul to offer anything less.

Rejection of Ungodliness

As the second part of Titus unfolds, we learn that God's grace is a *paidia*, a teacher bringing salvation and driving students toward godliness (Titus 2:11–14). This objective is what educators call "affective" rather than "cognitive," meaning that it deals with attitudes rather than knowledge. The training ministry of God's grace strives to bring believers to sufficient maturity, where dismissing ungodliness and worldliness becomes a distinctive act of the will.

Self-Controlled Godly Living

Verse 12 includes three adjectives—"self-controlled, upright, and godly." These words look inward, outward, and upward, as we focus on training Christian adults. The inward look means personal spiritual living, the individual Christian's walk with God. The outward look suggests upright conduct amid the ungodliness in the world, the context in which Christian living must be played out. The upward look requires dependence on God and His grace, which makes possible all this learning and living.

Waiting for Christ's Return

Paul dropped the theology of the Second Coming right in the middle of a practical family-and-church passage. Affirming the deity of Christ, the apostle observed that the context for living and learning is "this present age," but that it all happens while we anticipate the Lord's return (Titus 2:12–13).

Eagerly Doing Good

In verse 14 Paul reminded Titus that salvation brings redemption from both guilt and judgment, thereby allowing God's Spirit to produce righteousness in the lives of believers. Through the process God creates a new people of His own, people who are eager to work hard at doing good.

Did Paul offer Titus brief, specific, clear, and behaviorally oriented objectives? Without question. Paul's words linked creed and conduct, learning and life in a magnificent paragraph built around the model of the Lord Jesus Himself. What could be more relevant for the contemporary church?

CURRICULUM FOR ADULT EDUCATION

Having defined congregational needs and spelled out objectives, we now identify content for the learning process. Obviously Paul thought he had done this since he ended Titus 2 with the words, "These, then, are the things you should teach" (2:15). The "things" represent "sound doctrine" (healthy teaching), as noted in verse 1. Unlike the objectives, however, we cannot find the curriculum detailed in one or two verses adjacent to each other; it appears throughout the passage. Obviously everything taught to the different age-groups must be considered "core curriculum" as well as content necessary to fulfill the objectives described in verses 11–14.

Besides identifying three areas of behavior toward which this "curriculum" was directed, we might also think of them as targets toward which our adult-education programs should aim.

Heavenly Relations

As the diagram on the following page indicates, in providing content for adult learning, we do not start at the outside and work in, but rather aim at the bull's-eye and work out. This is the "core curriculum." People cannot get along with each other in families or congregations until they first get along with God. Pastors know from their hours of family counseling that the problems husbands, wives, and children often face are less initiated by their relationships with each other than by individual relationships with the heavenly Father. First the vertical, then the horizontal. Words like "reverent," "pure," "self- controlled," "upright," "godly," and the phrase "a people that are His very own" (Titus 2:3, 5–6, 12, 14) all indicate that biblical content aims to produce personal holiness in the lives of adult believers.

DIAGRAM 4—CORE CURRICULUM ON CRETE

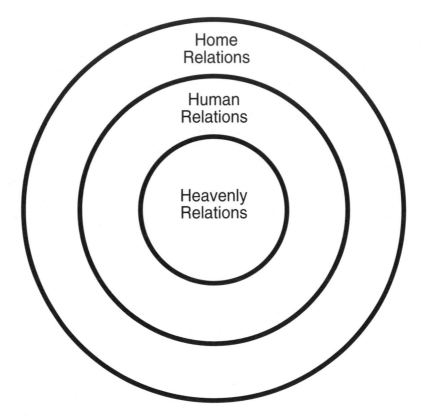

Home
Relations

Human
Relations

Heavenly
Relations

Human Relations

Each one of the five groups in Titus 2:2–6 was taught to relate to other Christians in some way. That's why we read about self-control, love, kindness, subjection, integrity, and honesty. In each of all five adult groups in Crete, we find some reference to the way they should relate to others in that congregation.

Home Relations

One cannot overemphasize the importance of family-life education in evangelical congregations. The obvious biblical emphasis surfaces right here in Titus 2 with direct instruction to younger women, an emphasis on children, husbands, and the extended family—all with respect for older men and older women. All these focus the spotlight of curriculum design on family relationships as a central concern in the first-century church—and the twenty-first.

As this book seeks to demonstrate, family-life education is a major adult-education component in any church. And if we use these three curricular elements in diagram 4 as a foundation, we could very well build other concentric circles on the diagram using words like "employment," "society," "cultural surroundings"—those things on which life is broadly based.

Having spent the last four decades speaking in churches around the continent, I'm quite convinced that the basic problems of the evangelical community have comparatively little to do with theology. We struggle more with the inability of people to get along with each other in couples, families, congregations, and wider social groupings. Many of the problems could be solved almost overnight if adult Christians would pledge allegiance to Paul's flag of unity which flies early in the epistle to the Philippians: "If you have any encouragement from being united with Christ, if any comfort from his love, if any fellowship with the Spirit, if any tenderness and compassion, then make my joy complete by being like-minded, having the same love, being one in spirit and purpose. Do nothing out of selfish ambition or vain conceit, but in humility consider others better than yourselves. Each of you should look not only to your own interests, but also to the interests of others. Your attitude should be the same as that of Christ Jesus" (Phil. 2:1–5).

LEADERSHIP FOR ADULT EDUCATION

As remote as a two-thousand-year-old chapter may seem, we enter the twenty-first century with thousands of young pastors not unlike Titus and thousands of congregations functioning in surroundings somewhat similar to Crete. In a day when people believe the most bizarre fiction is truth, Paul's description of a first-century culture sounds amazingly close to home. "For there are many rebellious people, mere talkers and deceivers, especially those of the circumcision group. They must be silenced, because they are ruining whole households by teaching things they ought not to teach—and that for the sake of dishonest gain. Even one of their own prophets has said, 'Cretans are always liars, evil brutes, lazy gluttons.' This testimony is true. Therefore, rebuke them sharply, so that they will be sound in the faith and will pay no attention to Jewish myths or to the commands of those who reject the truth. To the pure, all things are pure, but to those who are corrupted and do not believe, nothing is pure. In fact, both their minds and consciences are corrupted. They claim to know God, but by their actions they deny him. They are detestable, disobedient and unfit for doing anything good" (Titus 1:10–16).

The Pastor Is the Key

Rather than writing a general letter to the congregation in Crete, such as we commonly find in the New Testament, Paul wrote personally to the church's pastor. The apostle knew well that no effective adult education program can develop in any congregation unless it has the support and blessing of the pastor. Adult education in the church consists of talking, teaching, training, exhorting, instructing, and rebuking. The first and last verses of Titus 2 form "bookends" to describe the ministry of Titus: "You must teach. . . . These, then, are the things you should teach" (2:1, 15). One senses immediately that unless Titus carried out this role, Crete would see no effective adult education.

But we cannot construe pastoral leadership to mean teaching all the adults in the sanctuary during the Sunday school hour. The pastor may not be directly involved in an adult education class or the adult education committee, but his constant and visible support makes possible what we talk about in this book.

Discipleship Patterns Predominate

The popular term *discipleship* does not actually appear in the Book of Titus, but Paul surely emphasized discipling as a teaching technique. Notice 2:7–8:

"In everything set them an example by doing what is good. In your teaching show integrity, seriousness and soundness of speech that cannot be condemned." For the effective adult teacher genuinely concerned about biblical leadership, life precedes lecture and modeling replaces meddling.

Opposition Should Be Expected

Paul warned Titus about "those who oppose you" (Titus 2:8). To whom was he referring? Judaizers? Gnostics? Apostates? I like the way Hiebert leaves the landscape wide open: "Paul concluded his personal remarks to Titus with another purpose clause. The expression 'those who oppose you' is apparently left intentionally vague to leave room for all types of critics. (The original is singular: 'The opponent, one of the opposition.') When the objections are examined, the anticipated result is that the critic 'may be ashamed,' either feeling personally ashamed of his own conduct or made to look foolish because he is shown to have no case."[4]

METHODS IN ADULT EDUCATION

As already discussed, the teacher who functions as a facilitator can achieve more than the traditional knowledge transmitter. That principle leads us into methods that emphasize involvement and participation. But apart from specific teaching methods, Titus 2 does give us some clues on how to approach adult education.

Target Key Groups

Paul addressed older men, older women, young women, young men, and slaves—five specific groups of adults toward which the teaching program at Crete was to be directed. Almost every congregation today, regardless of size, includes the first four of those groups. If we apply the concept of the slave to employees today, we would find most of our adults in an age-related group (with its own distinctive needs) and a need-related group based on current work patterns. The more important question to ask is, What are the key groups in your church?

Emphasize Modeling

Paul reminded Titus that he must "set them an example by doing what is good" (2:7). The very emphasis of teaching by example requires constant attention to our own learning and spiritual consistency. Adult-education leaders and teachers model behavior, Bible study, prayer, serving others, kindness, and a host of other qualities we want to develop in adult learners.

Get Serious

The concepts of being worthy of respect *(semnos)* and being serious *(semnotēs)* characterize Paul's instructions to Titus (2:2, 7). *Semnos,* the second characteristic of Christian thinking in Philippians 4:8 is translated "noble." Perhaps too much Christian adult education in churches today offers food and fellowship without really preparing people for the serious spiritual battles of life or throwing the burden of productivity back on the learner.

In *The Seasons of a Man's Life,* Daniel Levinson emphasizes "individual life structure," which describes a man's conscious efforts to shape his own destiny as well as the unconscious unfolding of psychological and biological capabilities.[5] If Levinson is correct, every man passes through a sequence of stable and transitional periods, usually lasting four to eight years each. During these transitions he builds, modifies, and rebuilds the structures of his life.

The implications of biblical nurture in such a process stand unchallenged. Is it not true that many adults involved in learning experiences in our churches do not take them seriously? Might the sagging attendance in Sunday school generally and especially in adult classes indicate a failure to put viable learning and application high on a scale of importance for our people? Will we even admit to a general carelessness? By using the word "serious" Paul surely did not intend to say Christians should never laugh or have fun. I think he meant to say, "Titus, you must get serious about adult education, and you must make sure your adults get serious about it as well."

EVALUATION OF ADULT EDUCATION

Let's go back to the educational model (diagram 1, page 4). After we understand the biblical information, design objectives, and create programs, we need to ask how we are doing. Though nothing in Titus 2 specifically talks about evaluation, Paul certainly emphasized results. What happens when a congregation carries out its adult-education program correctly? In general we can say that church and home will support each other warmly and effectively; the church will design ministries to meet all known needs without overprogramming and demanding constant attendance at church meetings; and members of that congregation will show the results of what God's grace and God's Spirit teach them from Scripture. According to Titus 2, three results occur.

People will not malign the Word of God (2:5). In this context blasphemy seemed possible because of the unruly behavior of young wives. Presumably unsaved husbands (a well-populated group in the first century as well as today) might blame the gospel for causing it. The world judges any religion not so much by the truth of its doctrines as by the effect those doctrines have on the lives of its people. Certainly the New Testament indicates that the godliness of believers turns away criticism of the gospel.

Families will be strong (2:4). Again, the close link between adult education and family-life education need not be contrived. Years ago Lawrence Richards claimed that "everything in home life—parents' attitudes, conversations, examples—is educative. It is dangerous to consider Christian nurture simply as moments set aside for family prayer or Bible study. The whole pattern of home life should reflect essential harmony with the faith we profess. . . . We must relate individual church ministries to parental ministry. . . . We must administer our church programs to help rather than hinder Christian training in the home."[6]

The gospel will be attractive (2:10). If the behavior of young wives can turn away criticism of God's Word, so the godly behavior of slaves as the product of the church's adult educational program can make the teaching about God our Savior attractive. As suggested earlier, in application (not interpretation), the slave passages in the New Testament can be related to modern-day employees. This teaching, then, touches virtually every adult in the church. Imagine the impact on your community if every adult behaved on the job in ways that made teaching about the Savior attractive.

4

❦

How Do Adults Learn?

Suppose a church—let's call it Grace Church—wants to improve all its ministries to and by adults. They could form an adult-ministries committee that could begin by gathering curricular materials and information about adult-learning theory.

THE EDUCATIONAL CYCLE

One of the things that committee should note from the start is the educational cycle, a concept developed by Lois LeBar. Both Gene Getz and I picked up this idea in our writings on local-church educational ministry. The diagram on the next page is taken from my book, *Leadership for Church Education.*[1] The educational cycle is a way of programming integrated designs into an educational ministry system. The relationship of the components to each other and the sequence in the cycle are very important.

Biblical Imperatives

We start with axioms such as "Love one another," "Feed my sheep," "Pray without ceasing." For sincere believers these and other New Testament absolute requirements should be stressed in every church. In some cases they may be interpreted differently, but we would all agree we must be doing these

DIAGRAM 5—THE EDUCATIONAL CYCLE

things and teaching other people to do them. Notice how biblical imperatives stand apart in the cycle and are not subject to annual evaluation.

Biblical Objectives

For evangelicals, all education rests on biblical imperatives from which we then derive *biblical objectives.* Perhaps we could view this second step as a simple way of restating the imperative. "Love one another" now becomes "The student will learn to love other people in our church."

Alas, not all church members demonstrate consistent love toward others. Romans 12:5, for example, does not seem to work because the selfishness of the culture has turned people away from the idea that "each member belongs to all the others." Not only is the need obvious and the biblical foundation clear, but this is translatable into actual learning experiences for their adults.

Current Needs

Biblical imperatives do not change, but objectives change in the light of current needs. Churches need to recognize the futility of conducting an educational program for the twenty-first century based on needs diagnosed in the 1970s. So the idea of current needs focuses on a *core group* of believers faithful to the church's ministry; the contact group of people who come, perhaps even regularly, but have no involvement in ministry; and the community group which may be defined geographically in a larger town or city, but which could include all unchurched people in a small town.

Current Objectives

From current needs we move on to *objectives*. Biblical objectives, derived from biblical imperatives, serve as a general umbrella for ministry programs. Current objectives relate biblical objectives through the eye of current needs. This is a slight twist on the model presented in diagram 1 in chapter 1, but the end result is the same—interpreting and meeting needs in line with biblical truth. The reason for the difference? Here we have an educational cycle rather than a theological model.

Program and Curriculum

We must know what the Bible says; we must know what we want people to do about what the Bible says; and we must know how our objectives relate to the here and now. Only then are we ready to design a program and choose or create a curriculum. Curriculum comes up later in chapter 24, so here we simply call it a "course of study" since the Latin term from which we derive the word describes a racetrack. *Program* is an overused word, but it clearly communicates the idea of an organized effort to achieve certain goals.

Organization and Administration

From program and curriculum we move to structure and management. Organization and administration make programmed curriculum possible.

Somehow programs don't maintain themselves; someone must be responsible to make them work.

Methods and Materials

This takes us right into the classroom. Who will serve as leaders for our adult ministries? What kind of people can take on the role of facilitator rather than truth teller in a classroom? How will we train these people? What teaching methods will we recommend? Where can we get adequate materials that focus satisfactorily on what we know about how adults learn? This is where the action takes place. All the planning and programming, the organization and administration, are useless unless the soldiers on the front lines in the classroom or in study groups can make it work.

Evaluation

The last step in the cycle asks key questions: Does our program work? Does our program do what we designed it to do? Do we see evidence that people's needs are being met through this ministry program? Do we see evidence that the program outcomes are achieving the objectives we set? For the next year, what should we keep? What should we drop? What should we change?

Revised Needs

Finally, we look again at needs as we bridge from one cycle to the next. If a church chooses to use the educational cycle on an annual basis, it might see few changes in needs from year to year. However, those changes could have a significant effect on the array of family ministries. If a church starts a family program, its emphasis on participation and the meeting of needs could become so attractive that young boomers in their late thirties and early forties would start attending. This could call for starting a class of thirty-five to fifty-year-olds that would focus especially on people with children from middle school through college.

What they must remember however, is axiomatic to adult ministries: *In grouping adults for ministry, relationships are more important than age.*

To be more specific, a thirty-five-year-old married adult with no children is more like a twenty-five-year-old married adult without children than like a thirty-five-year-old with three children. Why? Because needs and social goals dominate our society.

The key for most churches is whether they can evaluate their educational programs, specifically adult ministries, through the guiding framework of this cycle.

ESSENTIAL QUESTIONS FOR TEACHERS

Perhaps this never happens to you, but I have a number of information items in my files which I cannot document. The following six questions are among them. The list may have come from Jerome Bruner, but I can't track that source.

What Do I Want Students to Learn?

We'll come back later to explore the different dimensions of learning. But specifically here we want to focus on scope. A number of churches offer adult-education classes in thirteen-week quarters, conducting both age-grouped and content-grouped (elective) classes. As each teacher prepares for his or her class, the question "What do I want students to learn?" should be a point of primary concern. In approaching the Gospel of Mark, for example, no teacher could cover every verse expositionally in any reasonable time frame. The focal point is not how far we can go, but what we want students to learn.

Why Do I Want Students to Learn This?

This question cranks up the difficulty level a bit. Ask any college teacher what he wants students to learn; he can drag out the syllabus and tell you with some precision. When you ask why this and not something else, the answers run the gamut from providing a prerequisite for another course (first-year Greek as a foundation for second-year Greek) to opportunity for the teacher to do research in an area of his or her interest. Every teacher must include some content and leave some things out. And that distinction can be more easily identified by answering the question, "Why do I want the student to learn this?"

When They Have Learned It, What Do I Want Them to Do with It?

In higher education we call this an outcome-based approach to education. If you teach a thirteen-week class on the Gospel of Mark, do you want your students to develop a basic foundation of the book so they can handle inductive study on their own? Do you want them to pick up the elements of evangelism and discipleship in Mark so they implement its teaching in their daily lives? Probably both—and a lot more; but objectives can't be spelled out until you have a good view of how students will carry information beyond the boundaries of a particular class.

When They Have Learned It, How Long Do I Expect Them to Retain It?

One body of research on classroom methods suggests that the more extensive goals we construct with respect to time, the greater the impact on the teaching process. To put it another way, if the limit of our learning goals ends at the close of a quarter or a semester, it doesn't really matter which methods we use. Teachers can lecture, ask questions, answer questions, conduct discussion groups, or show videos, but in short-term learning goals, which methods are used makes little difference.

On the other hand, if we are concerned that students retain what we teach them for five years or more after they leave the class, it makes a huge difference what methods we use. Here the participational hands-on methods score high, well above teaching-by-telling methods. This brings us back to what we earlier called andragogy. Adult-oriented learning serves both immediacy of adult need and long-range adult retention.

Are My Objectives Testable?

This may be a moot question for the adult-ministries program at many churches, since teachers do not expect to give tests—or do they? In a local congregation, passing written tests serves small consequence, though I have used them myself on numerous occasions. What really matters is changed lives—and that takes some time. If a church offers an elective adult class on prayer, it is quite possible that during the thirteen weeks of class time the teacher could actually see people growing in their prayer lives. Perhaps for the first time some folks would practice family prayer on a daily basis or show a willingness to lead in corporate prayer in a public meeting. Some have begun prayer journals to track God's answers to their requests. In some cases those changes will not be obvious and not likely testable.

What Provision Will I Make for Varying Learning Abilities?

Every time we face a class, we see people of different learning styles with different backgrounds and experiences and different learning abilities. For example, consider the *rate of learning,* how fast the student learns. Some people just pick things up; others take awhile to mull through new ideas and try to work out the details. Another issue is *mode of learning.* Some people learn best listening to someone talk; others learn better by interacting with others in a small group. We must also consider *motivation for learning.* In facilitating adult learning, it is not the teacher's task to bring motivation to the classroom. Instead his task is to unleash motivation based on the class members' felt needs.

Some recent research indicates that in addition to factors we have known for a long time—methods, background experiences, use of media—adults learn better when they like the teacher. I find that fascinating because we have applied that kind of thinking so often to children but rarely consider adults in the same light. When people adapt to a teacher and appreciate his style, they warm up to the content as well. We see examples of this all the time in seminary as some sections of a course fill up quickly. There is no difference in the content, the credit, or even the evaluation. Yes, different days and times could be a factor; but much more likely students want to study with a certain teacher.

THREE KEY CONCERNS

After we have reviewed the educational cycle and considered the essential questions for teachers, we need to take into consideration some other variables that always present themselves when we design a learning program for adults. This grouping of three is hardly exhaustive, but it affords a start.

Learning Environment

Teachers of adults need to understand how to create a learner-friendly climate in the classroom. Informality, comfort, regular use of Bibles, freedom to disagree, and a host of other ingredients make up the ambiance of a good adult class. Every teacher of adults must ask, What must happen for these people to learn effectively?

Content Organization

We keep coming back to scope and sequence. Think about a seminary class in systematic theology. Almost every seminary divides that broad subject into subcategories such as angelology, hamartiology, soteriology, eschatology, and more. Sequence asks, What should we study first? What should we study next? What should we study last? What class should follow or precede another in the lineup? Many theologians would argue that we begin with the doctrine of God because the Bible starts there. Another group insists we begin with the doctrine of Scripture because almost everything we know about God comes to us from the Bible. The faculty in the theology department and the teaching teams at local churches face the same challenge—how best to put the pieces of a learning program together.

Appropriate Awards

To discuss giving awards to adults may seem at first glance as though we jumped back into pedagogy, concerning ourselves with how to conduct a class of children. We already noticed in chapter 1 that adults are very interested in overt recognition. Not a trinket of some kind, but perhaps a certificate for serious accomplishment, or even a plaque. Some churches even give a diploma for the completion of three years (twelve courses) of study.

Let's review by reminding ourselves that adults are different, particularly educationally. Their different needs are based on developmental tasks, and, for educational purposes, a need is not a need until it becomes a felt need. Adults bring a wide and varied background of experience to every learning situation and those backgrounds color their learning. Adults bring different attitudes to a learning situation, and for most of them, immediacy of use is important.

Adult experiences create the needs churches must learn to address. For that reason, social and family issues may be studied as well. We approach teaching adults in a different way because of the independence and interdependence they bring to the classroom.

5

❧⟨❧⟩

Who Needs What—And Why?

*L*et's *keep our ears* at the door of the conference room where the Grace Church adult ministries committee meets. As they sort out how they will reconfigure their whole adult ministry, they have decided to take a hard look at needs and objectives since those concepts keep appearing in everything they read about adult learning. One of the members brought a copy of Malcolm Knowles's book *The Adult Learner: A Neglected Species* to the meeting and read his definition: "A learning need is the gap between where you are now and where you want to be in regard to a particular set of competencies."[1] The committee sensed immediately that this broad definition would fit almost all adult learning. It could apply to skiing, learning a foreign language, or an in-depth Bible study. It could describe the level of ministry skills a Christian adult develops in relationship to service for Christ. Of course, not every adult understands the concept of learning needs, nor can every adult develop or articulate personal needs. That's why we talk about "felt needs."

ASSESSING NEEDS

Felt needs become the "doorway to involvement" because they describe the way people understand their own needs and how willing they are to recognize those needs. In a sense, felt needs are problems to be solved:

(how to conduct effective family devotions; how to keep from losing my temper at work; how to understand the intricacies of the Minor Prophets; how to function effectively as an elder.) The problem or challenge becomes the catapult to an effective learning experience. So if someone asks how we motivate adults to learn, we simply answer that we help them understand their felt needs. Motivation, as observed earlier, is unleashed on the basis of what adults understand about themselves, in relationship to the ministry opportunities we afford them.

Prescribed Needs

Prescribed needs are based primarily in Scripture. They also come at us in numerous books on adult education. Jim Wilhoit identifies four needs of Christian adults with respect to how they approach spiritual formation in an alien culture:

- A commitment to the fact that being a Christian means living out of step with the dominant culture

- A recognition that the spiritual life can be mimicked externally

- The need to provide both spiritual support and challenge

- The importance of both finding patterns of devotion that fit "people where they are" and also introducing patterns that allow for deeper fellowship with God.[2]

Needs assessment in adult education can be demonstrated by the overlapping of the ovals in Diagram 6 that represent felt needs and prescribed needs. Notice what the model says: We deal with real needs only when felt needs and prescribed needs come together. In a model like this, we may assume that the ovals could be pushed together or pulled apart. The more they push together, the more we deal with real needs. The more they pull apart, the less likely we are to link our teaching efforts with something our adults really feel they need.

DIAGRAM 6—NEEDS ASSESSMENT IN ADULT EDUCATION

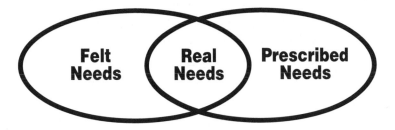

Felt Needs

Consider another area, very much a part of adult education—enhancement of family life. In a course I have taught for many years, students must survey their congregations with respect to a whole list of felt needs. In the most recent group of papers, the need to establish a daily quiet time surfaced on a majority of papers with almost astonishing regularity. We clearly know this to be a biblically ordained "prescribed need" so we can really get excited when we see the felt need overlapping that. It's rather like knowing your child is desperately weary and having her say, "I'm tired; I think I'll go to bed now."

Measured Needs

In addition to research in adult-education books, we can conduct surveys. The class project I mentioned above pinpointed at least ten areas of felt need, with responses varying from church to church. In this kind of research the quality of the survey document and the percentage of returns are important. We should ask clear questions which can be answered with precision and we should survey every adult in the congregation and aim for at least a 50 percent return.

That probably means handling the survey documents in a public meeting rather than mailing them out and hoping they come back. Although the survey should have open-ended segments, you probably need to list a group of prescribed needs as a starter in each category. At one church the adult-ministries committee created a sample questionnaire and asked each adult to take a copy home to fill it out with his or her spouse (or alone, if not married). That led to refinements which they could apply in the final document.

Some adults have effectively used a *critical-incident exercise,* something like a case study based on a hypothetical situation to ascertain felt needs. They ask adults about some issue to study, such as husband-wife communication, the fears and struggles of growing older. Adults respond by discussing the brief paragraph on one of these subjects, and as the committee listens they pick up information about how adults perceive the needs of a hypothetical person.

Sometimes a *forum* will work. Invite adults to the church for a fellowship dinner, and, as part of the program, offer interaction with the adult ministries committee to discuss learning needs. The usefulness of a forum as an information-gathering technique depends on the openness of the group and the skill with which the leadership team handles the situation. This is useful information since people's responses do not change that frequently. Certainly they vary from generation to generation, and sometimes even within blocks of time as brief as five or ten years. But to get started on an effective program of adult ministries, a forum can help a church gather a lot of data that will serve them well for long-range planning for the twenty-first century.

FORMULATING OBJECTIVES

In any well-designed educational experience, teachers and adult learners are always thinking about objectives. Educational objectives tend to unfold in three waves that are closely related but are different. We call them cognitive, affective, and conative objectives.

Without getting enmeshed in the inner workings of educational philosophy, we can at least glance at Benjamin Bloom's famous approach to learning objectives (see diagram 7). The first and lowest level is *knowledge,* which includes memorization, awareness, and familiarity with blocks of information. Bloom reminds us that knowledge, though enormously important, differs greatly from comprehension.

Comprehension (understanding) represents a higher level of learning.

DIAGRAM 7—BLOOM'S TAXONOMY OF
COGNITIVE OBJECTIVES

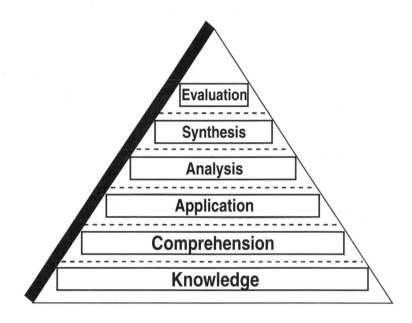

Many Christian adults can quote Bible verses but do not grasp their meaning. This illustrates knowledge without comprehension. When we find people locked in at the first level, we cannot solve the problem by dumping more information on them. We must help them move up the ladder.

The third level is *application*. This has to do with the correct use of abstract principles when no clear solutions are specified. Bloom suggests that many learners never get any higher than this.

Analysis is the ability to look at something and figure out what it means. This should be particularly interesting to those of us responsible for Bible teaching. The whole science of hermeneutics (interpretation) is based on analysis, because here learning focuses on breaking down ideas into workable parts so we can see relationships and patterns.

Synthesis means pulling parts together to make a whole. When a student writes a term paper or a pastor prepares a sermon, he engages in synthesis. The study for the sermon probably centered in analysis, but the prepared outline or manuscript represents synthesis.

Bloom calls the sixth and highest level *evaluation,* because the learner makes judgments about the value of ideas or concepts. An effective adult-learning experience requiring evaluation could involve reading and reacting to a textbook or handout. Class members could also give their opinions on their interpretation of certain problem passages in the Bible.

In all this we see important observations we dare not miss. *First, each item depends on the one before it*—no comprehension without knowledge, no application without comprehension, and so on. *Second, each succeeding item represents a level higher* than the one(s) before it.

Unfortunately many adult learning experiences have operated for years only at the knowledge and comprehension levels.

Affective Objectives

Most people who have no formal training in the educational process never think about affective objectives. Words like *knowing, understanding,* and *analyzing* seem well in line with how we understand learning. But the affective dimension has to do with attitudes and feelings. It describes a willingness to receive and pay attention to happenings in the classroom. Interest in other people as well as the subject matter fits in here, as does willingness to respond and become a part of the learning process. The key word is *attitude.*

Affective objectives also talk about value—how people accept a value and eventually commit to it. We would like all our adults to develop a value system that governs their lives. We design objectives in the affective as well as the cognitive areas so that learning deals with attitude as well as the transmission of information.

Conative Objectives

Yet another category of learning objectives we sometimes call *behavioral* (though I prefer the word *conative*). This term deals with skills based on performance abilities. To put it simply, cognitive learning deals with what the students know; affective with how the students feel; and conative with what they can do.

These three kinds of goals need to be balanced by thinking of the way learning goals and teaching objectives flow from the needs of the student. It doesn't come easily, but we must do it if we are to teach adults effectively.

We need to remember that goals and objectives operate on several levels. Basic goals can be developed for an entire adult-ministries program, but each teacher and or leader in that program must also design objectives for a *unit of study* (the length of which may vary) and *for each particular group meeting*. Those objectives should be brief, clear, specific, measurable, and worded in terms of student outcomes. Here are some samples:

1. The students will know the key salvation passages of Romans (knowledge).

2. The students will understand how the doctrine of the virgin birth fits into Christian theology (comprehension).

3. The students will apply their understanding of prayer in very specific ways over the next six months (application).

4. The students will analyze 1 John with a view to determining the biblical theology of that book (analysis).

5. The students will write a four-page testimony statement which can be used for witnessing to unsaved people (synthesis).

6. The students will evaluate an article that promotes cultic theology and critique it on the basis of God's Word (evaluation).

Examples in the affective category include:

1. The students will desire to know God more intimately and speak to Him more personally.

2. The students will love their families more deeply and actively than ever before.

Conative objectives could include:

1. The students will be able to lead a worship service effectively.

2. The students will be able to share the gospel with another person, utilizing tools explained in the class.

IMPLEMENTING THIS CHAPTER

The Grace Church adult ministries committee has been our example now for two chapters. The committee began by seeking to understand the needs of the their church adults, both prescribed and felt. To get information on prescribed needs, they researched educational books and examined some key Scriptures on this subject. Then they were involved in needs assessment. They used a carefully designed four-page instrument which took no more than fifteen minutes to complete. It was administered in every adult Sunday-school class by a member of the committee on the same day, and they received an amazing 74 percent response, a solid basis to move forward.

From there they climbed the scale of the model presented in the first chapter (see diagram 1). Understanding needs and the biblical implications of how to meet them, they moved systematically through philosophy, objectives, curriculum, organization, personnel, and methods. All this took nearly six months to achieve. Finishing in December, they thought it unwise to unleash a new program at the beginning of the new calendar year, so they waited until what most churches consider the beginning of the curriculum year (September 1). That gave them eight more months to write the important documents, order literature, find adequate leaders and classroom space, and complement the actual educational situations with other social groupings and activities beneficial to their overall goals. That year of planning may very well revolutionize the adult ministries of their congregation for ten or twenty years to come.

6

❦

Stay Tuned to the Discovery Channel

*M*alcolm Knowles tells an interesting story about his days as a student of Carl Rogers. Knowles walked into a class in adult education where the students already sat in a circle talking to one another. According to Knowles, it took him several days to identify the teacher. He probably heard the name, but because of the informality of the group, he could not recognize Rogers. Obviously, Rogers was a devotee of a classroom strategy that emphasized participation and independent learning. He was, in fact, a *facilitator* (see chapter 25).

Some will say that teaching Scripture with its timeless and absolute truth is so different from teaching any other content that one cannot arrive at learning through informal discussion. But Jesus in fact often did this very thing with His disciples. As long as we understand that involvement serves as the means to an end, we would find participational classroom strategy not only possible but preferable.

TWO APPROACHES TO TEACHING

Diagram 8 on the following page illustrates two different configurations of the same three components—teacher, content, and learners.

DIAGRAM 8—ADULT LEARNING: TRADITIONAL
AND CONTEMPORARY

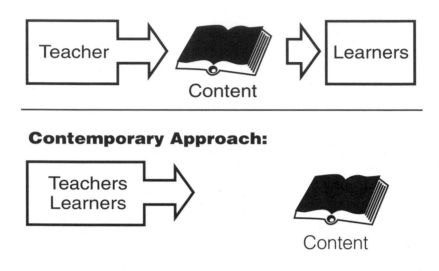

In the top half of the diagram we see the traditional approach in which the teacher studies content and communicates it to the learners. Can we agree that most learning groups in evangelical churches operate exactly this way and have for years?

Traditional Lecture

Dale Owen teaches young adults in this pattern. He uses his Bible, a printed curriculum with a teacher's manual, and a small podium on a table in front of him. He studies during the week, brings the content to class, and opens the basket of God's Word. Ninety percent of the time classroom technique takes the form of a lecture or some other one-way monologue. This traditional approach makes most of us feel comfortable; we believe this is the way teaching strategy ought to work.

Contemporary Involvement

The contemporary approach, however, requires Dale to study for thorough biblical understanding, rearrange what he learns, and ask his class members to approach the text with him. This does not mean that teacher and learner are equal with respect to what they know about the content. But on the basis of what we know about adult education, the interdependent approach with frequent applications of truth to life makes a lot more sense.

Multiple Applications

Don't miss the note about multiple applications. In the old system of classroom strategy, we began with the introduction and worked toward the conclusion which contained an application. But we hit constant snags when the time ended before the application arrived. Now we understand that a Bible teacher should apply some aspect of the lesson *about every ten minutes during the class period*. We dare not lose track of the three basic questions of inductive Bible study: What does the text say? What does the text mean? What should I do about it?

As Dale makes the transition from the traditional lecture format to emphasis on involvement and application, he has begun to enter the brave new world of discovery teaching. Teachers who are serious about their own Bible study practice discovery all the time; rarely, however, do they allow their students that joy. The next model unveils the elements of discovery teaching, showing how Dale can move from redesigning the atmosphere of his classroom toward the ultimate goal of integrated truth.

ELEMENTS OF DISCOVERY TEACHING

Friendly Atmosphere

Dale Owen wants to develop a facilitating classroom strategy. He starts with a nonthreatening atmosphere in which people can learn at their own speeds, focus on what they want to learn, and ask questions without fear of reprisal.

DIAGRAM 9—ELEMENTS OF DISCOVERY TEACHING

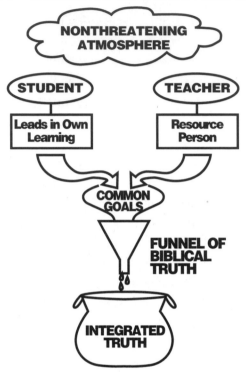

Revised Roles

We still have a student and a teacher, but now the student leads in his own learning, and the teacher serves primarily as a resource person. One could say that the student actually initiates learning, especially when choosing a topic for study and preparing for each class session. This represents a major switch from the passive learner we so often see in church classrooms.

Common Goals

Because of role revision, students and teacher can arrive at some common goals. This can happen only when students have clearly thought through what they would like to learn in any classroom experience.

Biblical Funnel

In the diagram above biblical truth refers to axioms we have learned from Scripture. As discussion takes place on any topic, students are encouraged, even pressed, to square their opinions and observations with God's Word. The funnel forms a protection device in the learning experience, guarding against human error and the countless spiritual fallacies of the pagan culture. The goal is to fill the kettle with integrated truth as we discover how Scripture fits into life, that is, how to use it effectively.

Integrated Truth

The first level of integration focuses on truth with content. Dale's class happens to be about parenting, and much of the background literature he is reading, even the resource book for the class, does not always specify biblical truth. So it becomes necessary for Dale and his class members to match up what they read with what they know of Scripture.

The second level has to do with integrating truth with life so that Dale's students can apply what they've learned long after the class finishes. Weekly he reminds them how they function differently as Christians because they know the Bible addresses certain major themes of their lives. Christians look differently at history, philosophy, and even theater and music. Certainly on a topic such as parenting the class can find volumes of biblical requirements and guidelines.

The third level of integration has to do with the student's involvement in this important process. Rather than being dependent on what the teacher says, students should drink at the well of the Scriptures so they can live their lives biblically without constant concern about what Dale says, what the pastor thinks, or what the church believes on a given subject.

As we noted, Dale has been struggling with this. He has used the traditional approach for so long that a transition to cooperative truth integration still seems beyond his grasp.

FOUR STEPS IN INQUIRY LEARNING

Adult ministry requires involvement and inquiry. Perhaps "self-involvement" would be a better way to state it. As Dale catches on to the principles of adult learning, he will want his students to acknowledge that the class is as much theirs as his, and they must take responsibility for learning outcomes, not just depend on him. This next model shows us four steps in discovery learning.

Asking the Right Questions

Whatever the subject matter, we want to arouse in students the right questions about the text or the content. Traditional teachers state questions and give answers. Teachers operating with a contemporary approach throw learning responsibilities back on the student, even if it means waiting a week for an answer that needs more research.

Suggesting Available Resources

Once students have asked the right questions, facilitating teachers must resist the temptation to give quick answers. To be sure, many students want just that and it would expedite class progress. But it doesn't teach students how to use their Bibles and other resources independently. When a teacher gives an answer to a question, that particular issue often closes. But answering a question with another question can help lead the student to a better understanding of truth.

Using Effective Means

On many issues, Dale finds himself stumped. He has a general idea of what the answer might be, but he needs to decide what resource to consult. Concordance? Bible dictionary? Bible encyclopedia? Commentary? The answer might just come through cross-referencing texts or following through on a word study. Dale is responsible not only for doing that but also for teaching his class members how to use those tools as well.

Evaluating Meaning and Application

Quite likely, secular education places too much emphasis on application to the detriment of serious content. Christian education, however, may suffer the opposite malady. We pour thousands of words of biblical information into a class period only to hope and pray that students will do something about it. Hope, yes. Pray, of course. But act as well. Follow-up assignments that make sense in life can help a great deal at this point.

THE TEACHER AS FACILITATOR

Much of the contemporary literature on adult education emphasizes this significant factor of the teacher's role. The word *facilitate* simply means to make easier. Dale's job is not to sound scholarly and confuse everyone with his deep research, but to open the text and let the Holy Spirit shine on the lesson of the day. We'll come back to this in chapter 25, but let's introduce the idea here.

What Facilitators Do

Facilitators create an environment in which people can ask questions because they feel comfortable. They design everything about the classroom experience to create the best physical and psychological climate for learning.

Facilitators also involve learners in mutual planning of methods and curricular decisions. They help class members diagnose their own learning needs, and no need is too nontraditional to be acceptable.

Facilitators encourage learners to formulate their own learning objectives. The word *encourage* is important because we don't want any forcing or pushing here. Facilitators also encourage learners to identify resources and devise strategies to answer their questions and meet their needs.

Facilitators involve learners in evaluating their learning, principally through the use of qualitative techniques rather than centering on the quantitative. In other words, "how well" rather than "how much."

Stephen Brookfield gives a helpful list of "Ways to Enhance Self-Directed Learning." If Dale starts implementing these steps in his classroom, he, too, can become an effective facilitator.

TABLE 2—WAYS TO ENHANCE SELF-DIRECTED LEARNING

1. Progressively decrease the learner's dependency on the teacher.

2. Help the learner to understand how to use learning resources—especially the experiences of others, including the teacher and how to engage others in reciprocal learning relations.

3. Assist the learner to define his or her learning needs.

4. Assist learners to assume increasing responsibility for defining their learning objectives, planning their own learning programs, and evaluating their progress.

5. Organize what is to be learned in relationship to his or her current personal problems, concerns, and levels of understanding.

6. Foster learner decision-making—select learner-relevant experiences, expand the learner's range of options, help learners see perspectives of others.

7. Facilitate problem-posing and problem-solving.

8. Reinforce the self-concept of the learner as a learner and doer by providing for progressive mastery, by giving a supportive climate, with feedback, competitive judgement of others and by using mutual support groups.

9. Emphasize participative instructional methods, and learning contracts.

—Adapted from *Understanding and Facilitating Adult Learning,* Stephen D. Brookfield (San Francisco: Jossey-Bass, 1986), 36–37.

Using a Lesson Plan

What is the purpose of a lesson in Dale's class? How valuable are his written objectives? As he becomes more serious about his facilitating role, he will want to enter each class with a brief lesson plan, which can guide him through the hour. Dale could start with a better understanding of adults, particularly young adults. He should get to know their growth stages, their personal characteristics, and develop effective learning strategies that will work with his class. He needs to pay particular attention to the *objectives* for each lesson, which should always appear on his lesson plan. *Methods* describe what Dale does (and what he encourages his students to do) in the classroom, and *evaluation* serves as a cooperative approach to checking the results.

All this culminates in *feedback*. Improvement in teaching comes as a result of what we learn in evaluation and feedback.

Dale has no idea what students have learned in his class. Occasionally, they will make a complimentary comment or thank him for the hours he puts into study, but he has no solid data regarding their learning. He has always assumed that every time he teaches the class learns, but we know from adult learning research that this is not always true.

Most teachers have seen numerous examples of a lesson plan so this is not a shocking new idea. I've discovered in my own teaching, however, that use of a common lesson plan for all classes helps me think through my priorities in the classroom. The simplified form that you see in Table 3 is built around the acronym COMMA, which focuses on elements we need to consider as we plan our classroom strategies: *Content, Objectives, Methods, Media, and Application.* Perhaps some mixture of these or an adaptation of the model will work better for you. But determine to enter every teaching situation with a lesson plan. Make it clear to yourself and your students that you have a map for the cooperative journey you will undertake.

What can you do about the information in this chapter? First, understand the difference between contemporary and traditional models. Yes, at times we must choose the traditional approach because of the learning level of class members or some other valid reason. But we cannot knowingly choose one or the other until we understand both.

Second, study the discovery teaching model in detail.

Third, become a facilitator. As you work through concepts of inquiry learning and learn how to write lesson plans based on a valid teaching model, you can transform your teaching and your class. Commitment to teaching deserves this kind of attention(and so does your class).

TABLE 3—LESSON PLAN SHEET

Lesson Plan Sheet

Date_____ Text_____ Number_____

Topic_____

Content Outline:

Objectives:
     1.
     2.
     3.

Methods:

Media:

Application (Assignment):

7

~∞∞~

Teaching with Style

S*teve and Cheryl* are at it again. Sunday after Sunday, sometimes over dinner, sometimes not until late evening, they discuss what they learned in Sunday-school that morning. Cheryl enjoys the class. Steve has serious misgivings. Cheryl brings home new ideas, talks often about the class to friends, and usually spends some time in study for next week's class. Steve has confidence in the teacher but somehow does not feel the class meets his needs or stimulates his thinking.

Cheryl and Steve seem very alike in many other ways. They both like tea instead of coffee. They seem to enjoy the same television programs. They even share the same favorite color—green. Why should a Sunday school class be a major point of difference in their lives? Because Steve and Cheryl are different types of learners.

ANALYSIS OF ADULT LEARNERS

Years before the recent research on learning styles, scholars talked about a difference in learning styles. One of those categories describes Cheryl quite well; another points at Steve.

Goal-Oriented Learners

Even the terminology fits the way Cheryl approaches the class, which, by the way, does not differ significantly from the way she approached classes in college. With clear-cut goals in mind, she aims for specific learning outcomes and expects the teacher to provide enough resources to get her there. Furthermore, she wants to achieve these goals as fast as she can and doesn't care what methods and approaches facilitate that kind of goal achievement. For example, several years ago she developed an interest in prophecy after hearing several radio messages on that topic. She checked books out of a church library, talked with the pastor about some sticky questions, and within two or three months became a serious student of Bible prophecy—even without any formal class. People who know Steve would tell you immediately that none of this sounds like him.

Activity-Oriented Learners

Steve cares about process. Yes, he has learning goals, but he cares as much about *how* he learns as he does about the final product. In fact, if he does not enjoy the process, he will often bail out before he ever gets to the end product. He couldn't understand Cheryl's interest in prophecy, especially her persistence in doing so much work on her own. Steve struggles with this present class because the teacher rarely uses a variety of methods, and the ones he chooses seem unappealing.

Content-Oriented Learners

A few folks in that same class are unlike either Steve or Cheryl. They seem to want education for education's sake. Their end goal is information and they are willing to stay with a situation until the information comes. When they learn the subject of the moment, they pursue information on another subject. This kind of learner can stay in school for a long time and often ends up becoming a professor, quite possibly in some heavy content area.

There is no problem with any of this so long as we recognize that learning styles exist and we take these into consideration in the way we approach adult ministry options in churches and Christian organizations.

Not only do we know much more about adult learning now than ever before, but we also have more demographic information about adults in general and particularly young adults. A declining work ethic appears to be one of the long-term trends affecting the United States, and focus has shifted from remuneration (salary and benefits) to the advantage work provides for the worker. That shift reflects the high priority of time over money as the number one currency of our society.

Another current trend is called "cocooning," a return to the home as the center of all life's activities and relationships, from running a telemarketing program for employment to playing Trival Pursuit or Pictionary on Friday nights. The question is, How will churches respond? How will we offer the Steves and Cheryls of our congregations learning options that meet their needs and relate to their personal learning styles?

LEARNING STYLE GRID

Although they are bright young adults, Steve and Cheryl don't even know they have learning styles and could never conclude that such a distinction would cause their differences in evaluating the class. But that is the most primary level of differentiation. Research by David Kolb, Bernice McCarthy, and others has identified four potential styles of adult learners.[1] But before we look at them, let's remember that when researchers speak of only two styles, they are probably talking about analytical and relational. Analytical learners interact best with content; relational learners interact best with other people.

Obviously a good bit of this is based on left brain/right brain research. Left-brained people tend to focus on facts, structures, and organization. Right-brained people lean toward more intuitive and participational approaches to thinking and learning. The term learning style affords no mystery or complication; it simply refers to some consistent way in which learners respond to educational experiences.

Analytic

Obviously all learners analyze, though they do it differently. This first group has also been called "convergers" or "thinkers." These largely left-brained people approach learning by watching, reflecting, and sticking strictly to a sequence of content. They enjoy the sheer joy of thinking through problems, quandaries, dilemmas, and so on, and need order and design in the learning experience. I can relate here. In my office everything needs to be where it should be with no piles lying on the desk or anywhere else. Disorder somehow upsets my rational equilibrium. When I listen to someone preach, I want the text dealt with in sequence, with point four logically following point three and a clear distinction made between them.

Learners like that are also time conscious. People in this category may not be patient with process because process takes times. That doesn't make process any less important, but thinking-style learners may not prioritize that part of the educational experience. We should recognize that people like this may learn with little concern for process. When they teach, they can overcome that inclination and assist other types of learners by emphasizing process. Leaders discipline themselves to do what is important and right even though it may not always fit their preferred behavior. Teachers of adults must constantly remind themselves that not all people in their classes learn the way they do.

What teaching strategies seem to work best with people like this? *Lecture* serves well because lectures are usually rational and sequential. *Analysis of problems* fits in this category, putting students in a position to study and draw conclusions on some problem or passage. *Question and answer* works also because it tends to follow a reasonable pattern. *Research, programmed instruction, memorization*—methods like these attract and retain the attention of analytic-style learners.

Dynamic

Other terms we might find here include "accommodators" and "sensors." These people are primarily doers, bored by sitting and taking notes. They tend to be skill-oriented (liking things because they do them well), present-focused, practical, and involved in the learning process. In leadership situations, analytical types need dynamic types on the team to complement their efforts. And that works both ways.

Learning strategies for this group include *case studies, group work, expressional activities, brainstorming,* and a heavy use of *media.* Already you see that comparing the first two categories has moved us from left to right in the brain department.

Innovative

The learning characteristics of this group differ dramatically from that of the analytics, less so from that of the sensors. This crowd is people-oriented, somewhat disorganized, loyal to authority, verbally involved, and concerned about keeping everyone happy. This last item is consistent with their concern with process in learning. Once again on a personal note, just as category one described me, this category describes my wife. How do people like her learn most effectively? *Personal sharing, small groups, stories, team activities,* and a heavy use of *visual media* are all important. Those same learning strategies will work with other groups as well, but they seem best suited to innovative types. Do not look for a fixed line of demarcation between any of these categories. Nevertheless, if learning-style research is valid, we need to recognize the important distinctions.

Intuitive

Sometimes called "assimilators," intuitive people tend to be private, independent, quite flexible, and change-oriented. In the learning process they are likely to take risks; they constantly look for new challenges; and they want application of their learning. Common sense is a major commodity in this group.

How does this group learn best? Since we already know that learning strategies are not distinctly unique to each category, we should not be surprised to see methods like *research, problem solving,* and *independent study* showing up again. Throw in a few *debates, experiments,* and just a dash of creativity and the picture begins to form.

Every reader may be saying about this point, "I don't see myself locked into any one of these." That's probably true. Most of us lean toward a combination of at least two, although some may feel that one of the four describes them quite accurately. If we plot all four of these on a quadrant model as in diagram 10, we get a better overall picture.

DIAGRAM 10—RELATIONSHIPS OF LEARNING STYLES

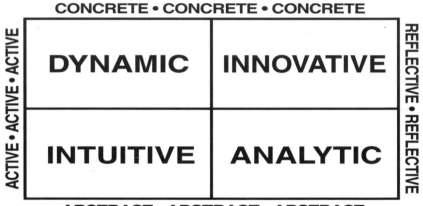

QUADRANT LEARNING STYLE MODEL

This kind of quadrant diagram is common in almost all fields of study, certainly in leadership and education. Notice the styles are identified the same way we looked at them above, with Analytic in the lower right quadrant, Dynamic in the upper left, Innovative in the upper right, and Intuitive in the lower left. Notice the words that surround the rectangle. Concrete thinking emphasizes dealing with firm facts and informational data we can count on—engineering would be an obvious example. The opposite type of thinking is abstract, pondering what angels might really look like or how sincere Christians come to various interpretations of various parts of the Bible. The left side of the diagram emphasizes an active learning process and the right side, a reflective learning process.

Suppose that in the last few pages you saw yourself as an analytic/intuitive learner. That suggests you feel comfortable dealing with abstract ideas, ambiguities, and that you are quite willing to wait until options make sense before you decide an important matter. Or you may see yourself across the top as a dynamic/innovative learner given to concrete ideas. In learning situations you want that kind of information. Reflective learners on the analytic/innovative side of the diagram want to think about ideas for a while. Not do anything, just think. People on the left side form the dynamic/intuitive team, a group who want active involvement in the learning process.

Just a word of warning at this point. Like a lot of research in adult education, these suggested categories have enough data to warrant our attention. But we should not view them as absolute; they are merely one possible way of looking at the way adults learn. We can start with this kind of information, assess ourselves as learners, and then move to the teaching role and ask how people in our classes respond and why. We might even get specific enough to wonder whether we can design learning experiences that meet the needs of different learning types within the framework.

An old question-cliché has stumbled around education for decades: What is the only bad teaching method? People sometimes answer "lecture," something they have seen too often in classrooms. But that is not the right answer. Lectures can be exciting and some learning types thrive on them. The only bad teaching method is the one we use *all* the time—whatever that is. When teachers use a single type of teaching strategy continuously, they probably overfeed a certain learning-style group and underfeed other learning-style groups. The best choice of classroom strategy for adult education emphasizes variety. Except in classes small enough to allow personally designed learning patterns that fit every individual style, facilitating teachers utilize several, a variety of methods.

So think about the adult Sunday school classes you have known. How many different teaching methods could you count in one class period? In a month? In a quarter? In a year? Sadly, one of the negative hallmarks of adult ministry in many congregations is a predictable sameness.

One more thought before we leave this section. Remember Steve and Cheryl? I have deliberately avoided categorizing them because I want you to do that. On the basis of what you know about them, and what you know about learning styles, where would you place Steve and Cheryl on the quadrant model? Take a pencil and write their names where you think they should go. Put yourself in as well.

MOTIVATING ADULTS EDUCATIONALLY

When students talk about what they want to learn in my adult-education courses, they usually get around to the issue of motivation—what prompts adults to get seriously involved in study. We can sit in committee meetings and complain over and over again how people should want to study God's Word. But veteran church leaders know that "ought" is far away from "will." People *ought* to come to church. People *ought* to study their Bibles. People *ought* to pray consistently. But in the real world, people don't always do what they ought to do—not even Christians. Furthermore, saying that people ought to do something provides not the smallest step toward motivating them; it is not a very useful way to spend our ministry time.

Virtually every aspect of adult learning, certainly including motivation, centers in unleashing an awareness of needs. What kind of needs? What do we know about this in general that we can apply to people in our own churches?

Relationship Needs

Not every adult will admit it, but many hunger for closer "belongingness." Once again, different learning-style types will respond differently to this need category, but generally speaking, confidence that some group of people cares about us, prays for us, and loves us with all our failings is something we all long for. The small-group movement is popular among evangelicals. Call them shepherding groups, cell groups, mini churches, flock groups, or whatever name you prefer—they work. Increasingly, congregations (especially larger ones), are moving toward small-group experiences that meet relational needs.

Recognition Needs

Besides loving us and praying for us, people in small groups recognize our importance. Everybody needs to feel a part of something, to be recognized by others. How rare to engage in conversation with someone who seems genuinely interested in us—but how pleasant as well.

But small groups can quickly degenerate into nothing but verbal therapy. Sometimes the group starts out with a clear focus on Bible study but ends up settling for coffee, donuts, and small talk. That places too great an emphasis on process and insufficient attention to product. Without ignoring the practicality and immediacy of adult learning, we acknowledge that solid biblical and theological content must be central to a church learning experience.

Reality Needs

I keep using words like "implement" and "practicality" because they genuinely describe effective adult education. *Adults learn by constantly inquiring why, not what.* Why this and not something else? Why now instead of later? Why two services instead of a daughter church? Why guitars and a worship team instead of the choir? A detailed explanation of the differences between the seraphim and cherubim may fascinate some, but most adults learn best when the content meets needs they understand, when they can activate what they learn as quickly as possible, and when they can assimilate lessons learned from the behavioral traits of a positive role model.

Roberta Hestenes, president of Eastern College, St. David's, Pennsylvania, has modeled adult education for years. After reviewing some of the basic andragogical guidelines we have talked about in earlier chapters, she addresses the issue of physical surroundings.

> The room itself must respect adult sensibilities. Many church classrooms smell old and stale. Some churches consign adult classes to a dungeon-like basement with cracked linoleum floors; cold, hard folding chairs; and children's Sunday-school posters from the sixties. Churches that feel inviting to adults give adult classes windows, sunlight, fresh air, clean bathrooms, fresh paint, attractive visuals, comfortable chairs—in short, the signs of a place that is alive and open. Another consideration: Do we put visitors on the spot? People in church cultures vary, but the older I get, the less I'm willing to enter a new situation and stand up and

talk about myself. If I'm made to feel uncomfortable in a given social climate, I tend to avoid it thereafter.[2]

Good advice. Anything that enhances our attention to adult needs, unleashes internal motivation, and activates learning styles should appear high on the priority list.

PART 2

Age Groups for Adult Ministries

8

The Millennials Are Coming!

The Millennials are coming! No this is not a new cult; it is a group of people born about 1980 who are now coming into adulthood. Sociologists tell us they differ greatly from the Sponsor generation, the Boomers, the Busters, (sometimes called Generation Xers), and just about every double-decade group before them. We'll talk about the Boomers, too, but we start with the youngest adult category because, like it or not, we must deal with them as adults who are no longer kids. William Strauss coined the term Millennials, and other sociological demographers describe them in interesting terms:

- This generation's pulse runs fast. Bombarded by frequent images, they are in need of continual "hits."

- The remote control symbolizes their reality: Change is constant; focus is fragmented.

- They have eaten from the tree of knowledge.

- They live for now.

- They are jaded, having a "been there/done that" attitude; nothing shocks them.

- They take consumerism for granted.

- They are a cyber-suckled community.

- They process information in narrative images (like Nike commercials).

- They've had everything handed to them.

- They don't trust adults.[1]

Mark Senter, long an expert on youth ministry, warns us that we had better throw aside our emphasis on entertainment, the "trickle-down strategy" (reaching leaders in hopes they'll attract followers), and the old patterns of assimilation. Those in this group will reach age twenty in the year 2000 and twenty-five in 2005. They are the new young adults. But before we emphasize one group too heavily, we should spread our thinking over the entire young-adult population, which I choose to group by experience rather than age, though the general age bracket for young adults can be viewed as eighteen to thirty-four.

FIVE YOUNG-ADULT GROUPS

Traditionally we have divided adults into specific age-groups, the larger the church, the more specific the group. Small churches might have just one adult class. Larger churches may have young adults, middle adults, and older adults (though they might not use those terms). Even larger churches might group by decade—adults in their twenties, thirties, and so forth. But as I have emphasized in earlier chapters, life experience and developmental tasks tend to be more important ingredients in the learning process than age.

College/Career Beginners

Obviously most Millennials would be in this group, though with increasing enrollments colleges are seeing older students, and many graduate schools report that their average student age is in the thirties. Most people in the college/career group are singles, but I want to return to that as a separate category in just a moment. Here we look at people still exploring career opportunities, looking for a job, selecting a life partner, perhaps preparing for marriage and learning how to manage money. Even though most of the young adults in your church who fit this experience category may also fall into the eighteen to twenty-two age-group, ages may vary significantly.

Young Couples

Young couples or young marrieds face a set of developmental tasks different from that of the college/career crowd. They may still be in the same age group, but a different set of experiences calls for different educational approaches. These people are learning to get along at work, adjusting to spouses, preparing for children, managing a home, and, perhaps most important of all, surrendering their independence.

Generations ago, graduating from college and getting married looked like twins; one took place within a few years of the other. Today we face a different world; that connection between graduation and marriage is no longer a norm among young adults, even though it does still occur with some frequency.

New Parents

As adults become parents, they move miles away from the first two categories of college/career beginners and young marrieds. Here we talk about family planning, development of parental skills, understanding children, developing family unity, and in some cases suddenly adjusting to a single income. Only one of those developmental tasks (family unity) faces either of the first two groups.

Parents of Teens

People in the eighteen to thirty-four age group are parents of teens only if they married early and became parents early. Parenting teenagers may very well fall completely into the next age bracket or at least straddle the latter years of this one and the early years of the next. Recently I talked to a friend whose adopted daughter will not be a teenager until after he retires! That may be an exception, but whereas parenting teenagers used to be a challenge for people in their thirties, in today's world it may occur more commonly during the forties. Regardless of age, adults in this group must deal with peer pressure, potential rebellion, sibling rivalry, and teens solidifying their own career choices.

Singles

This catchall category allows us space for adults who don't fit any of the other groups. We'll discuss single adults in a later chapter so we can bypass mention of their developmental tasks at this point. Most people in the college/career category are single, and every age group except young couples could contain singles.

Never-married singles may tend to move in and out of careers, trying to find just the right way to make a living. On the other hand, a thirty-seven-year-old divorced mother of three may be so locked into a job she desperately needs that life seems to have no variation at all.

KEYS TO YOUNG-ADULT MINISTRY

Perhaps my word choice is a bit dangerous since the word *keys* almost implies that some simple formulas might lie on the horizon. But some guidelines learned through research, experience, and even observation can help us approach ministry to this group more effectively.

Key Word

A key word that describes this age group is *intimacy*. But we must take it in its broad sense—intimacy with friends and with family, in some cases recaptured after years of alienation. Anyone who has worked with college students has had opportunity to observe how much their parents "seem to grow up" during the four or five years they spend in college. Sometimes those students even fail to acknowledge that the major change has come in their own lives.

Intimacy of friendships between adults is not only different but is greater than that of parent-child relationships. But do the Millennials admit this key need? They might not, but their denial doesn't make it any less so.

Key Problem

For many churches the key problem in this age bracket is the *newly married dropout*. Free from their parents, now on their own, paying their own mortgage, and buying their own cars, young adults suddenly feel free to shake loose from the ties of the past—even church. Their key life patterns are marked by variety and change—entering college, leaving college, taking a job, not liking that job, taking another job, moving several times. Those who have developed a genuine disciple-relationship with Jesus Christ will not be shaken into confusion and laxity during this tumultuous time of life. However, many who have come through the church do not have that solidarity and become dropouts.

Key Responses

Knowing that these adults face confusion and uncertainty, the congregation should respond with *acceptance* and *affirmation*. Affirmation of young adulthood. Acceptance of singleness. Affirmation of the importance of the church's ministry. At twenty-three, one can easily think the church is controlled totally by people over sixty who have no interest in young-adult opinions and no concern about young-adult needs. In some churches that may be true. Churches wanting to develop dynamic adult ministries will reach out and show people in this age bracket how they fit into congregational life.

Key Personal Problem

Especially among singles, but sometimes even for young couples, aloneness is a major issue. This is not the same as loneliness. Loneliness is a negative feeling, an emotion that could develop from aloneness. Aloneness does not necessarily imply social or emotional deficiency. And aloneness does not mean "all by myself."

Laura and Seth grew up in the same town. Their parents knew each other, and they went to the same church, met at the youth group, graduated from the same high school, and went off to the same college. Now married, they live four hundred miles away. They are not alone in any technical sense; they have each other. But the old friends are gone, and parents are far away. In new towns they feel like outsiders in their jobs, their church, and their community—aloneness.

Aloneness exists in college as well. Most college students grow out of it rather quickly, but the first few weeks can be terrifying for young people who have been close to their parents and raised in a somewhat sheltered setting.

Key Transition

All adult age groupings probably contain a key transition year (or years), and in the young-adult group it usually falls right around thirty, perhaps between twenty-eight and thirty-two. The mere crossing of the decade does not hold the terror it once did, though people in the thirty-something category often talk about how old they feel. There is a sense in which this transition forces us to leave "young people" behind and move on to something else. But we need to remember that age is not the issue. Experiences that accompany transition make the difference—marriage, first child, new job, and other major changes.

EFFECTIVENESS IN YOUNG-ADULT MINISTRY

One must constantly think through sociodemographic group shifts—like the Millennials, for example. So the following paragraphs attempt to deal with practical ministry reality in the late nineties and into the next century. These contemporary suggestions find their basis in traditionally prescribed needs of young adults, a menu worth reviewing here.

What kind of churches and what kind of adult ministry programs will be effective in the present and the future to serve young adults?

TABLE 4—GENERAL LEARNING NEEDS
OF YOUNG ADULTS

Familial

1. Choosing marriage or singleness
2. Learning to live in a marital role
3. Setting standards and values for the home
4. Preparing for the coming of children
5. Nuturing children and young teens
6. Growing in ability to manage a home

Vocational

1. Choosing and getting started in an occupation
2. Striving for status in a company or organization
3. Improving on professionalism and efficiency

Physical

1. Establishing wholesome standards of personal health and nutrition
2. Controlling sexual desires
3. Avoiding stress
4. Practicing intimacy with discretion

Social

1. Finding a congenial social group
2. Participating in constructive leisure-time activities
3. Achieving socially responsible behavior
4. Adopting motives and standards for social relationships—criteria for friendships

Economic

1. Achieving economic independence from parents
2. Living within family income
3. Facing the issue of a working wife and/or mother
4. Anticipating educational expenses for children

Spiritual

1. Evaluating conversion and spiritual growth
2. Developing a Christian world-view
3. Establishing effective worship patterns—public and private
4. Growing in Bible study and prayer
5. Increasing in ability to witness
6. Growing in understanding of theology

Churches That Meet Needs

Young adults in the twenty-first century will likely gravitate to churches that understand and do something about stability, identity, resolution, refuge, affirmation, and intimacy. That should be no surprise after what we've said about adults in general. We should expect that need-meeting churches will be attractive, and in my opinion this is a trend, not a trickle. Our society constantly drives people to ask, "What are you doing for me?" We can counter that by falling back on the "oughts," but that will do us and them no good. Instead, we can make some effort to unlock the motivational drives discussed in chapter 7 and determine that we will be churches that seek to meet our people's needs.

Churches That Unleash Motivation

Interestingly, certain identifiable factors unleash attendance motivation in adults. And sometimes they surprise us. We might want them to ask, "How good is the teacher?" But they may ask, "How good is the parking?" We might want them to ask, "Is the Bible seriously taught?" But they may ask, "How clean is the nursery?" Would you like to guess how many people stay away from churches because of sloppy nurseries? Broken toys may frighten away as many families as broken theology.

Part of this, of course, comes from Boomer attitudes and value systems, another topic still ahead of us in this book. If a couple drives to church in a Lexus because he practices law and she practices nursing and they bring little Melanie into a nursery that looks as if it hasn't been refurbished since 1950, we can see an identifiable factor that hinders motivation.

Churches That Understand Developmental Tasks

The felt needs of young adults tend to conform to those described by developmental researchers. To put that another way, what we see in the listing of developmental tasks for this age group tends to be borne out in their felt needs. Look again at the list of general learning needs of young adults. We want people in this age group to look at a list like that and say, "Yes, that's me. That's where I am. How can you help me?"

Churches That Provide Vital Relationships

Age-group isolation deprives people of relationships that might flourish in wider intergenerational settings. I have suggested several times that age might not be the best way to group people for adult-learning experiences. Age-group isolation also restricts people from making contact with others, and they lose a lot of life that way. Intergenerational learning (two or more generations studying together in the same group), is difficult to design, but when it works well, everyone benefits (see chapter 25).

Churches That Create an Opportunity for Intimacy Building

If intimacy is the key word, we need to figure out how to provide for it. Cutting-edge congregations provide young adults with opportunities to develop intimate relationships in which hopes and dreams can be shared without rejection; mistakes and sins can be confessed without judgmental criticism; moods and feelings can be revealed without a call for explanations. Yes, that could describe a marriage; but it could also describe a same-sex friendship (such as David and Jonathan). Certainly intimacy has potential sexual overtones, but genuine friendships thrive outside the boundaries of romance, sex, and marriage.

We still have much to learn about friendship from Scripture. Dennis Hiebert, a conservative evangelical scholar, observes, "It is possible that cross-sex friendship may be one of the more constructive means of finding interpersonal warmth in the 'chilly climate' of gender relations and interpersonal peace in the 'moral panic' of sexual correctness. We may still be a long way from having Christian social permission to phone our neighbor's spouse just to talk, or even to invite him or her to church. But cross-sex friendships at least provide men and women with an 'insider's perspective' to the other sex and an opportunity to bridge differences.... Bridging differences is what Christian community is about. The church needs to 'offer to the world models of deep friendships built on the character, the faithfulness of God.' "[2]

Churches That Create Structures for Mentoring Relationships

Primarily such relationships should develop between older adults and young adults. These structures could be widely varied: an elder developing an elder-in-training; a veteran Sunday school teacher working with a rookie; an older woman mentoring a younger woman in the pattern of Titus 2:3–5.

Yes, the Millennials are coming. And meanwhile, we still have plenty of GenXers in this age-group. So we rework our thinking and stick those keys in the doors in order to minister effectively to young adults in our churches.

9

❧⚜❧

Boosting the Busters

More than 46 million Americans were born between 1965 and 1983, the generation immediately following the Boomers. Normally we talk about demographic generations in the order of their appearance throughout the century—Sponsors, Boomers, Busters, Xers, and Millennials. But in this book we are working our way up the adult age chain, thereby encountering the Baby Busters next. In the year 2000 the oldest Buster will be thirty-five and the youngest seventeen. True, the seventeen-year-old will probably still be in high school and therefore not involved in the parameters of adult ministry. But by 2001 almost every Buster will fit our young-adult category and older ones will have moved into what we will call "middle adulthood."

Baby Busters represent the second largest group of young adults in U.S. history. They also became the first generation of latchkey kids, many of them the products of dual-career households. Thirteen million of them turned thirty in 1998. Demographers tells us they have created their own pop culture known as "grunge," meaning slovenly, asexual, and anti-fashion. Obviously such terms do not describe everyone in the group, but to grasp the accuracy of the generalization, one need only hang out at a mall anytime during the nineties and watch groups of teenagers pass by. As a cultural group Baby Busters tend to be somewhat angry, culturally dislocated, yet with a secret yearning to belong. They like to think they live life on the edge, and many do.

An insightful paragraph in *Business Week* tells us that "except for their collective sense of foreboding, busters have little in common with each other. Where boomers were united by pivotal events, such as the Vietnam war and Watergate, busters have been left largely unmoved by their era's low-cal war, Operation Desert Storm, and scandal-lite Iran-Contra."[1]

But like their Boomer predecessors, Busters have become more traditional with age. Part of that tradition is marriage, shaky and later in life though it may be. This chapter moves us from a general look at young adults to a more fixed focus on how to minister to young married adults. Keep in mind that the age may vary and, as in chapter 8, we are still looking at people in the eighteen to thirty-four age bracket.

HOW ARE YOUNG MARRIED ADULTS DIFFERENT?

That word *different* comes up often in a book like this. Adults differ from children and young people. Single adults differ from married adults. Young adults differ from older adults—and so it goes. Here we want to notice the marks of this particular age group as they stand in contrast to middle adulthood and older adulthood. To do so, we take a look at Stephanie and Brian. They belong to the thirteen million people we call young marrieds. If they attended your church and you wanted to minister effectively to them, what would you need to know?

Struggling with Repersonalization

Young married adults are people in process for whom change occurs with great rapidity. Stephanie and Brian are "becoming," discovering themselves individually and collectively. Repersonalization as a couple follows depersonalization in that long, arduous journey from adolescence to adulthood. Along the way they encountered the jostling experiences of college and career, the trauma of leaving one family and forming another, and the gap of aloneness so many adults go through in their twenties. Brian is a gifted young man and someday he will be very effective in ministry. Right now he has not yet found a spiritual identity, and his church seems unsure of how to help him.

Shaking Loose from Peer Pressure

In one sense none of us develops a total immunity to peer pressure. I happen to be one among thousands (perhaps millions) of men who wear ties only when cultural protocol demands it. We find no logical reason to twist cloth around our necks and then tighten it like a hangman's noose. It doesn't hold the shirt on; it can't protect from drafts; and the knot rarely comes out right the first time. To be sure, many tie-wearers consider themselves more properly dressed and "don't leave home without it." As I see it, such strange behavior can be attributed only to peer pressure—and some nefarious plot concocted by a French designer.

But most young married adults have intentionally shaken the influence that dominated their lives for more than a decade—other kids. Part of becoming a genuine adult lies in realizing that one does not have to do something because others do it. Nor does one have to pretend to be what he or she is not. As the old pop song put it, "I Gotta Be Me."

Learning Time Priorities

Many young adults begin learning time management in college, or perhaps even on their first job, but in both cases their priorities tend to be imposed by others. Adulthood means learning to utilize discretionary time. One finds little discretionary time in knowing that mom serves dinner promptly at 6:00 P.M., or that the college cafeteria closes its lunch line at 1:00 P.M. Few people can escape fixed time claims entirely, but moving into adulthood means guarding and caring about discretionary time. Stephanie gets home from work about six o'clock. She and Brian try to be in bed each night by eleven. Since her job doesn't require bringing home evening work, she has approximately five hours of discretionary time each evening. Since she recently became pregnant, a whole new pattern of time management will be required in a few more months.

Facing the Economic Bind

Obviously the spectrum of domestic finances can run from wealth to poverty. Throughout the nineties we have read about "instant millionaires," people who invented computer programs of some kind or perhaps own stock options in a company whose rapid growth put more and more money in their bank accounts. Most of us belong to the working class, which may mean moving from a rental apartment to a small house and learning to manage a budget. With a baby coming, and the possibility that Stephanie will stop working for a few years, the economic bind has become reality.

Finding an Adult Group

Unless people live in the same general area throughout most of their adult lives, the search for new friends is unending. Twenty percent of all Americans move every year—and they rarely take their friends with them. Amid all the other pressures they have faced, Stephanie and Brian need to make new friends—friends whose values will influence their immediate adult group during crucial years. Of all the life tasks young married adults face, perhaps the church can help most effectively with this one.

Developing a Dream

Brian and Stephanie have written countless lists over the four years of their relationship. For many young couples those lists about houses, cars, jobs, or income goals are dreams in the developmental process. Not all young married adults dream about retiring at age fifty with two or three million dollars in the bank. Some dream about an earned doctorate; others about serving God on the mission field; many dream about raising godly children. Dreaming is part of the age-group, and the more clearly their dreams connect to an awareness of God's gifts and His will for their lives, the more Brian and Stephanie will find spiritual and relational fulfillment in their marriage.

Starting a Career

Rarely do freshmen enter college with any understanding of what they will do when they graduate. One characteristic of our increasingly complex society shows itself in the changing of careers throughout adulthood. During those four or five decades American adults on average change jobs seven times and careers three times. Currently Brian works as a systems analyst and he is a good one. But he keeps telling Stephanie he would like to do graduate work in engineering, a dream they must explore in light of the coming baby.

Accepting Responsibility

So much of childhood and adolescence consists of taking; adulthood is a time to start giving. Married adults give to each other, to God, to the church, and to the community. Not just money, but a portion of themselves. Stephanie and Brian are about to hear a literal wake-up call to sacrifice the first night that baby comes home from the hospital.

PREPARING TO BE PARENTS

It seems as though Stephanie and Brian talk about little else these days. In some churches this dramatic moment in their lives might go unnoticed until the baby is born. Then after a few weeks of fuss and flurry, they could be on their own again. Most congregations need to gear up to help young married adults expecting and raising children. The program is so simple virtually any church could do it (see chapter 16).

Understanding Biblical Parenting

Through literature, classes, and some counseling, an effective church helps its young married adults grasp the true nature of children. Young parents learn to understand that the culture is wrong when it tells them children are essentially good until some external environmental force makes them bad. If young parents follow through on what they learn in God's Word, they can create a disciplined rather than permissive home for their new baby. This part of parenting education is rarely handled by churches.

Giving Unconditional Love

Parenting begins with unconditional love between husband and wife. Whatever happens in our lives, however far we might stray, however rebellious we might become, our heavenly Father cares for us, and we count on His unconditional love. Parents who know and walk in the light of that love can unconditionally love each other, and only then can they love their children unconditionally. Godly Christian parents love their children even when they misbehave in the worst possible way. God makes that possible because the Holy Spirit produces Jesus' love in the family.

Learning Sincere Forgiveness

Mutual forgiveness between children and parents is very much a part of Christian family living. Discipline and forgiveness go hand in hand, and either one without the other keeps us domestically crippled in dealing with our kids because children have an inborn sin nature. But they also carry the image of God, potentially redeemable by grace.

Providing Christian Day Care

As a pastor and Christian educator I have wrestled with this question through the years. In a perfect world, mothers would stay home and raise their children, and churches would take the responsibility to help them do so. Programs like Mothers of Preschoolers (MOPS) and Mother's Day Out have proven their value for many years. In addition, the church should reeducate today's parents about the sanctity of the home and the responsibility of raising their children as a heritage from God. Part of that education can focus on the potential dangers facing children who are constantly left at a day-care center.

But the world we live in is far from perfect. We know that an increasing number of parents are using some kind of childcare facility. Wealthy families might pay over $10,000 a year for an all-day preschool program. The new Early Head Start for children under three had only 22,000 slots for 2.9 million eligible children in mid-1997. According to *Newsweek,* "With federal welfare reform pushing more mothers of young children into the work force, demand is expected to reach record levels. More parents will have to patch together a makeshift sitter system. 'There is too much freelancing with these kids already,' says Ron Lally, director of the Center of Child and Family Studies in San Francisco."[2]

The magazine's same issue published a chart released by the U.S. Department of Education, showing the percentages of children in each age group in time spent away from their parents.[3] Of one-year olds, 24 percent are cared for by relatives, 17 percent are watched by paid baby-sitters, and 7 percent by day-care centers. But of five-year-olds, the percentage who are cared for by relatives drops to 15 percent and the portion cared for by sitters remains about the same as for one-year-olds. However, 75 percent of five-year-olds are cared for in day-care centers!

So many church facilities lie dormant for much of the week. Might Christian day-care centers be a whole new avenue of ministry and outreach? Yes. Some congregations already have effective programs in their communities, yet a national surge of evangelical day-care centers could provide safe, nurturing care for children from the congregation and an opportunity to share the gospel with many in the community. What would happen if a half million children were enrolled in day-care centers operated by evangelical congregations during the first five years of the new century? It seems worth thinking about.

Churches effectively ministering to young married adults today have something of interest and importance to say. Seminars and studies that show scriptural relevance can warm the hearts of the most detached Busters as they face the demands of an uncaring and dysfunctional world. As we approach the twenty-first century, there seems to be little normality in family life. Hundreds of people divorce because they find their spouses' personalities "incompatible." Hundreds more couples divorce because they do not agree on how to raise their children. Congregations that help adults during these crucial "becoming" years will have opportunity to disciple a generation desperately in need of spiritual nurture.

Effective churches offer instruction, modeling, and experience; they teach young parents how to reproduce these significant ingredients in their own families. In the affective dimension of learning, they work on developing biblical attitudes. They teach young adults and young parents how to communicate proper attitudes toward each other, the Bible, God, friends, neighbors, and society at large. Those attitudes form the atmosphere in which children learn about people. Everything parents say or imply about the Bible contributes to their children's attraction or aversion to scriptural truth. Passion is important, but so also is progression; first godly people, then godly partners, then godly parents.

ONE WAY

Worship

Public worship is important to young Christian adults. And we should make no assumptions about worship style, as controversial as that topic has become at the turn of the millennium. Many churches have chosen a blended worship program, including modern choruses along with traditional hymns. Both Stephanie and Brian love music so they look forward to Sunday as a highlight of their week.

Fellowship

This word means different things to our sample couple. To Brian it means the church softball team; for Stephanie it means Saturday morning Bible studies. For many young adults fellowship means finding a special group of friends we talked about earlier.

Instruction

Effective churches assess needs, set objectives, and proceed with a serious course of study that can bring their young adults "up to speed" in Bible knowledge and their ability to use it. Classes will be interesting, relevant, and participational in style. Brian and Stephanie are in for some serious discovery learning.

Service

This one word can describe that journey from taking to giving. Brian needs to be involved in the church in more ways than playing second base on the softball team. Though Stephanie may not be ready yet, she could someday become the teacher of the Bible-study group she attends. Within a few years these Busters may very well become productive growing members of their church family.

1O

❧

Caught in the Middle

When Dante was thirty-five years old and frustrated in his quest for a political position, he wrote the first lines of *The Inferno*. Many look back to those brief words penned in 1300 as the first recognition of what we today call midlife crisis.

> Mid way in life's journey I was made aware
> That I had strayed into a dark forest,
> And the right path appeared not anywhere.

What exactly is middle adulthood? When the American Board of Family Practice asked a random sampling of twelve hundred Americans when middle age begins, 41 percent said it starts when you worry about having enough money for healthcare concerns; 42 percent said it was when your last child moves out; and 46 percent said it was when you don't recognize the names of music groups on the radio anymore.[1] For purposes of this book we will put an age label on middle adulthood—thirty-five to sixty-five. With an increasing number of Boomers retiring in their early fifties and mid-fifties, those boundaries might be narrowed in the years ahead, but for now a thirty-year spread is about all we can handle. Obviously that puts all the Boomers right into middle adulthood as this book goes to print.

UNDERSTANDING THE BOOMERS

Born between 1946 and 1964, Boomers now clog the veins of middle adulthood. The first Boomer hit the age of fifty in 1996 and every seven seconds for the following sixteen years another Baby Boomer will turn fifty. By 2010, one in every six Americans will be over sixty-five as the Boomers move from middle to older adulthood.

What Are They Like?

Boomers tend to show low loyalty to churches, car dealerships, and stocks. They live in the world of what's happening now. If Honda comes out with a better product than Nissan, they think nothing of making an immediate switch. Dad, on the other hand, stayed a loyal Ford man all his life. Of course, he had limited options compared to his Boomer kids.

We have seen something of a trend reversal in Boomer attitudes toward church, particularly in the first half of the nineties. Wade Clark Rufe, a sociologist at the University of California at Santa Barbara, notes that a third of the Boomers never strayed from church, and another 25 percent are defectors who have returned but are usually less tied to tradition and less dependable as members. *Time* magazine tells us that "the returnees are still vastly outnumbered by the 42% of baby boomers who remain drop outs from formal religion . . . two potent events that might draw drop outs back to the fold are having children and facing at mid-life a personal or career crisis that reminds boomers of the need for moorings."[2]

Boomers are also people of *high expectations*. Boomers' parents lived through World War II, guided in turn by their own parents who had struggled through the Depression. Limited in experiences and possessions, they determined to make their children's lives just the opposite—and they grandly succeeded. Grandpa was glad to make a pair of jeans last another six months. Boomers, however, want the right label in a strategically visible place—never mind the cost.

Boomers represent *wide diversity*. On one hand demographers like to characterize them as a rather homogeneous lot, but one of the characteristics of the group tells us that Boomer watchers should be ready for preference swings one way or the other. The diversity shows itself in clothing styles, attitudes toward marriage and children, and behavior toward church membership. Many Boomers have turned away from the faith of their parents, while others have found new levels of commitment.

We're told Boomers are *politically pluralistic.* Throughout much of the nineties we had a Boomer president, and one would have expected to find he was elected largely by Boomer votes. But in fact a significant percentage of Boomers would consider their politics more conservative than those of the president, and Boomers as a group could hardly be credited with whisking Mr. Clinton from Little Rock to Washington.

Boomers are *significantly influential.* Not only the president but many of his advisers and official staff are part of this highly visible generation. Since they have now reached middle adulthood and have assumed leadership of corporations, churches, and culture, they will make significant political, financial, and religious decisions for this country for many years to come.

How Do We Minister to Boomers?

We start by designing *need-oriented* churches, just as we have described throughout this book. Boomers understand felt needs better than any adult age group in recent history, and they are quite prepared to make decisions on the basis of that awareness.

Transdenominational groups tend to do better among Boomers. They may want labels on their jeans, but rigid labels on churches seem less popular. Over the past two decades many denominations have taken out key words so that a former Westside Baptist Church now calls itself Westside Fellowship and an Asbury Methodist Church may have adopted the name Community Faith Center.

Geographically Boomers are essentially urban-centered. The type of employment they choose and the kind of lifestyles they follow favor clustering in the cities. There is still much to be done in rural and suburban churches. One could even argue that suburban churches are in a significant way "urban-centered." But churches that want to draw Boomers have to be where Boomers hang out and that will likely be near centers of culture, education, and ample white-collar jobs.

Up until recently Boomers wanted less emphasis on youth in church programs. That strange phenomenon came about because many of them married later and had their children later. A Boomer couple welcoming their first child at age thirty-two did not deal with teenagers until their mid- to late-forties. When Boomers reach that age, they will demand the same kind of youth-ministry opportunities their parents wanted for them.

How Do We Involve Boomers in Ministry?

Four answers clamor for attention here and two sound very much like the past. Congregations wanting Boomers to climb on board the service train need to *clarify the nature of God's call* in their lives. This has always been true among evangelical Christians but we have not always been required to define our terms quite as precisely. The other carryover from earlier days is to *equip properly*. True, that certainly means a great deal more in the twenty-first century than it did even twenty-five years ago. But if we want Boomers to involve themselves in ministry eagerly, they'll need the preparation and equipment to do it right.

Unlike the past we can *emphasize idealism,* that is, what the church can be if its middle-adult Boomers seriously support its ministry. We gave their parents straight doses of realism, often genuinely limited by meager resources. To put it another way, we did the best we could with what we had. Now having more has become part of the package.

But perhaps most important here is the *futility of guilt motivation* with the Boomer generation. We trapped their parents over and over again, scolding them into attending prayer meeting, nagging them into teaching Sunday school, always threatening that their failure to do whatever the pastor asked somehow showed a lesser love for God. That approach was wrong; today it is also useless. All the principles we already discussed regarding motivation in learning apply directly and significantly to these middle-life Boomers.

CHARACTERISTICS OF MIDDLE ADULTHOOD

Intimacy was our key word for young adults: What would serve as a comparable key word for middle adults? Doubtless such a question could be debated endlessly, but many adult-learning specialists would choose the word *career*. All the busyness and responsibility, all the change and trauma of middle adulthood, tends to center in career. A quarter of a century ago we could have described men that way; now we find no clear line of gender separation.

Let's remember, too, that this does not apply exclusively to Boomers. At the time I write these words, the oldest Boomer has not yet turned fifty-three, so we still face more than a decade's worth of younger generation folks holding down the older slots of middle adulthood. Some of the characteristics ahead sound different from what we have already said about Boomers; we can account for that by allowing the camera to pan a wider portion of the field, shooting all three generations that form a part of middle adulthood.

Satisfied Maturity

Folks in middle adulthood are finally really "adults." True, they crossed that line years ago, but the full weight of family, job, career, community, and church responsibilities usually doesn't settle in until sometime after age thirty-five. Middle adults are maturing adults; some haven't fully arrived, but they are well on the way.

Belonging Mentality

The belonging need keeps surfacing as we look at adults, and it will not go away even in the older age brackets. All that moving around during young adulthood, all those efforts to figure out who they are, where they belong, what God wants them to do, where they will live—all that and much more is largely settled after the age of thirty-five, even though lots of change still lies ahead. In this age bracket comes a feeling of stability and belongingness.

Security Consciousness

In middle adulthood security means paying a lot of attention to physical and financial safety for one's family. A man in his late thirties, for example, may finally decide his twenty-year-old dream of bungee jumping was never a good idea. The parents of two or three children have probably already begun saving for college and their own retirement. Increasing numbers of single parents now have fewer options in the present and the future.

Every serious parent wants to safeguard against danger and disease. Fathers who take that role seriously work hard to protect their families. Since the earliest *Star Trek* days, I've often told my family that I am their "Chief Security Officer." The years have not changed that sense of responsibility just because it now applies on a daily basis only to my wife and myself.

Relative Independence

This characteristic increases throughout this age group since adults are more independent at fifty-five than thirty-five. Empty-nesters no longer build their lives around soccer practice, piano lessons, and Little League.

But the adjective *relative* is important not only because independence grows through the forties and fifties, but because none of us ever becomes completely independent. For most people job responsibilities continue and perhaps even increase during middle adulthood.

Physical Transition

In terms of age the psychologically critical number is forty. Our culture has made leaving the thirties a major continental divide in life. The physical deterioration of the body, though varying greatly from person to person, usually comes about ten or fifteen years later. Men who played full-court basketball since they were ten discover they can't do it anymore as they approach fifty. Women struggle through menopause and send their babies off to college. Whatever the specifics, people in later middle adulthood will likely discover their bodies no longer allow what seemed so much a part of their lives in earlier years.

Achievement Disillusion

Throughout young adulthood everything seems possible. Money not available now soon will be. The mind begins to ponder—"They haven't made me manager of my department yet, but soon they'll see how important I am to the company. I've never been out of Nebraska, but someday I'll visit every country in Europe." Young adults can dream and plan anything—and well they should. By the end of middle adulthood, however, when retirement looms only a few years ahead, one begins to recognize what will not be possible. The nasty "what if" question clouds the mind and second-guessing life's choices becomes a hazard.

MIDDLE-ADULT HIGHLIGHTS

Beyond the financial concerns and physical limitations, above the pain pills and cancer scares, and after the joyous frustration of raising teenagers, we find in middle adulthood some happy flags flying.

Significant Stability

Middle adulthood may be the time of greatest stability in family life—economic, domestic, and vocational. If a relationship between husband and wife has been adequately nurtured in earlier years, they survive the departure of the children with full awareness that they mean more to each other than ever before. Careers are finalized, salaries are up, and reputations are built.

Significant Contribution

Young adults probably stuff more knowledge into college and graduate years than any other brief period of life, but wisdom comes with experience and experience has a strange way of linking itself with age. There is something about youth, even in adulthood, that flaunts every small success as world-shaking. We all suffer from the disease but none more than those who achieve goals earlier in life.

Halfway through this age-group, adults tend to think they've seen and done it all; but the greatest contributions God can achieve through us are not only unlimited by age (consider Mother Teresa), but will likely occur in late-middle and older adulthood. The wondrous blend of maturity and efficiency makes possible these significant contributions.

If all this is true, why does the widely researched "mid-life crisis" occur in middle adulthood? Think back to the characteristics of the age group, some of which can have negative implications. People come to a place at which anxiety turns into negative action. But why?

We can identify several factors, not the least of which is workload. Sheer physical exhaustion from the demands of the job may be the largest contributor to a midlife crisis. Because of the maturity and efficiency of older and middle adults, people take advantage without really intending to.

Running a close second is responsibility. If responsibility increases about 10 percent a year during this age bracket, one hundred tasks at age thirty-five explode to over six hundred by age fifty-five.

As already noted, physical aging is a factor that can contribute to midlife crisis. It doesn't have to come in the form of disease or illness; it may be that changing face in the mirror. Somehow becoming bald, overweight, and full of stress wasn't in the original plan.

Midlife crisis expert Jim Conway picks up on the work of Erickson and Levinson in observing the following:

> [A man's] third adult unsettled stage comes around age forty. This is even more intense than the one in adolescence or the one at thirty. This is the mid-life crisis. It may come at any time from thirty-five to fifty-five; generally, however, it appears in a man's early forties. . . . Following his mid-life developmental era, a man moves into a *third settling-down stage*, which starts in the late forties and continues to retirement. The man who successfully navigates his mid-life crisis will experience an increase in productivity, a decrease in competitiveness, a greater desire to be helpful to people, to enjoy leisure, and be comfortable with himself and his stage of life. His marriage will generally become more meaningful and satisfying to both partners. There will be an easy transition to becoming a grandparent and trainer of a new generation.[3]

Conway's book talks mainly about men but we will return to this crisis concept in the next chapter and speak briefly of women as well.

Robert Samuelson tells us that "the ordinariness of middle age won't suit a generation that demands to be different. Middle age is bound to be relabeled, if not reinvented. Well, why not? The concept of middle age, as Yale historian John Demos has noted, is relatively new. For most of our history, people pondered only the problems of youth and old age. The period in between was considered the prime of life. Who knows? Maybe they had it right."[4]

Everything in this chapter describes the way we must understand middle adults, and there is more to come in the next chapter. As Samuelson suggests, we cannot determine how Baby Boomers will change what we have come to know about these years. But one thing seems clear—spiritual and theological moorings must form the foundation, or the superstructure of life will eventually crumble.

11

The Best of Times—The Worst of Times

When *Charles Dickens wrote,* "it was the best of times; it was the worst of times," he could well have been describing middle adulthood. Caught between two generations, often attempting to care for both, people in the most crucial years of family responsibility face the continuing erosion of the family. Tom Morganthau warns:

> Nearly half of all American children will experience the break up of their parents' marriage before the age of eighteen. Single parenting, almost always by the mother, is on the rise among both blacks and whites: about a third of all American children now live in single-parent homes. Kids in single-parent households are twice as likely to drop out of school or get pregnant during their teenage years and the risk is just as high for kids from the "blended families" that result from remarriage after divorce. And because two-wage-earner households are now the national norm, intact families are under enormous stress as well. Kids in less affluent homes, where daycare and pricey after-school activities are out of reach, suffer from the lack of quality time.[1]

Steering the ship through three decades of this kind of social turbulence, middle adults need all the church can provide for their lives, families, and ministries. If research on developmental tasks is correct (and many

Christian educators hold firmly to developmentalism), the tasks to be met and achieved during these decades require a close alliance between individual families and the corporate family of God. Congregations must abandon blind faith that learning will somehow mystically take place if someone stands before a group of adults and talks long enough and loud enough. Adult-education leaders must provide satisfactory answers to many crucial questions, of which the following are only examples:

- How can we convince adults of their ability to learn?

- How can we stimulate a desire to study outside of classtime?

- How can we facilitate serious learning and application?

- How can we coordinate interests and needs for middle adults?

- How can we provide social and fellowship activities that support spiritual growth and family stability?

- How can we help adults build solid homes while at the same time effectively serving the church?

DECADES OF RESPONSIBILITY

How should we best group middle adults for learning activities? The needs of middle adults are less related to age levels than those of senior adults but are more connected than those of younger adults. Grouping by decades does give us some framework in which we can look at our educational responsibilities.

When it comes to actual teaching, we scan many variable activities to make good decisions on grouping: the size; the overall adult population in the church; the availability and quality of teachers; the curriculum; the space; and the congregational traditions which seem worth holding on to. All these are important, but none alone nor all of them together can approximate the importance of the crucial question, "How can we achieve our learning objectives for middle adults?"

Perhaps there is no best way to group middle adults, and certainly there is no simple answer to the various problems that stand between where your church might be now and where you need to go. One thing does seem clear. The evangelical community needs to pay careful attention to the development of this key group.

Decade of Adjustment: 35–45

Reasonably well established in a job, adults in this decade face some early career decisions and are still young enough to make those transitions. They are busy planning for personal growth—spiritual, professional, and cultural. Those who are parents struggle with improving child-parent relationships, particularly with teenagers. With responsibilities and adjustment comes the necessity for managing stress which, if unattended, can lead to the midlife crisis discussed toward the end of the last chapter. Jim Conway writes, "Because midlife crisis in men generally occurs in their early forties, it means that the average age of the wives is likely to be late thirties or early forties. At this age a wife is extremely threatened by her husband's crisis."[2]

In this age-group adults are also called on to assess their own personal worth and behavior. They ask, "Am I the person I really want to be?" Young adults ask what they want to *become*, which is a very different question. One issue has to do with how much we want to be like our parents. People in early middle adulthood look at their jobs, their appearances, the way they raise their children, and often see similarities with the previous generation. Interestingly, reactions differ widely, from amusement, to distaste, to appreciation.

All this raises another developmental task with which the church can help, namely, improving relationships with parents. We expect middle adults to have mastered the task of relating to their parents on an adult level. Often a "best friend" relationship develops. These are rich years which in many ways set the tone for the decades to follow.

Lest we think the stress and trauma of this decade is limited to men, let's have a look at Conway's observation about women, a concept more fully developed in the book *Women in Midlife Crisis.* "Let's assume that by her late thirties a woman has been married about fifteen years. She likely will feel hit with a strong need to reevaluate her life. About this time her last child goes off to school for all day. It is not the period of the *empty* nest, it is the period of the *quiet* nest. Yes, there are still children in the home, when they're not at school. She still has a role as a mother. But if she has chosen to be a full-time homemaker, there are long periods during the day when the house is quiet—almost deafeningly so. There is time to think about life."[3]

Without getting bogged down in the concept of "crisis," it is worth noting that churches that provide individual and group support during this decade will gain credibility in their efforts to provide learning and service opportunities. This book takes the position that only a vibrant, spiritually tuned, and Bible-teaching congregation can help adults achieve what Conway describes at the end of his chapter "Bewildered at Thirty-Five." "But it is from this crucible of the late thirties' midlife crises that we see a stronger, more self-assured woman emerging. It is her strength . . . developed through the testing fires of her own experience, that will enable her to help her husband through his midlife crisis." [4]

Decade of Responsibility: 45–55

Somewhere during this decade men and women tend to cross paths psychologically; men become more nurturing-oriented and women become more independent and aggressive. Some researchers suggest this is more biological than cultural, but one would think our society nurtures this very pattern. Much of it may have to do with the demands of child-rearing. For so many years men are asked to provide for physical needs and women to handle the emotional side of things and both may, as middle adults, have suppressed their own personalities. Then at the time of the empty nest their lifestyle patterns tend to converge and move in the other direction. Ronald Kessler argues that this decade is actually a period of reduced stress and anxiety, particularly the fifties. His biomedical research has discovered that between ages forty and sixty, people actually lose cells in the *locus coeruleus*, the part of the brain that registers anxiety, which may account for some mellowing toward the end of what we call mid-middle age.[5]

As the church turns to its educational task for folks in this decade, what developmental challenges must we help them face? These middle adults are moving from adjustment to a higher level of achievement and responsibility. Certainly a major focus for men and increasingly for women as well is *finding work fulfillment*. Assuming some job stability by this time, mid-middle adults may well have been in the same job or at least the same kind of occupation for twenty to thirty years. But does it bring joy? Do they see it as service for Christ or just drudgery? The Bible refers in a number of places to the role of Christians as employees, and we need to beat that drum loudly for this age group.

People in this decade also need to *learn how to relate to both children and grandchildren*, a very different relationship. It seems impossible to resist comparing one's grandchildren to one's children (we even call them by the same names on occasion), and part of the developmental task is recognizing a connection that has to be, in a sense, broken and then re-formed with grandchildren.

People in this group need to be working on enriching their marital relationships, though we could surely say that about adults in all age categories. Perhaps it becomes more necessary because people forty-five to fifty-five are approaching or entering the empty-nest syndrome. Once their kids are gone, there is nothing left but the partners, and the bond had better be solid. How often we hear people who struggle in a marriage say, "We're holding it together for the sake of the kids." When the kids are gone, that option is no longer available.

We also need to teach this group how to function as Christians by *enlarging their social and community relationships*. Since their responsibilities are greater and their roles wider, they are called on to stretch their contacts beyond the confinements of earlier years. This may mean greater responsibility and more money, but how does it open opportunities for new ministry?

During this decade people are required to understand their aging parents. As we said in the last chapter, they are "caught in the middle." At fifty-five we can understand twenty-five because we've been there. It seems much more difficult, however, to understand seventy-five. We can read about it and talk about it, but we can't feel it. We can't actually know what it is like to be seventy-five. There is no exact model of age ratio between middle adults and their parents, but if we use twenty-year segments as a guideline, we could recognize how crucial it is to assist people who are forty-five in understanding people who are sixty-five and right on up the ladder for the next ten years.

How interesting to notice how the various developmental tasks of adulthood relate to emotional maturity. Someone has said that maturity is the giving and receiving of affection while continuing to function creatively in life and society. Tensions in contemporary society cause people to react in withdrawal, anger, panic, or irrational confrontations of difficult situations.

In an older but still relevant book called *The Creative Years,* Reuel Howe argues that the development of modern adults has been stifled by preoccupation with security. He claims people are not adequately interested in present opportunities and that evidence of this preoccupation shows itself in gross conformity to society and the chains of technocracy. Maybe so. But one thing seems evident in our work with middle adults: "Present opportunities" will never be greater than during this thirty-year period. Howe is particularly helpful in providing guidelines for recognizing maturity.

1. A mature person is guided by long-term purposes rather than immediate desires.

2. A mature person accepts people and things the way they are rather than pretending they are the way he wants them.

3. A mature person accepts the authority of others without rebellion or "folding up."

4. A mature person can accept himself as an authority without extreme pride or guilt.

5. A mature person can defend himself from his own unacceptable impulses and from attacks from others.

6. A mature person can work without feeling he is a slave and play without feeling he ought to be working.

7. A mature person is able to accept the opposite sex and the relationship between the two in ways that are appropriate.

8. A mature person can love so satisfyingly that he becomes less dependent on being loved.

9. A mature person is able to accept his role in the larger scheme of things.[6]

What a lineup. And what a description for people in middle adulthood, particularly in this centerpiece decade.

Decade of Celebration: 55–65

Some writers call this period "later adulthood" and rightly see it as a bridge to older adulthood. As people live and work longer, older adulthood can be viewed as beginning at an ever later age. A hundred years ago people at age fifty-five would have been facing death, not the beginning of the last decade of middle adulthood. Why the word *celebration*? Because much of the achievement begun in young adulthood and realized in the first two decades of middle adulthood has now been actually attained. These people can celebrate having raised children and sent them out successfully to live for the Lord. They can celebrate having served a company or profession well, and for a long time. They can celebrate the stability of their marriages and, in increasing numbers, the quality of their health. So what do they need?

A ministry to fifty-five- to sixty-five-year-olds centers on applying the resources for living, making a successful transition into retirement, and coping with the deaths of friends and loved ones as well as their own. The key tense is the present, because even though the past carried both joy and frustration, the future is not very long. This is no time to talk about what we might do twenty years from now, but about how we can maximize our lives and service for Christ right now.

Invitations to weddings decrease; invitations to funerals increase. Many of our college friends are with the Lord, and reality requires that we recognize God grants us each breath to live in the present. How can pastors and Sunday-school teachers make this plain?

All this brings a new focus on health, with some anxiety about illness. Blood tests, heart monitoring, increasing use of medication—hardly the lifestyle of everyone, but much more likely in this decade than any that preceded it. Similarly, people in this decade generally avoid fast-food restaurants. The mere sight of a teenager preparing their dinner seems immediately odious.

People who have lived their lives well come to the end of middle adulthood with the feeling of distinct personal and professional accomplishment. It is our task in the church to help them realize all along the road how to walk in the will of God and to live as He wants them to live, thereby making it possible to arrive happily at this point. Perhaps the word *excellence* is worth reviewing here. Excellence is not perfection; it is doing the very best you can with the resources God has given you—and God has not given equal resources. To some He gives money, to others health, to others high intelligence. When adults in our churches come to the end of the active trail, we want them to be able to look back and say, "My life wasn't perfect, but I have lived it in excellence to the best of my understanding of God's will."

CENTRAL ISSUES OF MIDDLE-ADULT LEARNING

Throughout this book we have emphasized the importance of meeting needs, and I have focused nearly every chapter on that dimension. Wesley Willis reminds us to emphasize felt needs, not just prescribed needs. "Listen to what adults say they want. Unfortunately, educators often plan programs 'for' others, but neglect to consult them in the process. And while we think we may know what middle adults need, it is easy to miss the mark. Adults, and especially Baby Boomers, have opinions and are anxious to articulate them, given the chance. It is amazing how many adults who are competent leaders in other areas of life seem to shift into neutral when they enter a church building. We need to break through such cultivated passivity and create effective, relevant educational ministries. Do you want to know what adults want and need? Get radical; ask them!"[7]

If we do just that, what are they likely to say? Though the language would vary as much as the opinions, several crucial issues seem to surface in many surveys and conversations of this type.

Significance and Security

Some have suggested that if one were to name two words that describe the major concerns of men and women in middle adulthood those words would be *significance* and *security*. Men ask, "Why am I important? What is it about me and what I do that is useful and significant? How could I increase my productivity?" For women security—physical, financial, and emotional—seems to grab center stage. When a man loses his job he loses his significance, and his wife loses her security.

Conway suggests that "a man without a job is a man without an identity. He feels he has nothing to offer an employer. Unhappiness with his work or the fear of losing his job can cause physical and emotional effects such as ulcers, high blood pressure, colitis, impotence, or an emotional breakdown."[8] Perhaps one of our tasks at church is to help men be less dependent on their jobs, thereby avoiding the crash that comes when work problems increase or the job itself disappears.

One could argue the same about a woman's security and its dependence on relationships. Catherine Stonehouse says,

> In the interpersonal truths, self is defined in terms of relationships and not differentiated from them. The person is his or her relationships rather than having relationships. The expectations of others determine what one ought to be and have major control over the behavior of the self. Relationships and fulfilling the expectations of others give meaning to life. The person highly values inclusion (if asked, "Who are you?" the interpersonal self answers, "I am so-and-so's husband—or wife—and so-and-so's son—or daughter"). The person who has no identity beyond relationships is profoundly threatened if the other party in the relationship desires more space. If the relationship ends in death or separation, a major part of the self is gone.[9]

Purpose and Progression

The three decades we are grouping under middle adulthood take men and women from the setting of life purpose to the progression necessary to look back on achievement. For some that progression seems rather straightforward as they move up in the company, raise their kids, buy larger and more expensive cars and houses, and save for retirement. That pattern, however, may be more descriptive of men than women. Middle-adult women tend to see more of a mosaic pattern in their lives because there are more options. Should they work or stay home? If they choose work, should it be part-time or full-time? If they choose not to work, how much time should they give to the church and community activities?

Both can be upset by directional changes such as a job loss, an unexpected baby, or some crisis in the family, such as the loss of a child. Though all these directional changes affect both men and women, the church needs to recognize that the genders may react differently. Those reactions related to adult understanding of roles and goals are linked directly to the issues in this part of the chapter. When that unexpected baby comes to parents who have reached the age of forty-two, the husband may not get much sleep for a few weeks, but basically his job continues as it did before. But his wife's life is dramatically interrupted.

Identity and Self-Esteem

If men focus on significance, self-esteem is a huge factor and it usually comes from achievement. Church leaders can sit back and argue how men ought to be less concerned with achievement, but as stated earlier, we cannot build an educational program on "oughts." They simply will not support the structure. Focused on significance, men lay out that purpose, take aim at the progression, and expect to attain achievement. That accomplishment does not have to be in dollars; it could be in educational status, recognition for community service, or even in titles on the office door.

For women, we come right back to relationships. Their identity, as Catherine Stonehouse reminds us in the earlier-cited paragraph, will often come from human connection. Once again gender differentiation is important, since most learning groups in the church will serve both men and women together.

Fear and Frustration

We've talked much about gain and achievement in this chapter, even celebration. But in leading church ministries for middle adults, we would be unwise to minimize the reality of fear and frustration in their lives. As our chapter title suggests, middle adulthood can be the best of times and the worst of times. Repeated surveys suggest that fear and frustration center in loss even during a period of life when so much is being gained. Men fear financial ruin and, even more dramatically, impotence. Women fear loss of their beauty, their husband, a job, or even the home that they have cherished for so long.

And we can't serve middle adults well unless we understand how they respond to what they perceive as loss, because that's when fear turns to frustration. With men we can expect anger. Perhaps internal and controlled, but maybe public rage. Women are more likely to struggle with depression, the feminine parallel to masculine anger. While we teach that neither is an acceptable response for mature Christians, we recognize the stark reality of both. Conway directly connects depression with loss when he writes, "Psychological depression is always connected to a loss."[10] And then he identifies relational loss, loss of material things, lost time, lost opportunities, and loss of control or choice. He concludes the section by saying, "Loss, then, in any area of life, may cause us to have feelings of depression. We must identify the sources of loss and make necessary adjustments—then the depression will lift and we can move on with living."[11]

Middle adulthood—so much to gain, so much to give. As I look back on my own life, the central decade of middle adulthood was probably the best period of that length I can recall, surpassed only by years I spent in college. Baby Boomers by sheer demographic attention have controlled social norms in recent years. Since almost all of them are now in middle adulthood they need to look ahead and see the preceding generation, which is going back to school in record numbers, forging new careers or making great strides in their old ones, and enjoying longevity heretofore unknown since the days of the Old Testament.

As we teach and serve them, let us also show them how to teach and serve. A variable approach to middle adults, one with built-in flexibility represents our best choice. Stonehouse reminds us of this:

> In adult Christian education, does one "size" fit all? Not when the particular differences of either men or women are ignored. Adult education in the church will contribute most to the life and ministry of God's people

when it understands the strengths, concerns, and the needs of both women and men. Out of those understandings will come some gender-focused specialized ministries. But much of Christian education will continue to involve men and women learning together from one another. Life and ministry is enriched when all perspectives and concerns are respected and the insights of both women and men are utilized in building God's kingdom.[12]

12

❦

Wisdom Available: 1-800-Seniors

Every day NBC's Willard Scott receives over fifty requests for birthday greetings offered on the *Today Show* to Americans one hundred years of age and older. Sometime in the mid-1980s the Social Security Administration listed over thirty-two thousand centenarians on its rolls, and as early as 1990 the U.S. Census Bureau counted 35,808 people at least one hundred years and older. Whatever else those numbers mean, they surely remind us that we live in an aging population.[1]

DEMOGRAPHICS OF AGING

John Nesbitt calls the present and future age wave "the most important trend of our time."[2] In 1985, for the first time, the number of people in the United States over age sixty-five exceeded those under eighteen. Some demographers project that as many as one million Baby Boomers will reach the age of one hundred.

Graying of America

The average life expectancy in 1950 was 68.3 years; in 1985 that figure jumped to 74.7; and for 2020 it is currently projected at 78.1 years. The 1984 U.S. Census Bureau report observed that the number of Americans sixty-five and over doubled in the previous three decades and could account for 20 percent of the population in the next millennium. That would mean sixty-four million "elderly" Americans by the year 2030—all of whom already live among us.[3]

That last figure stands solid, though the percentage of the overall population may vary. Demographic projection can be interrupted as it was in the early nineties by another baby boom. Demographers suggest that by the year 2040 the over-sixty-five population will number eighty-seven million, conceivably as much as one-fourth of the total population. In that year, life expectancy for males could be eighty-seven years and for females, ninety-two—amazing numbers.[4] How can churches plan a ministry for people over sixty-five?

Looking toward 2020

Most church leaders find it impossible to project a ministry strategy for fifty years, or even thirty. So let's pick the year 2020—scarcely more than a generation from the publication date of this book. True, we can't do any kind of specific long-range planning that far ahead, but we can anticipate what evangelical congregations should be doing to understand older adults.

Demographers project that in 2020 people sixty-five and over will make up 17.3 percent of the U.S. population and pension and health-care payments will reach 11.8 percent of the National Gross Product. No wonder we hear cries out of Washington regarding the status of Medicare and the Social Security system. If these have been mismanaged, as some allege, the forthcoming needs will require every bit of competence we can muster. Already the retirement age has been increased by incremental levels, a decision of consequence to the church.

Challenge of an Aging Nation

How do older people feel about all this? What primary concerns do they express? Even though nursing homes are opening in America at the rate of one a day, most older people report their health is good. Even among those eighty-five and older, fewer than half (45.4 percent) need assistance with everyday activities. That number drops to less than 10 percent among people between the ages of sixty-five and sixty-nine. Still, *health* is the primary concern.

But *finances* also ranks high on all the survey lists. Of course income varies greatly among seniors, but in general they have more assets than their younger counterparts and the poverty level among those over sixty-five dropped from 35 percent in 1960 to 12 percent in 1990.

A third issue centers on *retirement location,* and lest we think all seniors rush to Florida or Arizona, it may be worth noting that more than 75 percent of people over sixty-five don't move at all; of those who do, half stay in the same county. Fewer than 5 percent of retirees move to a different state. We'll come back to needs a bit later in this chapter, but as a prelude to looking ahead, let's pause to look back and see how this nation has greeted aging in the past.

THE ROAD BEHIND

Historian Martin Marty calls the following historical periods "cultural antecedents to aging," and this portion of our study offers a mere cursory overview of his research.[5]

Pre-Colonial Era (1492–1607)

One finds very little to report in this time frame. The continent saw an era of adventure and plundering individualism, with people dying very young and others having little concern for ongoing relationships. That describes the European settlers; Native Americans, on the other hand, had developed rather dominant patterns of caring for older citizens.

Early New England (1607–1750)

Several patterns began to develop in the seventeenth century. As generations multiplied, families began to trace lines back to original immigrants. This brought more positive attitudes toward aging, and the position of older people improved during this century and a half.

The Enlightenment (1750–1800)

Along with a new spirit of pioneering, a new generation of geniuses arose in fields such as literature, education, and science. But there was still no commitment to social help. One could never have predicted in 1800 that the independent society of those days would become to some extent a welfare state today. Improving status for older people in the nineteenth century can be largely credited to family care, not government funding.

National Period (1800–1860)

Marty calls this era "the righteous empire period." Anyone remembering high school American history will know why the period stops where it does—the bloody and disruptive Civil War. That horrendous conflict dashed people's dreams about a lot of things, including education. It stalled the lives of thousands of younger Americans who could have and should have provided care for aging parents in the years beyond. But before the Civil War the nation experienced a new religious intensity and spirit of revivalism. Perhaps for the first time people began to see the social implications of the gospel, the recognition of doing something for other people as a demonstration of faith. Organizations like the YMCA began to spring up.

The Take-Off Era (1860–1918)

After the Civil War the attitude of the nation toward older people changed dramatically. There were more seniors, and we didn't know what to do with them. Both North and South rebuilt, an emerging social gospel took over, and liberal theology dominated the church. People talked about immigration, urbanization, modernization, secularization—the golden age had arrived. Churches began to teach that humanity is essentially good and that sin had been grossly overstated. Inventions and discoveries overwhelmed the country, and while theology suffered, society and social concerns ruled both church and state. It was a tough time for evangelicalism with its message of the cross, discipleship, and the coming of the Lord. Then World War I crushed everything, including global confidence. Who could have known in those awful years that it would happen again?

A New Deal (1918–1950)

The nation had little chance to catch its breath as World War I was followed by the Depression and then by World War II. The United States entered the Second World War in 1941, and the national metabolism was jolted again. Under the leadership of Franklin D. Roosevelt, Washington took control of guiding and rebuilding the nation. Social Security, for example, was a part of his "New Deal." Initiative for care fell for the first time into secular hands, given over by both family and church to the government.

The Age of Retirement (1950–)

Obviously before 1950 people "retired," but now the Social Security system encouraged retirement at age sixty-five. For over half a century we have watched entitlement programs, advocacy, ombudsmen, and the vast power of the American Association of Retired Persons (which one can join at age fifty with or without retiring). Then came the Age Discrimination and Employment Act guaranteeing nonmandatory retirement. Businesses had to change policies, and the "retired" populace became a specific social grouping.

Now retirement is the third stage of life (after childhood and adulthood) and attracts enormous political influence, and along with it, an emphasis on lifelong learning and the economics of aging.

Some leaders tell us the twenty-first-century church must rethink ministry to older adults, recognizing that seniors are and will be more physically vigorous, more interested in adventure and experience, and more involved in ongoing learning. Of primary significance is the need to acknowledge that we can no longer simply think of seniors as a population to be ministered to, but must recognize that they are experienced and often wise members of the body of Christ who have much to offer.

DEVELOPMENTAL TASKS OF SENIOR ADULTS

Tim Stafford quotes J. B. Priestley, who at seventy-nine described himself this way: "It is as though walking down Shaftesbury Avenue as a fairly young man, I was suddenly kidnapped, rushed into a theater and made to don the gray hair, the wrinkles, and the other attributes of age, then wheeled on-stage. Behind the appearance of age, I am the same person, with the same thoughts, as when I was younger."[6] The same person with the same thoughts, perhaps, but not the same body in the same environment, and not perceived by others the same way one perceives oneself. What challenges face senior adults? What tasks must they undertake just when they thought they had left tasks behind?

Maintaining Self-Esteem

I write these words within less than a year after my own "retirement," and I am not yet quite sure how to handle it. But one thing seems sure; leaving an established and titled position carries with it enormous adjustment. When one adds geographical relocation, the sheer physical and emotional trauma of it all can be overwhelming. Complicate all that with health problems or financial turmoil, and the impact of change can be shattering. Above all the physical and emotional changes looms the question, "Who am I now?" Most seniors who have led active and productive lives will find good answers to that question, but answer it they must.

Adjusting to Decreasing Strength and Energy

One could argue that this ongoing condition follows people through most of adult life, and that would be true. But the diseases that haunt our culture and the nagging frailty that chips away at good health tend to be considerably more complicated for people in this age-group.

Living on Reduced Income

Obviously not all retirees face financial problems. Corporation executives and political figures will have taken care of themselves well before age sixty. Millions of others, however, watch blips in the stock market and wonder who will tamper with Social Security next. Even some folks in ordinary jobs do much better than their peers. A close friend of mine left his position at age fifty-two with full retirement, full salary, and full benefits. The company wanted to make some adjustments, to bring in some younger people, and they offered him a "golden parachute," an early retirement package he couldn't refuse. He went on with his life, never missed a paycheck, insurance coverage, or other benefits. But that's not common. In addition to the paltry sum Social Security allows retirees to earn, the financial picture essentially consists of three components—a Social Security check, an employee pension check, and investment returns. The sad reality here is that all three depend on one's earlier income.

Establishing Peer Relationships

One need not move into a retirement community to recognize the importance of peer relationships. Some people in their sixties have stayed close to many of their friends throughout the years, and the gang grows old together. Others have spent their entire time with their children and have no idea how to link up with people who aren't two or three decades younger than themselves. Often friendships center around recreational activities. If you've played tennis or racquetball all your life, shuffleboard does not look like a happy alternative.

Establishing Comfortable Housing

This item depends largely on both health and finances. Many adults work decades to pay off the mortgage and happily retire "at home" without those nagging monthly payments. Others would like to do so but never paid off the mortgage and therefore can't keep the old place. But what happens to those who have no financial problems but just can't physically keep up more than two thousand square feet of house and a half-acre of yard? What are the options? A condominium? An apartment? A smaller house? A retirement community? Any of those choices might work, but each requires a tough decision. Making and implementing it represent a significant developmental task.

Finding New Ministry Roles

Finally there is time to serve on elder or deacon boards or do some short-term missionary service. If God allows health and opportunity, senior adults could be the most productive members of the entire Christian community. But we'll return to that theme in the next chapter.

HONORING OLDER ADULTS

Honoring older adults is a responsibility of younger generations which is not only important to God but is also commanded by Him. Numerous Bible passages clamor for attention here, but let's take a quick glance at just a few. "Honor your father and your mother, so that you may live long in the land the LORD your God is giving you" (Exod. 20:12). "Rise in the presence of the aged, show respect for the elderly and revere your God. I am the LORD" (Lev. 19:32). "Listen, my son, to your father's instruction and do not forsake your mother's teaching. They will be a garland to grace your head and a chain to adorn your neck" (Prov. 1:8–9).

We quickly aim the Exodus passage and even the Proverbs passage at children and teenagers, but God also expects such behavior of respect and honor from adults in their twenties, thirties, and forties.

How Can We Honor Adults?

Perhaps *respect* is the first step in this long walk. When I hear a nineteen-year-old receptionist call an elderly patient to the inner sanctum of a doctor's office by using his first name, something rattles in my bones. Certainly she intends no disrespect, but perhaps no deliberate respect either. What passes for comedy in our day often pokes unkind fun at the frailties and weaknesses of people who have earned society's highest respect. This is hardly a respectful society.

The second step is *care*. Paul's words in 1 Timothy 5:3–4 should hardly surprise anyone who has studied the Old Testament: "Give proper recognition to those widows who are really in need. But if a widow has children or grandchildren, these should learn first of all to put their religion into practice by caring for their own family and so repaying their parents and grandparents, for this is pleasing to God." God commanded the Israelites to care for widows, orphans, and strangers, a requirement that obviously didn't change as the gospel spread around Asia Minor. On reflection, we could probably argue that the earliest New Testament church structure arose from a congregational effort to assist widows (Acts 6:1–6).

Third, we can *compensate for older adults' weaknesses and faults.* When they stumble and stutter, we can assist and affirm them. The rage of a rebellious teenager and the whispers of careless adults should bring us up short. They should remind us of passages like Proverbs 30:17: "The eye that mocks a father, and scorns a mother, the ravens of the valley will pick it out, and the young eagles will eat it" (NASB).

Honoring older adults does not come naturally to sinful humanity or it would not require so many biblical commands, like the reminders in 1 Timothy 5, the prayer of the old man in Psalm 71, and the warning passages of the Gospels exemplified by Mark 7:10.

How Do We Dishonor Senior Adults?

We dishonor older adults when we deny them the three positive avenues mentioned above; but the negative list seems to have no end. How does this culture dishonor senior adults?

- By stereotyping them, forcing them into roles in which they don't belong

- By attributing esteem only on the basis of productivity, so that people without titles or jobs may be considered less important

- By forcing them to live on the economic margins of society

- By compelling them against their wills to live where they don't want to go and to accept what they don't want to do

- By denying hope in this life as well as the life to come

- By remembering them and reminiscing about them only after they are gone

Somehow the church of Jesus Christ must rise above the culture around it in this as well as virtually every other aspect of life. The Bible gives little support to the idea that protecting children or the unborn is more important to God than protecting the elderly. As a congregation respects and cares for senior adults, it may very well discover that what appeared on the surface to be a burden, another complication, a biblical duty, in actuality becomes a blessing. We must tap the rich resources and the wealth of wisdom this rapidly expanding, increasingly active group of people can bring to any church. Stay tuned—that's what the next chapter explores.

13

❦

The Last for Which the First Was Made

Cliff and Agnes have it made, or so it seems to most of their friends. They live in a mortgage-clear home in an active retirement community and enjoy relatively good health for people approaching seventy years of age. They enjoy riding their bikes, taking long walks, and traveling to areas of the country they never had time to visit before. Their children and grandchildren all live within one day's drive, and the family gets together at least twice a year. But Cliff and Agnes have a problem—church.

Before moving to their retirement home two years ago, they had spent most of their forty-five years of married life in the same Midwestern city. Cliff worked as a plant supervisor for a major electric company, and Agnes was a nurse at the county hospital. Their church could be called "traditional," and its congregation included a wide variety of ages spanning several generations. Cliff served as a deacon and Agnes taught in the early childhood department of their Sunday school. Now everything has changed.

Two people who faithfully attended and served in a local congregation for decades are still church hunting in their new location. So far they have found three types of congregations within the boundaries of their doctrinal perspective:

1. The time-warp church: They have visited several congregations that seem untouched since 1950. Songs, programs, preaching—all preserve the memory of post–World War II evangelicalism.

131

2. The desperate church: Several congregations with fifty or fewer members have nearly begged Cliff and Agnes to join. They could plunge in immediately and each hold several ministry positions. In doing so, however, they would miss the fully developed worship program, learning experiences, and especially fellowship with people their own age they had appreciated so much in their former church.

3. The cutting-edge church: Seeker services, worship teams with booming percussion, and folks attending church in jeans and shorts characterize this type of church, but none of that holds any appeal for Cliff and Agnes. Churches like this are scratched from the list after just one visit.

What are they looking for? They know they can't reproduce their former congregation in a new location, but there are some specific things they are looking for in a church. In that search they represent thousands of seniors across the continent. They want to worship with dignity in ways meaningful to them. They want to study in serious learning opportunities that build on all the years of Bible study now behind them. And they want to serve, perhaps in a more limited capacity, but in positions that make good use of their gifts and experience. How can we make room for people like this in our congregations?

Actually, much of what this book has already said fits here. We should determine the specific needs of senior adults in our church and community. Certainly some information on "prescribed needs" will be helpful but church leaders need to know the specific makeup of a given congregation. In some cases church leaders may need to tell senior adults that they may find a more comfortable situation elsewhere. But suppose you want to develop a ministry to older adults, where should they begin?

BASIC TEACHING ASSUMPTIONS

Just as we have made assumptions about adults in earlier age groups, so we can do it again here. The general guidelines rest on our understanding of who seniors are as a group, how they function, and what they need.

Aging Is Normal

We dare not confuse the normality of aging with the old line that death is just a part of life. Death is not a part of life; it is the ending of physical life by a force of Satan's making rather than a part of God's creation design. But given the realities of sin and its effects, aging has become a part of the way human beings live out their lives, and though all seniors age, they do so in different ways. Someone said senior adults can be grouped into three types—go/go, slow/go, and no/go. Cliff and Agnes would place themselves in the second category.

Aging Does Not Cause Illness

True, older people may be more prone to illness because of the breakdown of bodily tissues and functions, but we all know people in their eighties and nineties as physically and mentally capable as people two decades younger. David Enlow claims that the "results of a study made up of 400 noted people brought a startling revelation. Thirty-five percent of the world's greatest achievements were accomplished by people in the 60–70 age bracket."[1]

Aging People Influence Three or Four Generations

My sister-in-law has just become a great-grandmother at the age of sixty-four. She is healthy, active, heavily involved in her church, and dramatically influential among people in her own generation, her children, her grandchildren, and now her first great grandchild. To achieve all that during a life of service to Jesus Christ demands the attention of the church and the honor addressed in chapter 12.

Aging People Can Learn

Cliff and Agnes are not opposed to change, even though a stereotype of their age group often implies that. These vital human beings want independence and self-direction. And what they want is certainly no greater than what they offer, the vast resource of wisdom and experience so urgently needed by younger men and women in virtually every congregation.

Can we agree on the assumptions? They hardly seem revolutionary, and given the proper consideration, they can propel church leadership to the next level, helping us design learning situations best suited for older adults.

RESPONSIBILITIES OF TEACHERS OF SENIOR ADULTS

Some churches assume seniors must be taught by another senior. Certainly that may work well, but it's hardly a necessity. Any serious Bible teacher who can stay out of the past tense and avoid using clichés (e.g., "golden years" or "sunset years") and focusing on disability can work well with seniors. Primarily that teacher must avoid any indication that older people have reached a point of uselessness—even when they themselves hint at that false analysis in their own conversation. When we find a good candidate to guide seniors in a learning situation, we train that person to do the following seven things.

Focus on the Present

Older people idealize the past for obvious reasons, and there's probably little harm in that at the conversational level. When it comes to the application of Scripture to life, however, we want them to understand what God has for them now and in the *future*—and a forward-looking learning facilitator can do just that.

Utilize Seniors in Class Leadership

Remember the experience factor; seniors bring to the table collective experiences well beyond what one teacher can offer. At this level, churches should organize classes with presidents, vice presidents, social leaders—anything that gets seniors involved in their own self-directed learning and fellowship activities.

Adapt the Learning Schedule

A wise teacher of seniors will develop compensating activities to fit the abilities and interests of people in the class. Two days before beginning this chapter, I visited a church that offers numerous kinds of ministry opportunities every week, all of them in the daytime. This is helpful for seniors because many of them don't like to drive after dark. Their schedules are open during the day, so why force them into church patterns designed for people who spend their days on the job or in school?

Offer Ample Public Recognition

Evangelical congregations are usually good about applauding every minor achievement of teenagers. We all understand that; positive reinforcement can produce additional positive behavior. But the contributions of teenagers can't compare to what Cliff and Agnes have done for the body of Christ for half a century. They, and others like them who have been faithful to the Lord and still want to give and serve, deserve all the public affirmation and applause we can give them.

Organize the Learning Group for Ministry

The four elements we all want in church life are accentuated among older adults—worship, learning, fellowship, and service. In some churches fellowship and service activities may be separately organized by an associate pastor in charge of senior ministries, or perhaps a lay leader charged with that task. In many cases, however, it falls to a Sunday school teacher or learning facilitator to pull together peer groups that offer vital and viable fellowship and service opportunities.

Emphasize Dependence on God

This is hardly a novel idea for Christians of any age. But now that Cliff and Agnes are summoned to funerals of their friends and find themselves waiting more frequently in doctors' offices, trusting God's work in their lives becomes more crucial. Certainly at the death of a spouse every congregation should rally to the support of the survivor, even when the death may have been expected for months.

Focus on Attitude and Meaning

All adults are more likely conceptual learners than factual. Older adults especially have declining interest in informational trivia (they neither need it nor can remember it), but they respond well to biblical teaching that applies to their own needs and offers obvious usefulness in their lives.

SENIOR COGNITIVE DEVELOPMENT

One of the ugly clichés of older adulthood has to do with mental process and intellectual disability. Words like *senility* and *early Alzheimer's* enter the conversation every time someone over sixty can't remember where he put his car keys. Now we have new research available to show us how Cliff and Agnes will learn when they find a church that gives them the opportunity to learn. We will analyze the three parts of cognitive development—attention, memory, and intelligence—by noting how they operate in older adulthood.

Attention

Selective attention (one's ability to focus on another person) does not seem to decrease with age. *Divided attention,* on the other hand, describes an activity such as a family-room discussion in which several people may be speaking at the same time. Educators must remember that senior adults have diminishing capacity to receive input from the wider group, but not necessarily diminishing of selective attention.

This important observation may be related to some hearing loss which can make multiple simultaneous sounds resemble a cacophony of noise. This concept of "processing capacity" suggests that researchers are unable to determine whether the difference between selective and divided attention centers in hearing loss or in the ability to absorb and apply learnings. Very likely, both play a role.

This observation alone suggests guidelines for teaching. Whereas teenagers might do well in small groups scattered around a room in which six or seven voices can be heard at the same time, that would not be an ideal learning situation for seniors. Something as simple as asking people to turn and address the larger portion of the group with a question or observation could make a major difference in the mental participation of others in the group. The wise teacher of older adults will make good use of selective attention and not force learners into divided attention situations.

Memory

Both short-term and long-term memory show a slight dropoff during aging. Consider some typical senior frustrations: Where did I put my glasses? What did I have for lunch? Where did I leave my car? True, this is not a problem unique to seniors, but research reveals that it is more common in that age-group and is a factor clearly related to learning.

Despite memory loss, however, older adults experience a sharpening of what researchers call flashback capability. God gives older people an amazing recall of details in experiences that occurred decades earlier. There is something about the way our minds function in later years that enables us to reproduce the most insignificant trivia about childhood or events of teen years. Memory hasn't vanished nor has it been injured; it just operates differently.

In the early sixties I wrote a biography of Walter L. Wilson, a popular pastor and evangelist in the mid-twentieth century. Dr. Wilson was eighty-three years of age when I began the book. He had started a college, a local church, and a mission board, so I went to those organizations and gathered what documents I could find. But the documentary research would never provide an adequate biography; there simply was not sufficient information. So I went to his home with a tape recorder and discussed his life with him, asking questions I had written in advance. I would write a chapter, return, and read it to him. As he would hear a paragraph of some event that occurred in his early years of ministry, he would sometimes stop me and say, "No, that happened in 1892, not 1893." To be sure, Walter Wilson had an unusual clarity of mind, but that experience reflects flash-back capability.

Intelligence

Researchers distinguish between fluid and crystallized intelligence. Fluid intelligence describes general mental capacity apart from formal school-ing. Sometimes we look at a four-year-old and say, "Isn't he a bright boy?" We have seen no IQ tests, and there is no GPA to check. The conclusion is based on observation alone. Crystallized intelligence, on the other hand, describes acquired knowledge and skills, what we would call *schooling.* Researchers tell us that intellectual decline seems to occur in the area of fluid intelligence but not crystallized intelligence.

That surprises me; I would have thought genetic mental capacity would last longer than acquired learning, but that is not the case. At issue here is the discipline of the mind, not just capacity at birth. This should fasci-nate educators at all levels. It appears that the longer one participates in organized learning experiences, the more intelligent he or she will be in the later years of life. People who have no background in study, reading, or other mind-challenging activities end up with atrophied intelligence, watching endless hours of television and going for walks.

A major factor seems to center in how cognitive development pro-gressed before older adulthood. Study habits formed in early adult years, a love for learning, accumulation of a library, commitment to research—all these seem to make a significant difference in one's ability to utilize intelligence in later years. I have never seen this as an argument for not dropping out of college, but it could certainly be used that way.

Earlier in the chapter I quoted from Enlow's book, and in that same section of his opening chapter he lists some examples of intellectual prow-ess in later years.

- Benjamin Ririe, a Canadian member of the China Inland Mission, retired from missionary service at age seventy. He learned Greek at eighty. He took refresher work in Greek at ninety. He still brushed up on the language while traveling on the subway at age one hundred.

- At seventy, J. Oswald Sanders became principal of Christian Leaders Training College in Papua New Guinea.

- At eighty-nine, Michelangelo was producing sculpture masterpieces.

- Guiseppe Verdi wrote operas after he was eighty.

- Alfred Tennyson was eighty-three when he wrote "Crossing the Bar."

- Some of Victor Hugo's finest writings came after he was eighty.[2]

Facilitating Senior Learning

Back to Cliff and Agnes. Assume they visit your church and wonder whether it will provide the kind of ministry opportunities they need at this point in their lives. What have we seen in chapters 11 and 12 that could help you track and serve senior adults? Perhaps the best way to answer that question is to return to the discovery model (diagram 9, page 60) presented in chapter 6 and focus on it for a senior learning group.

Learning Experiences

The instructional class that aims to teach content to older adults in a teacher-directed, fact-focused environment does not offer the best option. Yet that describes a rather large percentage of adult Sunday school classes and other learning experiences in which involvement is only visible by some kind of attachment to truth sources. Student-oriented and need-focused learning experiences look very different in a class for seniors than for teens.

The diagram also shows us that involvement which focuses on engagement of the mind with truth forms a major part of the learning experience. This is a contrast rather than a comparison model. Instead of asking people to attach to truth sources, we want engagement through truth experiences. That doesn't make the sources any less important, and it certainly doesn't minimize the role of the Bible in class. However, for many senior adults, content absorption presents a constant problem, and they end up focused on knowledge rather than application and behavior.

Like any other group of Christians, older adults incarnate Bible truth by actually serving other people. When we utilize their experience and wisdom, and show them how to demonstrate to others that God has made a significant difference in their own lives, then they have reached engagement through truth experiences. What happens (as stated repeatedly in this book) is that the instructional class gives way to the discovery class, an andragogical approach to learning.

Learning Environment

Again review. Teachers who create a warm and casual environment for learning, who demonstrate patience, graciousness, and biblical love to their students, set the stage for serious study by serious seniors. Such teachers adopt a slower pace to allow for slower responses. They keep in mind the cognitive processes discussed earlier in this chapter. In the learning environment they also communicate clearly, and, if necessary, they repeat questions and comments, making every effort to allow seniors to connect with truth important to their lives.

Not everyone can work comfortably with senior adults. The Holy Spirit gives no specific spiritual gift for serving senior saints, but some certainly have an ability and perhaps even a calling to this kind of ministry. One would think it likely that people who have worked with teenagers and college students—and do well at it—might not be effective with older adults. Ultimately the teacher's attitudinal framework contributes negatively or positively to the learning environment.

A group of senior adults is just as diverse as any other group. The members reflect a variety of needs that must be addressed and an almost limitless supply of interests and concerns.

GROWING GODLY GRANDPARENTS

Remember those multiple generations influenced by people in this age-group? Strategic to that intergenerational lineup is the role of seniors as grandparents. Some readers may wish to review my chapter on grand-parenting in *The Christian Educator's Handbook on Family Life Education*,[3] but here we'll just look at five basic roles of grandparenting.

Historian

Grandparents guarantee the family heritage. As biographers of earlier years, they provide a connection in family relationships. In many cases they have traditions observed by their children and grandchildren and are called on to explain and even help preserve those important family behaviors. Furthermore, they know things moms and dads don't know because they were around when those things happened. As we enter the twenty-first century, grandparents will be able to talk about World War II, the assassination of several important public figures, and the techno-logical revolution. Their grandchildren know nothing of cars *without* seat belts, air conditioners, tape and CD players, and airbags. In many cases they know nothing about the poverty many of today's grandparents lived through to reach senior adulthood. The role of family historian is highly significant.

Mentor

In chapter 3 we talked about the example of older women teaching younger women according to Paul's instruction in Titus 2:3–5. We need not limit that instruction to theology. Showing grandchildren how to fish or play basketball offers useful mentoring experiences. When my oldest grand-son was six, he turned to me in the middle of an evening meal and asked, "Poppy, which is better, Jesus' blood or heaven?" How would you answer that question? Where did it come from? Obviously in his Sunday-school class he had heard about the importance of both. Clearly he understood that both of them are important, but which is better? Every grandparent could share multiple examples of such questions which provide teach-able moments, golden opportunities for grandparent mentoring.

Role Model

How does one learn to be a grandparent? Is there a grandparenting school? Can one earn a doctorate in grandparenting? Like almost everything else in family life, we learn to be grandparents by watching our grandparents. Without good grandparenting models, this strategic function of family life would fall on hard times. The time one invests in grandchildren is a gift with no obligation because grandchildren cannot repay time and money.

Nurturer

In God's plan for the family, the primary nurturers of children are their parents. In our day, however, some children spend more time with their grandparents as both parents work. In single-parent families grandparents may well serve as substitute teachers of spiritual truth. At the very least, they can and should augment what Christian parents are providing; one can hardly imagine Christian children in this godless society becoming "overnurtured."

Wisdom Resource

Grandparents who spend time with their grandchildren are wizards whose wide experience can sometimes astonish them. I've been trying to teach one of my grandsons how to balance a cane on one finger, a feat considerably more impressive to him than my writing a book. True, this is not a human activity one uses often, but it establishes credibility. Perhaps an adult who can balance a cane on one finger might be able to answer questions about Bible interpretation as well.

I hope Cliff and Agnes find a congregation in which church leaders minister to older adults, teach older adults to minister to each other, and then send out those seniors to minister to others. Golden years? Maybe not, but certainly productive years. Seniors who bring a wealth of wisdom and experience to the altar of Jesus Christ and His church demonstrate in day-by-day living "the last for which the first was made."

PART 3

The Family and Adult Ministries

14

❦

Swinging with the Singles

As the United States entered this last millennium, married adults made up nearly 95 percent of the adult population, and singles accounted for only about 5 percent. Blips occurred during World War I, the Great Depression, and World War II, which narrowed that gap considerably. Then the post–World War II baby boom hit, and the nation saw a 97 percent married-adult level, while the single-adult level dropped to 3 percent. From that point singles began to climb and marrieds began to decline, reaching a 50-50 level about 1992. The latest statistics suggest that in 2000 the single-adult population will outstrip the married-adult population by about a 60 to 40 percent ratio.

We talked about single adults in chapter 8. Now they deserve their own chapter since they have become a dominant demographic group facing the church. In one sense this is a bridge chapter leading us from the section on age groups to the section on family life. Singles come in almost any age, and though their needs vary, their singleness forms an overarching factor in ascertaining needs and interests.

When I ask my students in adult-education classes to describe singles, many are talking about themselves at that moment, while others have little difficulty remembering back to that time in their lives. They use words like *varied, independent, transient, exuberant, vocal, energetic, unattached, dating, anticipating, going, seeking,* and *busy.* These are fascinating terms when used by people to label others. When I ask those same students how they think singles feel about themselves, I hear words like *isolated, content, optimistic, uncertain, pessimistic, insecure,* and *confined.*

Whether the singles we want to describe are eighteen or thirty-eight, the issues of meaning in life are written all over the words we use to describe them. Many of the terms listed above indicate the idea of transition. Spiritual transition: How can I focus my spiritual formation now when I may have more time than later after I marry and become a parent? Relational transition: If I'm such a transient person, how do I develop lasting relationships? The single experience presents us with a phenomenon in adult life previously unknown to parents of Boomers who married just out of high school or college. One could call it a definitive baby boom, complicated by the hippie era, the women's movement, and the so-called new morality. There were 65 million single adults in America in 1990 and that number will rise dramatically by the year 2000.

A caveat: This chapter does not deal with single parents; they will be discussed in chapter 15.

FOUR BASIC GROUPS

I do not intend to suggest here that the following four are the only groups of singles, nor is this necessarily even the most efficient way of grouping singles for ministry. But they help us sort out this montage of 75 million or so people to see whether the need groups can be designated more specifically than just "singles."

Never Married

This is the main focus of the chapter, though other groups will fit in as well. Let's remember that never-married people may hold that status by choice or by circumstance. Increasingly we find people choosing to spend their entire adult lives as single persons; others, however, have never met the right person, have never been asked, or have some physical or mental handicap that precludes marriage.

Formerly Married/Spouse Alive

Obviously this category includes people who are either separated or divorced. In legal terminology "formerly married" may refer only to divorced rather than separated people. But as we deal with them in the church, it often makes little difference whether those final papers have been signed. A pastor friend of mine in Georgia invited me to conduct a family-life conference in his church. In one session we discussed the issue of divorced people in the church and how one ministers to them. He turned to his wife and said, "If we decided that all the divorced people in our church could not hold any ministry posts, we wouldn't have anybody to do anything." A deliberate hyperbole to be sure, but an accurate description of a growing problem facing many churches. Though it is not the purpose of this chapter to discuss what the Bible says about divorce, each congregation must determine how this category of single adults fits into congregational life.

Widowed

We can use two helpful subcategories here as well: widowed because of death by natural causes (an awkward phrase meaning one's spouse died at an appropriate age and with reasonable warning) and widowed prematurely. One of my students was left with two small boys when his lovely wife died of a brain tumor in her late twenties. He became a single parent, and therefore technically discussion of his case belongs in this chapter. But as we segment out this need group we need to see his situation as different from that of a widow who buried her husband of fifty-five years, a man in his late seventies.

Spiritual Singles

Here we look at people whose spouses are not believers. At home and church they function like singles—coming alone to church, to Bible study, groups, and to opportunities of service for Jesus Christ. Obviously people in this category could be singles without children, but they differ from the never married in many significant ways.

FOUR CAUSES FOR GROWTH

Why has this population group has increased so dramatically? Certainly newfound independence and freedom among Boomers and Busters figure in here. But we dare not forget those decades of the sixties and seventies when sociologists complained about overpopulation. While I have no specific research statistics to support the view, it would seem that many were influenced by that emphasis to marry later and either to have no children or to have their children later. One can also imagine that the recently revived nuclear threat hanging over the world during those years complicated the problem.

Overpopulation Propaganda

As recently as 1997 the Associated Press syndicated an article by Charles Hanley entitled "Have We Reached the Limit?"[1] Hanley described a 1972 report put out by the Smithsonian Institution, and they compared it with data twenty-five years later, in 1997. The now-famous 1972 "Limits to Growth" report said the world population would almost double from 3.8 billion to 1972 to 7 billion in 2000. Instead it will barely reach 6 billion, and its growth rate has fallen from 2 percent a year to 1.4 percent. Few singles today would consider this reason one of importance, but over the past twenty-five years it has had its impact.

Society's New Freedoms

Some years ago while pastoring a small church in Dallas, I interviewed a young couple who had visited our congregation and wanted to join the church. I quickly learned that though they were not married, they had been living together for some time. When I raised the issue, they were astonished that any pastor in 1985 could consider this in any way out of line. We resolved the problem amicably, but it reminded me again how the thinking of singles has changed so dramatically in just three generations.

Climbing Divorce Rate

Obviously the single category has been elevated by the divorce rate. According to sources quoted by Hazel Ruth Bell in *Search,* however, high divorce rates do not indicate disillusionment with marriage itself. The story the statistics tell seems to be one of couples disenchanted with their present marriages, searching for the ideal marriage somewhere else, with someone else.[2] Most divorced singles remarry, but many do not. Whether we must serve them in a permanent single state or only temporarily until the next marriage occurs, divorced people form a major portion of our singles group.

Fear of the Future

Some of the words we noted earlier—such as *uncertainty* and *pessimism*—suggest the unsettledness that many singles feel with respect to where the world is going. That may have been more of a concern before the Berlin Wall came down, but even today many singles apparently conclude that marriage and parenting will be too difficult to face in the world ahead.

FOUR GREAT NEEDS

What are the essential needs of single adults? As we explore that question, let's remember that these are not necessarily the same as general needs felt by young adults, because age is not the issue here.

Acceptance

Singles are a special-need group, but they don't want to be viewed as handicapped in some way, or, in today's vernacular, domestically challenged. Churches wanting to minister effectively to singles must confirm their single state as not only normal, but biblical. However one understands Paul's various statements about marriage, it would seem that neither he nor Barnabas ever married. Serving God as a single is a perfectly biblical option, and those who choose it deserve no harassment from their brothers and sisters in Christ.

Loneliness

Here we move from our earlier word (*aloneness*), used to describe young adults, to a genuine loneliness. Patricia Chapman, a mature Christian single who is widowed, identifies this as the most dominant need from which many others spring. She writes, "Singles can connect for jobs and careers, but often have difficulty making the kinds of social connections they need to keep them from becoming lonely. Related to this is depression, a major reason people enter hospitals. This leads to another need—relationships. All three are closely related. It seems that singles constantly look for ways to fill a void in their lives, the void created from lack of intimate relationships, or not being significant in the life of another."[3]

Self-Worth

Perhaps this represents the greatest concern among two single groups: the recently divorced and the elderly widowed. Divorced singles face the problem of guilt and blame whether children are a part of the mix or not. Elderly widows and widowers often discover that their concepts of self-worth were so heavily tied up with another person that the loss of that person lowers the survivor's esteem to dangerous levels.

The church has not compiled a very good record in dealing with the divorced and widowed. We have miles to go before we can say we are successfully meeting these needs of acceptance, loneliness, and self-worth—and this is also true of the next need.

Integration into the Local Church

It makes little difference whether we're talking here about a twenty-one-year-old college student relating to a local congregation in a college town or a church dealing with a divorced person of either gender, pondering how that person melds into a congregation which knew him or her only as a married member of the community. Each congregation must design its own procedures for dealing with singles, and particularly divorced singles. And those procedures must be built on sound interpretation of key biblical texts.

FOUR CONGREGATIONAL RESPONSES

Chapman observes that "today's church has a rare opportunity for dynamic ministry among singles. Many large congregations across the U.S. now include a pastor to singles on their paid staffs. If the church wishes to meet the needs of unchurched singles and single parents, it must take off the blinders and really understand them. A place to belong, people that care, wholesome activities, and positive Christ-like role models all make the church which promotes them more attractive to lonely singles."[4]

Rather than dwell on past failures, let's gear up our ministries to accommodate singles in the future. The Bible does not specifically address ministry to single adults (except for widows); however, it makes no distinction in gender, age, or marital status when it reminds us so frequently that we should be caring for each other. Consider the following passages:

"Let us therefore make every effort to do what leads to peace and to mutual edification." (Rom. 14:19)

"Let us not become conceited, provoking and envying each other." (Gal. 5:26)

"Carry each other's burdens, and in this way you will fulfill the law of Christ." (Gal. 6:2)

"But encourage one another daily, as long as it is called Today, so that none of you may be hardened by sin's deceitfulness." (Heb. 3:13)

"Let us not give up meeting together, as some are in the habit of doing, but let us encourage one another—and all the more as you see the Day approaching." (Heb. 10:25)

"Brothers, do not slander one another. Anyone who speaks against his brother or judges him speaks against the law and judges it. When you judge the law, you are not keeping it, but sitting in judgment on it." (James 4:11)

"Therefore confess your sins to each other and pray for each other so that you may be healed. The prayer of a righteous man is powerful and effective." (James 5:16)

These representative passages clearly suggest that singles represent a need group for which every serious Christian congregation must be designing ministry. How do we do that?

Recognize Its Legitimacy

Perhaps this point repeats the acceptance factor noted earlier, but here we're talking about what the church provides, not just what the single adult needs. *Congregations should stop telling single people they have to be married to walk in God's will.* As we've already observed, several key Bible characters carried out their entire ministries without being married. When we look at the history of missions, we might well ask ourselves where the international church would be today without single female missionaries. Claiming that people must be married to have fulfilled lives and walk in the will of God distorts the picture dramatically. Many congregations will not hire an unmarried pastor, but their reasons are probably more sociological than biblical.

Develop Relational Support Systems

Since single adults are socially and emotionally motivated (rather than theologically), the relationships of which Chapman spoke in an earlier citation loom very large. Discipling, mentoring, and small-group opportunities all provide some kind of support group to help meet the needs we have already discussed.

Carol King talks about a survey conducted in conservative and fundamental churches in a population center of nearly one-hundred thousand people. Few churches reported any significant number of singles in their congregations. Most of the churches had a ministry aimed at older adults—some with Sunday-school classes and some with a senior citizens group that met regularly. Many of these churches had college and career Sunday-school classes to meet the needs of those who had recently graduated from high school or college and had not yet married. However, fewer than five churches had a program designed to meet the needs of the single adult over twenty-five. In fact, of the two-hundred and eight churches in the Yellow Pages, only one (a church from a well-known mainline denomination) made any reference to a ministry for singles. Phone calls to area pastors turned up a few more ministries to single adults, although they were not publicized, and an individual could find out about them only by word of mouth.[5]

Affirm the Value of Singles

This has to do with both attitudes and programs in a local congregation. The first step is to show singles how useful, valuable, and important they are in the ministry of the church. But the other dimension of this response intends to prevent them from becoming some kind of isolated clique. Too often in large churches the singles group becomes a church-within-a-church, never reaching that integration level mentioned earlier in the chapter. All this has to do with congregational motives that underlie a singles ministry of any kind. If just a few singles in a congregation have been mainstreamed, there may be no need for a specific singles ministry. In any case the affirmation/acceptance factor is crucial.

Develop Spiritual Leadership

People grow in the Lord somewhat proportionately to the way they get involved in ministry. Social programs are essential for singles and are relatively easy to design. Serious Bible study which develops spiritual leadership takes much more creativity and effort. I recall speaking several times at Park Street Church in Boston, one of the oldest churches in America, located right next to the Boston Commons. This historic evangelical congregation actually consists of two congregations. At the morning worship service, one speaks to a normal mix of people, quite intergenerational and reasonably reflective of any church its size. On Sunday evening, however, Park Street hosts a totally different group. Since few congregants live in downtown Boston, they stay home in the suburbs on Sunday evening as the singles invade the service. Many of the latter were not present Sunday morning since the pizza party Saturday night didn't wind down until about two or three in the morning.

Please read this as a noncritical observation of a demographic phenomenon in one specific place. Because of its uniqueness, I doubt Park Street Church would want to be considered a model in singles ministry or perhaps anything else. Nevertheless the need to mainstream singles into the local church remains a challenge for every congregation.

FOUR COMMON MYTHS

Hazel Ruth Bell, whose article I referred to earlier, reflects on a major problem in evangelical churches: Church leaders have made false assumptions regarding singles and the way they should be treated in the church.[6] What are these common myths?

Singles Are a Threat to Marrieds

Bell suggests that churches worry whether married people might find the freewheeling single lifestyle more attractive, or perhaps one of the singles more attractive than a current spouse. The old song does lament, "I wish I were single again," but if this problem exists in any congregation or small group it is usually not initiated by the singles.

Most Singles Follow a Promiscuous Lifestyle or Are Homosexuals

Certainly professing Christian singles can get caught up in promiscuous or homosexual lifestyles, but that should hardly be considered the norm.

Most Singles Are Down on Themselves and Are Irresponsible

We have already talked about low self-esteem, which can breed immaturity leading to irresponsibility. But this may very well be more a factor of age and lack of experience than marital status. Furthermore, the opposite motivational scheme might come into play, whereby single adults serve with more vigor and enthusiasm to try to prove themselves worthy of acceptance in the church.

Most Singles Have Plenty of Money Since They Do Not Have Family Responsibilities

Some singles do seem to communicate that notion, and financial commitments are usually greater for heads of families. But singles have many of the same responsibilities as family people—mortgage payments, car payments, education expenses, food bills—and divorced singles may very well be considerably less financially secure than married adults.[7]

The group addressed in this chapter includes a wide age span. Perhaps it helps to think of singles not only as twenty-something but also as seventy-something. In a divorce-prone society, churches will have increasing opportunity to minister to middle-adult singles facing issues of job security, boredom, self-reassessment, physical changes, and health issues. Single-adult ministry means service for real people, by real people, and to real people. It is the task of the entire congregation, led by the pastoral staff and lay leaders. It works best when we target specific need groups, understand the concerns of singles, and when necessary, develop an interchurch community network to serve this strategic unit of the adult population.

15

❧ ❧ ❧

Flying Solo in the Family

At thirty-four, Allison's life bears no resemblance to what she anticipated fifteen years ago. She has one apartment, one car, two children, one
goldfish, and no husband. She suffers from loneliness, fatigue, disap-
pointment that sometimes borders on depression, and the empty feeling
that this frustrating life will continue without improvement for many
years to come.

Allison finds little comfort when reading that the number of single-
parent homes is growing rapidly. Nearly half the children born in the
midseventies will spend time living in one-parent homes before they are
age eighteen. Some estimate that more than half the children in all the public schools in America live with only one parent—in most cases, the mother.
One third of all divorced fathers never even see their children again.

But the church faces a new challenge unrelated to divorce. Nearly a
quarter of never-married eighteen- to forty-four-year-olds (four million)
have had at least one child. This trend goes back to the mid 1970s, when
women started making enough money to support children without husbands, but in the late 1990s this phenomenon has become widespread.
Furthermore, the most rapid rise in single motherhood shows up among
educated professional women.

How can your church help Allison, a divorcée, and many other men
and women who are single parents for a variety of reasons?

COPING WITH LONELINESS

All the research we have done—formal analysis of technical surveys on divorced people and single parents, as well as informal discussions with friends and acquaintances like Allison—indicates that loneliness rises to the top of the pile of problems for single parents. When it occurs with the sudden jolt of an unwanted divorce or unexpected death, the shock intensifies.

Lonely people who have been through divorce tend to suffer from a low level of self-esteem. One of the biggest struggles after a divorce is dealing with feelings of rejection, worthlessness, and failure. Allison's divorce came about because she could no longer tolerate her husband's abuse of her and her children. However, one of her closest friends, JoAnne, was divorced by her husband when he decided he wanted someone else. They both feel that they should have done things better or differently in order to have stopped these tragedies. The sting of rejection has made JoAnne feel like a complete failure as a woman.

This is just as hard emotionally on men. After nearly twenty years of marriage, Roger's wife decided she didn't want to be married anymore. He battles his need to forgive her and make a life for his two sons against his own feelings of failure for not understanding her emotional and personal struggles. Though single fathers will never outnumber single mothers, Roger is hardly alone. Men accounted for 15 percent of single parents in 1991, a total of 1.2 million households in the United States. Furthermore, half a million children are being raised by fathers who have never been married, a number that contrasts dramatically with the 32,000 who fit that description in 1970.

Nowhere will this chapter suggest easy answers. These kinds of agonies usually take a long time to heal. One of the first steps, however, sends us right back to the concept of grace. In God's eyes Allison, JoAnne, Roger—and all His children in similar situations—stand completely forgiven and totally loved. Somewhere along the line each will have to take the important step of accepting that forgiveness and leaving behind the self-condemnation that almost invariably accompanies a divorce. Jesus Christ, the Prince of Peace, can break down the walls between warring parties and can help suffering people to rest their internal struggles.

The Need for Belonging

People are peculiar. Just when the formerly married most desperately need the fellowship of the family of God, they are most tempted to separate from Christian friends who might be judgmental or at least uneasy about their status.

Loneliness and insecurity surrender their terrors not only to a *sense* of belonging but also to the *behavior* of belonging. Churches often ignore single parents, and these parents feel excluded from involvement in the ministries of the church. Walls of rejection still impede their struggle for acceptance.

The Need for Affirmation

Crucial to coping with loneliness stands the genuine affirmation that postmarital singleness is legitimate in the sight of God. This chapter does not present views of divorce and remarriage; there are excellent books and articles by competent evangelical theologians on that subject. We want single parents to hear and understand their role in the building of God's temple and to become a part of that spiritual construction (Eph. 2:21–22). The family may be incomplete at home, but it can be extended and increased through that family of families we call the church.

COPING WITH THE CHILDREN

Broken marriages inflict trauma and crises on more than a million children every year. We know that divorce presents children with one of the most serious and complex mental-health struggles they will ever experience.

But the ripple effect beyond the day-by-day struggles only complicates the issue. More than twenty-five thousand children a year are snatched or hidden from one parent by the other, and kidnapped children not found within six months probably won't be found for years.

Allison doesn't find this information about children very encouraging. She already feels guilt over the difficulties of handling her children. She can't seem to find the balance between personal fatigue and the need to spend time with her children. There is no secret formula or final solutions, but here are some suggestions single parents have found helpful.

Minimize Stress

The many daily experiences single parents face create psychological or emotional stress. Much of the pressure can be blamed on *domestic stress*. It invades the homes of single parents because their children struggle to adjust in school and probably have problems with peer relations.

Sometimes domestic stress gets tangled up with *financial stress* because of limited income. The necessity to work full-time, often during afternoon and evening hours, makes effective parenting almost impossible. Can this kind of stress be minimized? Only if we don't compound it with the internal emotional stress of guilt and failure. But how can we help single parents minimize these awful struggles?

We can encourage them to take their children into their confidence as much as possible in discussing how to solve family problems. We can teach them how to work out schedules together, how to utilize the resources of friends and parents, and how to let the kids describe where they hurt and what they need so they can at least pray together about the family situation rather than pretending it doesn't exist. We can encourage them to practice the truth of Matthew 11:28: "Come to me, all you who are weary and burdened, and I will give you rest."

Provide Role Models

Children with missing dads require a Christian male role model; those with missing moms, a female role model. (Boyfriends and girlfriends are not the answer here). If grandparents are still young and active, they might serve well. Or maybe uncles and aunts can help plug the leak. Sunday-school teachers, youth leaders, pastors, or other godly men and women at church all provide a talent pool of examples. It's hard to imagine an organization more equipped to meet this felt need than an effective church-education program.

Expect Improvement

Too many single parents simply anticipate that things will continue to get worse even when there is no justification for such a conclusion. How long does it take a child to adjust to divorce? It varies, of course, with the age of the child, the stability of his life both before and after the divorce, and the way the remaining parent handles the situation.

Generally speaking, we can assume that the situation of all family members involved in a divorce will get worse before it gets better. That's bad news. The good news is that even though the situation may seem to continue deteriorating, it can improve very suddenly. In one study psychologists found that five years after their parents' separation, a third of the children seemed to be resilient, an equal number seemed to be muddling through, coping as they could, and the rest were bruised, looking back to life before the divorce with intense longing.

But that research dealt with people who do not have supernatural answers to such problems. The help of Christian friends and family, the support of a godly, loving congregation, and the direct work of God's Holy Spirit in the lives of family members can dramatically change those statistics in favor of a healthy single-parent family.

With the help of fellow Christians in a caring church some single-parent families will not only survive, but they will thrive. Research comparing the percentages of sixth- through twelfth-grade young people in single-parent families who thrive with those who experience problems has uncovered at least six assets to thriving families: support, control, structured time, educational commitment, positive values, and social competencies. In every case we would have to agree these are areas in which the church can assist single parents in developing "thriving qualities."[1]

COPING WITH THE FUTURE

Besides having domestic and financial stress, Allison also finds herself constantly in *social stress*. Should she date? Should she think about remarrying? Can she still spend a lot of time with married friends without others becoming critical of her developing improper friendships?

In addition to coping with her own loneliness and the problems of her two children, she also has to cope with how to handle her life and their lives over the years and decades ahead. Allison knows she has to look ahead, and she's doing that by considering certain critical areas of concern.

Accept Singleness

Allison has accepted her singleness and is learning to live with her frustrations about getting remarried. Marriage may come sometime in the future, but she's not trying to make it happen nor will she worry if it doesn't happen. She's determined to be "whole" with or without a husband, and she is asking God to keep her from longing for marriage. She is fortunate to have a uniquely supportive family, and they help ease some of the loneliness. She tries to follow the advice of Ann Li Puma, who counsels single women to develop confidence, growth, and progression. "Equipped with the right balance of these, women will ultimately be able to transform this overwhelming need into something more realistic— more livable. Once that happens, we can all get on with our lives and perhaps even feel fulfilled, with or without a man."[2] Li Puma speaks for women, but the principle is the same for men.

Take Control

Neither JoAnne nor Allison had handled the family finances before their divorces, but they've decided to learn how to do them well, rather than living in fiscal fear. An accountant in their church showed them how to set up budgets and has graciously given them needed advice.

One of Roger's sons has a learning disability, and his wife had always taken care of medications, doctors' visits, and educational evaluations. Now Roger has no choice but to learn about those things himself.

All three of them had to change their household routines in order to make them workable. JoAnne had to lower her housekeeping standards since the necessity of working made it impossible to keep up her routine at home. Roger turned the meal-planning and grocery-shopping over to his oldest son. Allison contacted a neighborhood mechanic, who, for reasonable fees, would help keep her aging car running as smoothly as possible. In time these new skills and routines gave each of them a much better sense of personal control and competence.

Trust God

All three of these people have significant unmet needs in their lives. The issue of forced celibacy looms high on the list. Opportunities abound to meet that need in nonbiblical ways, but each has made a commitment to seek God's will. Not only do they not want to dishonor God, but they also want to model the kind of lifestyle they want their children to emulate before they marry. It's proving to be a major struggle, especially for Roger, and one that requires a moment-by-moment choice to trust God.

Seek Help

Biblical principles for parenting with grace do not change whether children are being reared in a single-parent family or surrounded by a large extended family. In all cases problems may arise that cannot be handled well within the family unit itself. JoAnne's oldest child, six when his parents divorced, was not doing passing work in the second grade. His teacher recommended counseling and therapy for him. This does not make JoAnne a failure as a mother; it does mean that her son needs help to deal successfully with the trauma in his young life. How will your church help her?

Choose Service

Allison has committed herself to becoming a person who serves. Yes, to a certain extent she will have to be served by others. The church will help her; relatives will help; friends will help—and she'll be grateful for all the help she can get. But she wants to be a helping person too. Her first line of ministry, of course, is to her own children. But she expects God to give her opportunity to talk to other single mothers and perhaps establish a network of people like herself in her church or community. She plans to discuss that with her pastor and solicit his support.

Allison will make it; many others will not. She'll make it because she understands the problems, believes they can be solved, and knows that the only real help comes from the Lord and His people. Recently she met several strong Christian adults who have been the products of broken homes. She had always assumed that missionaries, pastors, and Christian leaders came out of model families where both parents taught them the things of the Lord all their lives. What an encouragement for her to meet Christians who never knew their own fathers or whose parents abandoned them when they were very young.

Allison has set high goals. By God's grace her children will be loving, committed servants of Jesus Christ, leaders in their churches, godly marriage partners, and biblical parents—even if she has to give her life to that single goal. And that may well be the cost. How can your church design effective support ministries for Allison, JoAnne, and Roger?

Any congregation inherits a certain number of single parents, and in designing a ministry for them we must link truth and grace as Jesus did so beautifully in His life on earth. For traditional evangelical congregations this is a tough call. How do we offer grace without sacrificing truth, and maintain truth without sacrificing grace?

Perhaps all singles, including single parents, are drawn into a congregation through something of a funnel model (see diagram 11). At the top of the funnel we find church activities that clearly meet felt needs—support groups, child-care, social activities, singles classes. The problem comes when churches stop at that point and think that because singles have entered the funnel ministry the church has done its job. But the second level of the funnel as it narrows involves singles in worship, small-group Bible studies, and service projects. Eventually long-term commitments and serving in various offices must become a part of the process.

In all of this, obviously, we are striving for integration into the normal life of the congregation rather than isolation as a "problem group." Caring congregations help singles find a place where they belong. They assist the Allisons, JoAnnes, and Rogers in their search for normalcy. We can't pretend single-parent kids have two parents, but we can help them past the difficulties of their home situations. In a caring congregation divorced single parents are less likely to choose the worst possible option—marrying the wrong person and making the same mistake all over again.

All of this deserves the very best expertise and attention any church can give. God does not want us to shun people who have needs because of mistakes or even sin in their lives. And there are few people with needs as obvious and pressing as those of single parents—people who are struggling to force life to make sense once again when it seems to be total chaos.

DIAGRAM 11—FUNNELING SINGLE PARENTS

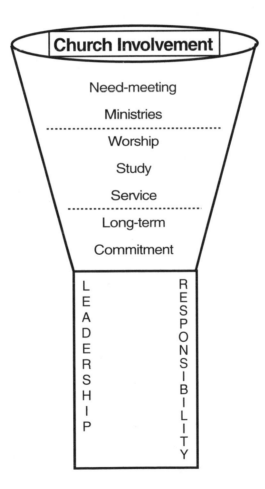

16

❧

Partnering with Parents

Family ministry is church ministry," announces the headline of the first issue of *Family Matters*, the newsletter of the Center for Family Life, founded and directed by my longtime friend Charles Sell. And because of the family's central importance the next six chapters focus on how congregations can help families.

The following figures present a most unenviable statistical portrait of present-day family life:

- Nearly half of all children live in single-parent families.

- 90 percent of one-parent families are headed by mothers.

- 30 percent of all children born today are born out of wedlock.

- 30 million children spend their early years in day-care centers.

- 100,000 children in America are homeless.

- 58 percent of mothers with preschoolers work outside the home.

- 14 million American children live in poverty.

- 25 percent of American teenagers drop out before finishing high school.

- 77 percent of all child abuse in America is initiated by parents.

In mid-1997 one of America's news magazines reported that childcare is the biggest job for men and women. Citing research from Penn State University, *Newsweek* indicates that men claim they spend 17.4 hours a week in childcare, and women 35.1.[1] America's families are desperate for help, and that help will not come from "a village"—it takes a church.

Charles Sell writes, "Family ministry is church ministry; it is at the heart of the church's spiritual and moral mission. To understand this, we need to define properly the term family. In sociological terms family is a 'social institution' which refers to the ways and customs of societies as they organize themselves to meet common needs."[2] Sell identifies seven needs (we could even call them developmental tasks) of families: reproduction, sexual expression, socialization, status, economic cooperation, emotional satisfaction, and social control.

Some would argue that social institutions have taken over many of these roles, but I contend that the biblical pattern requires parents to raise their children within the framework of a loving, supportive congregation. When that happens, many of the statistics cited above can take on very different patterns. Sell concludes his editorial by saying, "Many Christian leaders have been urging churches to recognize the critical relationship of churches and families. It is the Church's business that people live in Christ-like ways in their families at all stages of life."[3]

The church that does not meet the family needs of adults clearly fails to carry out its educational task for well over half the people in any congregation. Our purpose here is to deal with the way we can develop relationships and responsibilities (particularly as they relate to parenting) in all the homes represented by our congregations.

Source, the newsletter of Search Institute, suggests that adult education should turn to the business of strengthening families. Search researchers argue that children have eight needs: support, empowerment, boundaries and expectations, constructive use of time, commitment to learning, positive values, social competencies, and positive identity. Evangelical church leaders might use different terminology and offer solid biblical support, but it is difficult to disagree with the general premise of the Search Institute: "Responsibility for children does not end with the provision of external assets. There needs to be a similar commitment to nurturing the internalized commitments, values, competencies, and identity children need to guide their choices and create a sense of centeredness, and purpose. Adults who model these assets when children are young lay the foundation for children to observe, learn, and gradually internalize these assets."[4]

QUALITIES OF A STRONG FAMILY

We have all seen the lists—some religious, some secular—that identify the marks of strong families. And most of them represent solid research, not just some idea that occurred to an author or reporter. What follows is something of a summary of the kind of things churches should develop in their family-life education programs.

Commitment to Family

The next chapter will pick up this theme, but we must mention it here. Strong families are committed not just to each other but also to the concept of family itself. When it comes to the principal players, mom and dad, we know *it is not the love that sustains the marriage, but the marriage that sustains the love.* Christians commit themselves to each other and that commitment nurtures their love. Strong families do not stumble around trying to explain why things don't work; they make things work. And when they make things work at home, we have some hint that they may be ready for leadership at church.

Growing Intimacy

We have spoken on intimacy in relationships beyond the boundaries of family. But in the context of the family it takes on a much more significant meaning.

Family intimacy means sharing not only attitudes but feelings and emotions. Family members watch each other laugh and cry, smile and pout, joke and sulk. They not only share feelings about themselves on an intimate level, but also feelings about each other. Strong families don't turn an evening meal into a brawl just because one member tells another the truth about how he feels. Family intimacy is cultivated; it is a developing process that takes years. It may begin with two young people in love; then that immature but deeply felt emotion acts as the door to a workshop in which we will hammer out tools of intimacy on the forge of daily struggles.

Time Together

Strong families find a way to spend time together—and they don't cheat on that requirement by talking about "quality time," one of the great domestic excuses of the last decade. Strong families try to make *all* their time together "quality time."

Expressed Appreciation

Strong families say, "Thank you," "I appreciate you so much," "I'm grateful to God that you are a part of our family," and "I'm proud of you." We have talked about the affirmation that comes from jobs and social institutions like a church or a civic club. But none of that can even approach the level of affirmation needed at home. When it comes to expressed devotion, the boardroom is no match for the family room.

Good Communication

If you never saw a list of the qualities of strong families, you could have guessed this one. Good communication takes place when family members have learned how to talk to one another. Not just husband and wife, although that is where it must begin, but parents to children, children to parents, in-laws to out-laws, and others.

Biblical Awareness

Strong Christian families study the Bible together because it helps them draw closer to God. They discuss Scripture and talk about interpretation;

they apply the Bible to life and make it the ultimate measure of family behavior. The "good communication" we talked about above takes on important new dimensions as God speaks to Christian families through His Word and they respond in obedience and prayer.

Congregational Involvement

Strong families understand they are part of the church, the body of Christ, and of a local congregation. They help us minister to them by declaring and living out their allegiance to the church. Make no mistake; we can never expect quality service from a family that has not first received quality ministry from its church.

FAMILY OF FAITH

Let's take this church-home partnership business a bit further. When we compare the family of faith at home to the family of faith that gathers in a church building, we note immediately how marriage compares biblically with salvation. Christ is the Bridegroom and believers are the bride. Through evangelism God procreates new believers and we call it "new birth." Then we talk about *nurture*, a horticultural term describing how people take care of plants and a spiritual theme especially common in the writings of the apostle Paul.

The security of the family reflects the provision of the church for needy people. As Luke wrote in Acts 4:34, "There were no needy persons among them." Both family and congregation represent dynamic support groups, both paying special attention to needy members. What an unstoppable team—the family of faith at home and at church.

Theological Concepts

Nearly twenty years ago educator John Westerhoff suggested that congregations "become the central most important unit of societal life, that they become the fundamental social unit in our modern culture. . . . The issue for the church, therefore, is not how to humanize or help the family and the state to be humane, but how to reform its life so that it might become a 'faith community' for the humanization of persons and social life."[5]

Westerhoff turned to German Lutheran theology for support, picking up the concepts of *Gemeinschaft* and *Gesellschaft*. Martin Luther had contended that the church can be faithful only if it is more like the former than the latter, though both words could be translated by the English word *community*. A *Gesellschaft* tends to be more like a voluntary association in which persons play a greater or lesser role and participate in communal activities. Performance and contribution to the group certify the value of its members. Perhaps we could compare it to a local YMCA where our children or grandchildren play in the soccer league.

A *Gemeinschaft*, on the other hand, is more like a family where one gives whatever love requires and the value of the members centers in their being a normal and natural part of the group. Perhaps better English words for *Gemeinschaft* are *brotherhood* or *fellowship*. Westerhoff develops four ideas that mark this faith community in its sense of common life, qualities we would hope are found in both family and church.

Common Memory

In a family, common memory centers in the wonderful traditions built up through the years. Photos, slides, and videotapes reproduce for us things we did together ten or twenty years earlier. The Christian family with its mutual commitment to God carries over into the congregation with its "common memory" centering in the history of God's work in the world as we know it from Scripture.

Common Vision

Sound families and churches not only understand the past; they are committed to a future together. How can this be when we are such a transient society? Westerhoff tells about a Dachau survivor who asked a pastor how such a catastrophe could have happened in the land of Luther and Bach. The old man responded, "That is easy to understand. The Christian church had become concerned with the here and the now; it had lost its visions and forgotten what the Bible teaches."[6]

Common Authority

In both church and home the common authority is Jesus Christ and the Word of God. Far above governmental rubrics or the requirements of a constitution and bylaws, evangelical believers hold to the authority of Scripture in an intense effort never to forget what the Bible teaches.

Common Rituals

Here Westerhoff has in mind "repetitive symbolic actions expressive of its memory and vision." Family traditions fit well into this *Gemeinschaft* category, as do our collective celebrations at church—baptism, the Lord's Supper, Christmas Eve, or Good Friday, and many other marks of our collective life together. These are rituals of the family of faith. As Westerhoff puts it, "It is only because of our life in our church that we can be Christian alone, in cultural families, or in society."[7]

Educational Concepts

How do we make this work? How do we design adult-education ministries to produce the kind of family life the Bible calls for, the behavioral patterns discussed in chapters 16–21?

Parent counseling represents exactly what it appears to be—counseling by the pastoral staff or other church leaders with quarreling spouses, rebellious children, or parents struggling with a variety of parenting issues. *Parent education* focuses on everything from weekly Sunday school classes, which will occasionally deal with family matters, to parenting classes designed in their totality to achieve the kind of goals we have set for them. *Parent conferencing* refers to "off-campus" events such as seminars, retreats, or family camp. *Parent participation* simply means that people in families are a part of what the church does on a regular basis—Sunday school, youth activities, preaching, social events.

Parent counseling, the first of these four, generally requires more expertise. But parent participation, the last of these, calls for minimal staff time (virtually all church ministries are staffed by volunteers) for serving the largest possible number of people. Family counseling, although necessary, will become less urgent if more parent participation and parent conferencing are done.

But none of it will happen without a strong component of family-life education in adult ministries.

THE MODELING CONGREGATION

Modeling takes place whether we design it or not. In the family, fathers and mothers have no choice except to model well or to model poorly; modeling itself will happen. So in the congregation, even when people may not specifically think of church leaders as family role models, the Bible calls for this kind of responsible behavior. What must a congregation do to be an effective and positive role model for the family?

Take a Biblical Approach to All Cultural Issues

The positions a local congregation adopts on matters like abortion, homosexuality, divorce, and a host of other societal problems must be defended biblically. No congregation should ever adopt a theological view on these issues merely because its denomination has done so or because society at large seems to be swinging in a certain direction. Certainly biblical texts are capable of different interpretations. However, this is one area of family modeling which does not derive much help from tradition. Orthodox answers may work at an ordination council, but the realities of life require a warm biblicism. The famous rich young ruler was orthodox, and Jesus commended him for that. But he couldn't answer the penetrating question, "Who is my neighbor?"

Teach Parents to Function at Home

We can never do the whole job at church and shouldn't try. Pastors and Sunday-school teachers are only parents to their own children, though every congregation does some surrogate parenting with the offspring of unbelievers. Biblical congregations don't keep multiplying ministry programs to take the place of what parents don't do at home; they focus their energy and attention on how to help parents take up their own responsibilities.

Correct Traditional Failures

Too often the church has been judgmental rather than redemptive with respect to family struggles. We have often overprogrammed our ministries, stifling family life for people who want to be faithful to everything that goes on at the church building. Except for the past twenty or thirty years we have paid little attention to family life (and especially family-life education), apparently assuming that parents would figure things out on their own. Only the major breakup of the family in the late twentieth century jolted the attention of evangelical Christians.

Be Sensitive and Courageous

Sensitive to need and hurt, but courageous for the truth, we find ourselves back at the need for balance between grace and truth. When parents can see church leaders and teachers functioning in this kind of biblical balance, they will be more able to respond that way at home with each other and with their own children.

SEVEN WAYS TO DEVELOP A FAMILY-ORIENTED CHURCH

We still have chapters ahead which deal with adult-education programming and family-life goals, but here we'll quickly mention some ways churches can demonstrate their commitment to stronger families.

Preach about the Home

Certainly this should be done on special days like Mother's Day and Father's Day, but preferably more often than that. Expository preachers who preach through Bible books need to make room for those special days as well as emphasizing all the significant family passages found throughout the Bible. No need to reach out for family emphasis as a false gesture; just don't neglect it when it appears in the text. The pastor approaching Acts 16, for example, might very well stop at Paul's decision to add Timothy to the ministry team and talk about the kind of family support that helped prepare Timothy for serving in such a role.

Program with Families in Mind

Most churches are doing much better at this now than two or three decades ago. Such programming leaves nights open and suggests time for the family to be at home rather than at church. It recognizes the struggle of double-income families with long commutes and arranges its programming around the family rather than forcing the family to reorganize its life around the church.

Popularize Family Life

We can find many creative ways to do this—bulletin announcements, a "family of the week" emphasis, prayer for families by other families, and many more. Be careful here. As we popularize family life, we do not want to make singles feel uncomfortable. But a balance is not impossible to achieve.

Prospect for Families

Biblical programs of evangelism and outreach aim at families, not just children. Whatever else "household salvation" means in your theology, it surely means God does not want us to separate any family member from the others, if at all possible.

Sunday school bussing isolates children from their parents. Though we are all grateful for the thousands of children who heard the gospel because churches ran bus fleets all around their counties, the concept has virtually no biblical support. That big Sunday school bus rolled up in front of a house and its very presence said to parents, "Go back to bed; we'll take your children to Sunday school."

Prayer for Families and by Families

Most congregations look for creative ways to conduct public prayer. In one church I attended, the midweek prayer time centered on families, with a focus on one or two each week. The pastor introduced families by name, asked the congregation questions about the family to see how well they knew them, and asked the family members (especially the small children) questions about their parents. It was a delightful time and genuinely centered the interest and prayer focus on families.

Provide for Families

Provide whatever they need to do the job. Do they need some guidelines for family worship? Do they need a book on strong-willed children? Do they need Christian videos to help their children learn Bible stories? Provide it—that's what churches are for. That's what family-life education does.

Purpose to Be a Serving Church

Congregations committed to family-life education determine that they will serve their families. In reality, this seventh suggestion makes possible the first six. A church actively determined to serve its families will find ways to do so.

Yet there are still church leaders whose view of the family centers in the demand that the family serve the church. "Guilt-trip theology" seemed a hallmark of many evangelical congregations just after World War II. Somehow we need to back away from such thinking, review what unleashes motivation in adults, and apply that to our efforts at family-life education.

As Charles Sell wrote, "A church that facilitates robust family life is ministering morally and spiritually, tasks God intended for it. Family ministry is church ministry, something essential, not optional. By enriching and sustaining family life, the church is nurturing itself."[8]

17

Developing Biblical Homes

In Thorton Wilder's play *The Skin of Our Teeth,* Mrs. Antrobus says to her husband, "I didn't marry you because you are perfect. . . . I married you because you gave me a promise." She takes off her ring and looks at it. "That promise made up for your faults and the promise I gave you made up for mine."[1] Two imperfect people got married; the promise made the marriage.

All marriages include promises. Much of family life rests on how well they are kept—not only between husband and wife, but between parents and children and among the varying relationships in any family group. But unfortunately, our society is not given to promise-keeping. The enormous popularity of the men's group Promise Keepers indicates something of the felt need for a higher sense of loyalty and stability, especially in the family.

Statistics about family breakup and divorce are bounced around and used to support varying viewpoints. But we do know that the family faces a state of disintegration in Western culture. For decades it has been under fire from a variety of powerful enemies. Somehow, however, we want to believe that there ought to be exceptions to the statistics—the families who attend our churches. Surely men and women dedicated to Jesus Christ and to each other can stem the tide in a society seemingly determined to destroy the family.

Unfortunately, an informed analysis of evangelical churches does not support that notion. Divorce, separation, delinquency, drug use, abortion, marital unfaithfulness—all the problems that contribute to family breakdown in the society at large have found their way into the Christian community as well.

But we see mounting evidence that committed churches are rededicating themselves to enhancing family stability. Like pockets of resistance in a war-ravaged country, they have determined to follow through on God's design for the family and to support Christian homes. What does it take? What are the marks of a Christian family?

Biblical People

Christian homes can only be created by biblical people—people who have chosen to build relationships and determine their actions according to God's plan. Remember the progression: Biblical people become biblical partners who can then become biblical parents.

What do biblical people look like? Does some special quality make them people who somehow live on a plane inaccessible to the average person? In truth, becoming a biblical person is like everything else in life worth developing: It takes hard work and a series of increasingly complex commitments. Certainly it helps to have grown to maturity in a home that modeled biblical living. However, since many who seek help with parenting problems have not had that privilege, we'll describe the process through the lives of two people without it.

Two Sample Christians

Let's start with twenty-five-year-old Pam, a graduate of a large Midwestern university with a degree in computer science. Pam didn't grow up in a Christian home. She trusted Christ through a parachurch campus ministry at her university and launched into a promising career as a programmer in a startup high-tech company.

Her parents are extremely proud of her; neither of them attended college. They owned and operated a print shop with modest success, so Pam had to plough through her education on scholarships, loans, and part-time jobs. Though her parents were not Christians, they had formed a stable marriage, characterized by mutual respect and support during both good and bad times. This model has given Pam something positive to work toward, and she thinks she can build on it in her own commitment to Christ.

Although she is in many ways still in spiritual childhood, Pam has recognized that she needs to be part of a nurturing group of Christians and has joined a large church with a reputation for ministry to singles in her new city. There she met Scott, whom she has dated for the last six months.

Scott's family background bears little resemblance to Pam's. His parents divorced when he was only two years old. Because his mother was an alcoholic, his father had full custody of him and his older brother, then eight. His father has since been married and divorced twice more. Although his father's profession permitted financial comfort, Scott has struggled with personal insecurities along with unresolved feelings of anger and bitterness about his upbringing. His older brother, following in his father's pattern, has been twice married and divorced.

Despite his marital woes, Scott's father did see to it that his sons attended church regularly, and he encouraged their participation in the youth-group activities. A caring youth leader introduced Scott to Christ and helped give him some stability during his teenage years. His college years proved difficult at first. He found it hard to choose a major, and he dropped out for two years to work with a relief agency in Central America. During that time, he became proficient in Spanish and found he had a genuine affinity for teaching young children. He returned to college, earned his teacher's certification, and now works with at-risk children in an urban school district.

Scott sincerely loves Pam, but his family background makes him very reluctant to guarantee a long-term commitment. One thing he knows: Despite his material comfort, he does not want his children brought up the way he was.

What decisions do Scott and Pam have to make to give birth to a new home that is genuinely Christian? How can these very different members of your congregation find some answers at church?

Four Basic Principles

Adult educators understand that no rigid formula, followed without deviation, can automatically produce a perfect family. These chapters contain guiding principles based on Scriptures, years of parenting practice, and years of interacting with others through their family and parenting experiences. Pam and Scott need to consider four initial commitments as they think through the possibility of marriage:

- A commitment to God's will

- A commitment to each other

- A commitment to family

- A commitment to lifelong love

No one of these commitments stands independently from the others. The initial commitment, however, needs to start with the source of all: a loving Father who desires the holiness and Christlikeness of His children. Pam and Scott know they are, separately, God's own; now they must be willing to entrust their relationship to God as well. As they continue to get to know one another, we must also teach them how to place their relationship before the Lord for His direction.

Serious adult educators know that the kind of love expressed so beautifully in 1 Corinthians 13 comes from the commitment to love, not the romantic feelings that accompany it. Traditional popular music makes it sound as though romantic love can be sustained endlessly and effortlessly. But this is a juvenile myth. Lasting marriages protect and develop loving relationships.

Any program of family-life education cultivates the desire to be biblical people. Only through this foundation can a man and woman seek to fulfill the biblical purposes of marriage.

Biblical Purpose

Because of Scott's background, Pam sometimes feels they have little in common; the distance between them seems insurmountable. Not because of Scott's personality—he's lots of fun, gentle, attentive, and he goes to church with Pam every Sunday. But is this enough to fulfill God's purposes in marriage?

Pam spends many sleepless hours wondering why God created marriage in the first place. The complications seem overwhelming. Scott, as we know, has his own hesitations. Having seen no healthy models of marriage, he wonders if a good marriage is even possible.

What is God's design for marriage? What priorities does He want His children to follow?

Complete Companionship

Companionship stands as the primary purpose of marriage. In spite of all the wonderful things God created in the Garden of Eden, Adam alone was incomplete. None of the animals, splendid as they must have been before the Fall, could provide a fitting companion for him. So "the LORD God said, 'It is not good for the man to be alone. I will make a helper suitable for him'" (Gen. 2:18).

The strategic role of the husband-wife relationship in marriage draws a bull's-eye on the family target. Everything else is secondary. Everything else takes a lower place, because when companionship doesn't work, the family can't function.

Sexual Fulfillment

The early chapters of Genesis contain no specific account of the sexual attitudes and activities of Adam and Eve. But throughout the pages of Scripture it seems clear that in Christian marriage, physical sharing flows from spiritual sharing. The mutual responsibilities of husband and wife are noted in 1 Corinthians 7:3–5: "The husband should fulfill his marital duty to his wife, and likewise the wife to her husband. The wife's body does not belong to her alone but also to her husband. In the same way, the husband's body does not belong to him alone but also to his wife. Do not deprive each other except by mutual consent and for a time, so that you may devote yourselves to prayer. Then come together again so that Satan will not tempt you because of your lack of self-control."

To people like Pam and Scott we emphasize that sexual fulfillment in marriage is part of God's design, never to be used as a tool of manipulation. Sexual ploys open lives to temptation by Satan. Biblical people practicing biblical purposes understand the meaning of Hebrews 13:4: "Marriage should be honored by all, and the marriage bed kept pure, for God will judge the adulterer and all the sexually immoral."

Because of their strong physical attraction to each other Pam and Scott naively assume they will have no problems here. But sexual problems rank very high on the list of primary causes for marital discord. It takes a great deal of time, a lot of trust, and maybe some teaching for young couples to learn to please their mates sexually.

Planned Parenthood

Like many other people in their generation, Scott and Pam will be in their late twenties when they marry. If they want children, they will need to plan how God's purposes can be fulfilled in their young family.

The crowning glory of children in marriage provides the theme for a song of praise often sung in the pages of Holy Scripture. In Psalms 127:3–5 and 128:3 we learn that children are a reward from the Lord. The command to "be fruitful and increase in number and fill the earth" came to both Adam and Noah (Gen. 1:28; 9:1, 7). God's miracle of procreation continues as a mystery of grace to expectant parents.

But this purpose cannot be filled by every parent. In some cases God wills people to be childless, often despite trying all medical options. The Bible doesn't ask us to be passive in accepting childlessness nor aggressive in building large families. The Bible's gentle, patient tone simply suggests that husbands and wives seek God's will together.

Scott and Pam haven't said much about this yet, but they had better get it on their agenda soon. Pam will probably find herself pregnant within a year if they choose not to use birth control. An unexpected "surprise" may delight them; it may also devastate them if they feel emotionally and financially unprepared.

Family planning is certainly a luxury of recent generations. The issue before Pam and Scott is not one of morality but practicality. Both came from small families, Pam an only child, Scott one of two. Would they prefer the same for their family, or would they enjoy the challenges of rearing several children? What spacing between children would work best? Because Scott's profession is not particularly high-paying, should Pam continue to work during their children's preschool years? If their church helps them address these kinds of questions up front, it can spare them many arguments and misunderstandings later.

Family Unity

Shortly before he died Moses reiterated the Law for his nation and emphasized the Israelites' responsibility as parents (Deut. 6:4–25). The home has always been God's primary place of nurture and growth. In designing marriage the heavenly Father created a system in which children can be nurtured in wisdom and faith.

God doesn't give babies to school systems or church congregations; He gives them to families. The very process of reproduction stamps on parents the responsibility to nurture their children until they become adults, and then the cycle begins all over again. In that domestic context, now as then, God wants to see the kind of unity and harmony that reflect the Holy Spirit's presence in the living and loving of people in our congregations.

Church Symbolism

The primary metaphor for the New Testament church centers in the human body (Rom. 12; 1 Cor. 12). But in Ephesians 5, Paul drew a comparison between husband-wife and Christ-church relationships. What is the church like? Like a family. How do we understand what the church is supposed to do? We watch godly husbands and wives relating to each other and to their children, and we learn what God intends in the congregation.

Some Christian families become the only "church" unsaved neighbors ever see. As they watch husbands and wives nourishing and cherishing each other and their families, they learn something about the way the Lord nourishes and cherishes the church. As they see children treat their parents with respect, honoring them with obedience, they learn how God's people respond to the Lord of the church. Christian families are to be a microcosmic demonstration of the body of Christ in the world.

Churches develop intricate plans for neighborhood evangelism—and sometimes they even work. But the daily behavior of a godly family offers consistent witness of God's grace wherever people watch them, almost as though He is playing and replaying a video of His craftsmanship—in the yard, at a neighborhood Christmas party, in restaurants, at a Little League game—unfolding the story of a family representing the church.

Biblical Principles

Marriage is for adults only. As Pam grows in her own Christian life, she hopes Scott can keep up. No doubt about his salvation; but sometimes his lifestyle and comments seem out of sync with biblical values. As their relationship develops, they have begun to make commitments to each other, and Pam is hoping and praying that this will all sort itself out after the wedding.

Biblical people ready to embark on a biblical purpose must maintain a level of maturity that can handle the different tasks of family relationships and apply biblical principles in those relationships. Your church will want to teach numerous biblical principles for marriage and family living, but here we look at only four.

Monogamy

How can our teachers handle Old Testament passages telling us that David and others had multiple wives and yet were greatly loved and blessed of God? After all, David is called a man after God's own heart (1 Sam. 13:14; Acts 13:22)! Looking at the flow of God's truth through both Old and New Testaments, we see God's initial design was for one man and one woman in the Garden. Then sin entered the world, and all kinds of aberrations became common.

In speaking to the Greeks about idolatry Paul said, "In the past God overlooked such ignorance, but now he commands all people everywhere to repent" (Acts 17:30). As the New Testament opens and the church takes form, it almost seems as though God starts over again with His plan for Christian families. Joseph and Mary offer the purity and beauty of monogamous godly marriage. Amid the paganism of Greco-Roman culture, the early church stood committed to several basic and absolute truths, including the purity of marriage relationships.

Fidelity

Whatever happened to "till death do us part"? In Romans 7 Paul used that concept as an illustration of the law in Christian living. His illustration emphasizes the finality of the marriage bond: "For example, by law a married woman is bound to her husband as long as he is alive, but if her husband dies, she is released from the law of marriage" (7:2). Sometimes we talk about marriage being "eternal," but that is not a biblical concept. Heaven has no marriage (Matt. 22:30)—its termination at death is a part of God's plan.

As much as we talk about committing ourselves to each other "forever," we really mean until death. The fancy language in marriage ceremonies comes not only from years of church tradition, but also from a solid biblical base. Yes, sometimes things go wrong and marriages don't last. In those agonizing experiences we turn people to God's grace, not to judgmental harshness and finger pointing. They are not perfect people any more than their church leaders. But that is no excuse for not working hard to help them apply biblical principles in their homes.

Heterosexuality

Just a few years ago it would not have seemed necessary to emphasize heterosexuality in marriage, but "homosexual marriage" reflects the perversion of contemporary culture. Overwhelming biblical evidence condemns homosexuality. We know of only one episode in history in which God singled out a particular sin and destroyed two entire cities because of it, the sin was homosexuality, and the cities were Sodom and Gomorrah (Gen. 19).

Though Christians do not entirely agree on this subject, the recognition of a homosexual or lesbian union as a "marriage" clearly falls under biblical censure. It surely does not diminish our emphasis on God's grace and forgiveness to suggest heterosexuality is God's only plan for marriage. Once again, church education must handle social issues biblically and courageously.

Mutuality

Scott and Pam are both excited. They worked through the problems, set the date, and are planning their wedding. They talked about how to blend their careers, share responsibilities in homemaking and parenting, and take lifetime responsibility for each other. They seem well on their way toward a positive partnership and committed service to Christ in their church.

Mutuality in marriage requires the willingness of each partner to unite two lives and take equal responsibility to make the marriage work. Some claim marriage can't be a fifty-fifty arrangement because such a marriage would have no "boss." But headship in marriage is another matter. The concept of mutuality means sharing responsibility for outcomes and consequences. A solid Christian home is not built on a "fifty–fifty" marriage. It should be more like a one hundred–one hundred arrangement.

Scott and Pam have a lot going for them. They love each other, and they are intelligent, cautious, and optimistic. Even with Scott's dysfunctional family background, their dependence on God and each other can launch them well into marriage and give them a good chance at establishing a Christian home—with the help of their church.

But they'll have to beat the odds. With single-parent families rapidly on the increase and second and third marriages more common than ever in history, Scott and Pam will have to practice the principles set forth in this chapter to achieve God's best for them.

Remember, this is not a formula—marriage is not mathematics! As they develop their love and God honors their commitments, the happiest years of their lives lie just ahead.

18

❧❦❧

Establishing Godly Standards

S*andy and her friend* Kim have just turned fifteen. Last week they went
to their first "real" party, a get-together of about twenty kids after a basketball game. There was no parental supervision; they were allowed, perhaps
unwisely, to go with their dates, who were two or three years older. And
though both girls are Christians, most kids at the party were not.

The loud rap music and dancing offered no surprise, and they expected heavy beer drinking, even by members of the team. But late in the
evening something happened that changed their lives. Their dates took
them to a bedroom at the back of the house and invited them to try some
cocaine. As the powder was passed around, they said no, stuck with it,
and paid the price in harassment for the rest of the party. But that evening
proved a significant milestone in their spiritual growth—they each made
a personal, independent decision regarding right and wrong.

Why would they make a decision like that? Why not run with the crowd?
More important, what kind of family and church support provided them
with the resources to make the choice most Christians would consider right?
Christian parents and evangelical congregations struggle to identify and
teach absolute standards of biblical morality and ethics without superim-
posing their own particular interpretations or peculiarities on what the Bible
says. But morality often seems a moving target. The key word is *absolute:* a

principle or truth that does not change. Our society has virtually thrown over absolutes, particularly in the realm of morality and ethics.

On certain subjects Americans have simply changed their minds. Gambling used to be widely condemned. Now churches run Bingo games, and many states operate lotteries. At one time, consumption of alcohol was widely condemned. Now nearly two-thirds of Americans drink at least occasionally. Churches are called by God to help parents teach their children and teenagers to live godly lives in a culture designed to make them ungodly.

CONFLICTS IN THE BATTLE FOR STANDARDS

Whatever Sandy and Kim would have decided that night, one thing is sure—they faced internal conflicts arising from standards taught in their families and church. But even more important, the Holy Spirit in their hearts would constantly remind them of the difference between right and wrong. Once we help adults understand the human tendency toward sinning, and recognize the reality of the battle, we can also help them begin to sort out the conflicts and teach their children some guidelines.

Between Product and Process

Most Christians agree to some extent on the kind of product they would like to see come out of their homes after eighteen years—but they often disagree on the process. Parents abuse Proverbs 22:6 when they take it as an ironclad promise rather than a guideline. Parents need to recognize that the rules of parenting may vary with each child who enters the home, whereas biblical standards do not change.

Between Society's Standards and Family Standards

Should Christian young people be allowed to smoke? Should they go to rock concerts? Is social drinking in the Christian home harmless or harmful? Christians don't agree on the answers to these questions. Regardless of the positions your church takes, children will be playing and talking with youngsters from families with widely varying sets of standards. Strict legal codes of what we "do" and "don't do" are not adequate. Instead both parents and teens need to develop convictions and standards arising from the teaching of God's Word.

Between Parental and Youth Values

How democratic can a family be? We can teach participatory family leadership and we should; but there are always certain things that parents alone can determine. Kids may petition their parents about certain issues—but Christian parents cannot abdicate God-given authority in basic decisions that affect the family.

However, God-given authority exercised lovingly in a participatory setting does not mean absolute control over the lives of family members. As we teach parents to talk out various problems and issues, discussing the biblical principles behind their decisions and guidelines, children begin to grasp the idea that mom and dad have their best interests in mind. They will not always agree with the decisions, but we can help parents try to maintain fairness with their children.

Let's take another look at Kim. Already under a pile of classes, yearbook responsibilities, drama club, and dates, she comes home and announces she wants to try out for cheerleading. Should her parents agree? Should they "protect her from herself" by not letting her get involved in too many activities? What should we say to our church members to prepare them for real-life situations like this?

Morality and ethics do not figure into this question, so it becomes a matter of what is best for Kim at this time in her life. Wise parents will steer toward a mutual decision, one that takes into consideration her grades, the amount of time she would have to invest in cheerleading, and what family sacrifices might be necessary if she makes the squad. Key question: How does Kim handle the commitments she already has?

Giving Kim some responsibility for decision-making will increase her self-respect and her commitment to the family and will probably enhance the value of the decision. But do her parents know that?

Between Legalism and License

In Paul's day the Galatians had no problem accepting God's grace for salvation, but they wanted to write a whole code of Christian conduct based largely on Old Testament teachings. Paul pointed out that living for Christ after salvation is just as much an act of faith and grace as salvation itself (Gal. 3:1–5; 5:1).

The opposite of legalism is license, and Peter addressed that problem clearly: "Live as free men, but do not use your freedom as a cover-up for evil; live as servants of God" (1 Pet. 2:16). Liberty provides the joyful biblical balance between legalism and license. But we only live in freedom when we behave in accord with the principles (standards) of God's Word.

CONVICTIONS IN THE BATTLE FOR STANDARDS

The development of godly standards is a proven step toward crisis prevention and may have been the difference between standing and falling for Sandy and Kim. *Convictions are valued beliefs that can be translated into behavior.* Sure, they are learned from adult mentors, but the ones that work stem from the inside, not from someone else's faith system.

Paul wrote a lot about Spirit-motivated behavior. Here are five of the many principles he advocated.

Body Control

Everyone faces body-related temptations—drugs, alcohol, obesity, anorexia, bulimia, illicit sex—and God has given some instructions regarding the use of our bodies. First Corinthians 6:12–20 is one such passage. The *Living Bible* renders verses 19–20 as follows: "Haven't you yet learned that your body is the home of the Holy Spirit God gave you, and that he lives within you? Your own body does not belong to you. For God has bought you with a great price. So use every part of your body to give glory back to God, because he owns it."

That's clear, isn't it? Properly applied, this biblical standard could eliminate many controversial questions about behavior. When we teach adults that Jesus lives in us, we help them take a major step on the road of sanctification. Every Christian of any age has to realize, "God lives in me; where I go, God goes; what I read, God reads." The text deals with immorality, but general application aims at Spirit control of one's entire body at all times.

Self-education

Paul wrote this about freedom: "Everything is permissible—but not everything is beneficial. Everything is permissible—but not everything is constructive" (1 Cor. 10:23). This standard states that Christians ought to be doing things, thinking things, going places, and acting in ways that will build up their lives and make them more like Jesus. Standing guard against things that can harm us is only half the battle. Paul urged us to go one step further and to ask, in essence, "How does this help me as a Christian?"

Habit Freedom

Christian living can't be legislated, but it can be learned. In 1 Corinthians 6:12 Paul wrote, " 'Everything is permissible for me'—but I will not be mastered by anything." So freedom from habits is a question not of rules but of responsibility. Does alcohol master people? Yes. Do drugs master those who take them? Yes. What about homosexuality? Anger? Bitterness? Envy? Depression? Answer the questions yourself, and consider the importance of communicating principles of "habit freedom" to both parents and children in the Christian home.

Life Testimony

First Corinthians 8 presents an argument leading to the final and key verse: "Therefore, if what I eat causes my brother to fall into sin, I will never eat meat again so that I will not cause him to fall" (8:13). What about the television shows parents watch when guests are in their homes? What kind of language or attitudes do parents display around their children? The standard is clear: I *am* my brother's brother or sister and must take responsibility for behavior that causes him to fall into sin. That's a tough standard in a society constantly looking out for number one!

When Sandy reflects on the party after the basketball game, she whispers a prayer of thanks to God for giving her the courage to live up to her convictions. Opportunities to share her faith and explain why she does or does not behave certain ways have dramatically increased since that night. What she first thought might bring ostracism from the group, God turned into credibility. Sandy has a developed a reputation as a "genuine" Christian.

Preeminence of Christ

Effective adult-education ministry teaches parents to work at the Lord-disciple relationship so essential to Christian living. Describing the supremacy of Christ, Paul writes, "He is the head of the body, the church; he is the beginning and the firstborn from among the dead, so that in everything he might have the supremacy" (Col. 1:18). Dedicated disciples practice the brief but poignant life philosophy of John the Baptist: "He must become greater; I must become less" (John 3:30).

COMMITMENTS IN THE BATTLE FOR STANDARDS

Sometimes in the parenting process parents want to be committed to a nice quiet padded cell somewhere. We can offer them few "once and for all" finalities in parenting. With each new state, each step of growth, they recommit themselves in each of the following areas.

Patience

Parenting takes patience. We're trying to move children from dependence to independence. Some freshmen enter college unable to handle even the smallest decision because they were refused the opportunity to question and reason at home. Their parents forced them into a position of dependence too long.

The opposite problem surfaces when parents offer independence too soon. Students given too much liberty tend to adopt a general attitude of rebellion and a growing distaste for authority. The solution? Patience and willingness to spread the process from birth to adulthood.

Perseverance

Consider emphasizing to parents in your congregation that great verse in Hebrews: "Therefore, strengthen your feeble arms and weak knees. Make level paths for your feet" (Heb. 12:12–13). The words almost seem alien to the context, but they follow a major section on God's discipline of His children and also the discipline by earthly fathers of their children (12:5–11). I think the passage is indicating plainly that such things don't come easily. Too many parents make a good start but never finish because they simply can't stick with it.

Trust

Certainly parents can condition their children to behave in certain ways. That has potential for both positive and negative outcomes. But in the final analysis the standards that last on into adult years are rooted in belief systems planted in the hearts of children by the heavenly Father Himself. Godly parents trusting the power of the Holy Spirit and the dynamic of the Bible, bathing the entire process in prayer, can win the battle.

When my children were young, my wife and I made decisions for them—carefully selecting television programs and providing close supervision when they played with certain neighborhood friends; we regulated their bedtimes, what they ate, and when they went to church. We did not consider such issues open for discussion.

During their preteen and teenage years, however, we engaged in a great deal of dialogue with our children. They actively involved themselves in the decision-making process. We encouraged and valued their opinions. However, final authority still rested with us as their parents.

Now, with both of our children married and establishing their own Christian homes, we watch with joy as they make decisions based on the principles of God's Word. The root was planted many years ago, and the plants watered regularly. Now it's our turn to see the fruit grow and ripen.

Yet in many churches one can find godly parents with broken hearts because their children, now young adults, have apparently departed from everything they were taught in earlier years. Tom and Ruth have three children now in their late twenties or early thirties. Their oldest daughter, Jan, serves as a missionary in Hong Kong, where she lives with her husband and two children. Tom Jr., and his family live near his parents and are active in their church. But the day young Mary walked out of her home to go to college marked the beginning of an era of rebellion and bitterness that continues to the present. She has verbally denounced the faith of her parents and apparently turned her back on all Christian values.

How sternly does God hold parents responsible for such behavior? Without contradicting the enormous responsibility they have for their children while they live at home, we find an interesting balance-wheel passage in Ezekiel 18. The prophet quoted an ancient proverb, "The fathers eat sour grapes, and the children's teeth are set on edge," and then he related God's message: "You will no longer quote this proverb in Israel" (18:2–3). What follows is a specific and detailed outline of the relationship between a responsible adult and God. *The Bible seems to teach that God holds parents responsible for their children's behavior during childhood and teen years but gives young adults the option to make their own choices.*

At that point the Lord holds the new adult responsible, assuming the parents have done their part in raising him or her for Christ while they had influence in the home. Ezekiel addressed this matter of personal responsibility in 18:19–20. "Yet you ask, 'Why does the son not share the guilt of his father?' Since the son has done what is just and right and has been careful to keep all my decrees, he will surely live. The soul who sins is the one who will die. The son will not share the guilt of the father, nor will the father share the guilt of the son. The righteousness of the righteous man will be credited to him, and the wickedness of the wicked will be charged against him."

Let's take seriously the task of developing in our adults these internalized standards so that when their children come to adulthood they will voluntarily choose the righteous path God places before them. But if they choose otherwise, and if we have been faithful in bringing them through the process of developing godly standards, remember that God has absolved us of guilt in their behavior. They must answer before the Lord. As Christian educators we can hardly offer our congregations less.

19

❧❦❧

Preparing People to Be Parents

For a variety of reasons people in our day marry and have their children later in life than their parents did. In the past young people tended to marry in their early twenties or maybe even late teens. Preparation for marriage was almost nonexistent. Before the availability of effective contraceptive devices, children often followed within the year. Young adults who wait until their mid- or late-twenties to marry and then invest time getting to know each other before children enter the home often do better at effective parenting.

Joel and Amy are awaiting their first baby. Eagerly waiting and planning for the arrival, Amy fixes up the nursery while Joel buys little toys. Although several of her close friends are expecting as well, Amy's baby will arrive first. They think everything is planned well. They enjoyed their childbirth classes, practiced breathing techniques, and packed the requisite overnight bag. The closet bulges with boxes of disposable diapers and the crib has an educational toy already attached.

Finally the day comes, and the long wait ends. Labor turns out to be considerably more extended than anticipated, and last-minute fetal distress prompts an unexpected C-section. Nonetheless the baby, a boy, is born healthy. After a few days, Joel takes Amy and the baby, Jeremy, home—and then the problems start.

Their lives as parents are simply not what they expected. Jeremy takes a lot of Amy's time. He cries many nights, fights colic, and sleeps fitfully if at all during the day. Amy's mother stays for a week to help, but then has to return to her job. Joel feels neglected and thinks Amy is doing a poor job managing what should be simple duties. Amy, exhausted beyond anything she has experienced before, feels like a prisoner in her own home and resents the fact that Joel wants to resume sexual intimacies when all she can think about is grabbing a few extra minutes of sleep. Their uneasiness creates an atmosphere of tension rather than the loving climate Jeremy needs during his first crucial months. Sound far-fetched? Only to people who have never gone through it. The adjustments often prove much greater than anticipated. When the second and third children come, the situation often becomes even more challenging.

And what happens to Jeremy's formative mind during those early days? A baby learns love, trust, and security from the firm but gentle hands and arms that hold him and minister to his needs hour by hour. Joel and Amy need to find a way to satisfy Jeremy's physical and emotional needs without neglecting their own. Who should teach them that? TV talk shows? I think not. Such vital information should be available at church.

UNDERSTANDING BIBLICAL PARENTING

My wife, Betty, and I once asked a young man of our acquaintance what questions would first come to his mind if he found out he were soon to be a father. In order they were: "Where do I buy disposable diapers?" "How much do they cost?" and "Will Mom come take care of the baby for us?" Apparently he had never thought through what parenting really involved. What do parents really need to know? What basic understandings should your adult-ministries program provide?

How to Cope with the True Nature of Children

My college friend Bill used to argue that babies are born with a neutral nature. Leave them to their own devices in a positive climate, he said, and they will develop good behavior. Then Bill and his wife, Claudia, had a baby daughter and within two years their theology changed! Amazing—

they didn't have to teach the baby to scream at bedtime or hit her parents in frustration over a denied wish. In fact, they spent much of those early years trying to handle behaviors created by a sinful nature lurking behind those blue eyes and rosy cheeks. Sometimes after a particularly rough day, they would gaze at their beautiful daughter as she slept and say, "What happened? She looks so angelic!"

Viewing children as essentially good leads to a permissive rather than a disciplined family environment. Bill and Claudia assumed that their daughter, because she was being brought up in a loving environment, would naturally choose right over wrong. It was quite a disillusionment to discover that what their daughter considered "right" rarely coincided with their own ideas.

In truth, the Bible teaches that children are neither good nor neutral at birth (Ps. 51:5; Eph. 2:3). They possess a sin nature that must be controlled and ultimately changed by the power of God. This difficult concept dawns slowly on those expecting their first child. Those darling newborns do look innocent, and when clean and sweet-smelling, with full tummies and a good nap, they are nearly irresistible. But only when parents understand the concept of an inborn sin nature can they exercise with confidence a benevolent authority given by God.

How to Give Unconditional Love

Whatever happens in our lives, however far we might stray, however rebellious we might become, God cares for us (1 Pet. 5:7). Little kids see Jesus when their parents show them loving care. Their first, and generally their lasting, concepts of a heavenly Father come from their parents. People who had loving, accepting, forgiving parents usually have an easy time transferring love for them to a joyous love for God. But suppose they had an abusive father who had no control over his temper? Suppose their mother had no emotional warmth for them? Like it or not, those early experiences probably affect response to God. What kind of God-image can we portray for young parents?

Consider how much the Lord has given us. We need only review John 3:16 and similar passages to see the generosity demonstrated in God's sacrificial love. Certainly sometimes parents give too much of themselves or attempt to substitute material gifts for personal love and intimacy. Earthly parents never model perfectly the image of our heavenly Father. This responsibility ought to cause humility, and the recognition that our faults necessitate reliance on the grace of God. We must help parents understand they will often have to ask their children to forgive them for failures.

How to Forgive Children

Just as children will need to learn to forgive parents (and children do grant this forgiveness readily when asked in humble sincerity), moms and dads will also need to learn to forgive their children. Boys and girls will misbehave at the most inopportune moments. They will definitely embarrass us from time to time. They will not necessarily live up to our expectations. They vomit on our nicest clothes, break our most precious heirlooms, and tell our most private secrets in the most public places!

Most readers will be too young to remember the Ink Spots, but those who do can't forget the old song, "You always hurt the one you love, the one you shouldn't hurt at all." That's certainly true in the family. Perhaps because the family offers the greatest opportunity for hurt, it also offers the greatest opportunity for forgiveness, but not as a substitute for proper discipline. All three coexist within the framework of a healthy home when parents both discipline effectively and forgive completely. As Jesus taught His disciples, we pray, "Forgive us our sins, for we also forgive everyone who sins against us" (Luke 11:4).

How to Respect Children

We briefly noted the inborn sin nature of children. Now we must spend a moment considering their innate dignity. Jesus died for the least of us—and for our children. Each of us carries the image of God marked indelibly on the deepest parts of our personalities. Small wonder the writer of the Book of Hebrews recalled the dramatic language of Psalm 8, "What is man that you are mindful of him, the son of man that you care for him?

You made him a little lower than the angels; you crowned him with glory and honor and put everything under his feet" (Heb. 2:6–8). Believers are children of God (John 1:12). That means that parents should behave toward their children with never-failing respect, characterized by kindness, gentleness, and self-control. Our goal is to help people parent with awe that God should entrust them with one or more of His little ones.

KEY QUESTIONS ABOUT PARENTING

Joel and Amy are learning, sometimes painfully, that marriage and children force us to constantly redefine and nurture relationships. Compatibility, mutuality, affection, and partnership are qualities necessary for a healthy marriage and family. Many of the crucial questions that haunt the marriage relationship surface only after the wedding and as the family begins to grow. Both Joel and Amy know that the final decisions must be theirs, but they hope their church can help with some information.

How Many Children Should We Have?

Wouldn't it be nice to open the Bible and have some verse leap out to tell us exactly how many children we should have? Well, it won't happen. Each couple must answer this question for themselves after prayer and plenty of discussion. Although they may be influenced by arguments about population control, and grandma and grandpa's desire for more grandchildren, the decision must be their own.

How can we help them here? Before Joel and Amy decided to conceive their first child, they had to ask themselves, "Why do we want children? How many children will be best for us? How is the Holy Spirit leading us in this matter? When do we want our first child? How soon will we really be ready to be parents?" No hard-and-fast formulas exist to answer these questions. Amy knew long before Joel that she felt ready for parenthood. Joel reached that point a full two years later. Fortunately, Amy had enough maturity to hold off until Joel would walk in harmony with her. She knew his financial concerns were legitimate, and those extra two years gave them time to work through some other problems.

Somewhere along the line they should hear a church leader discussing passages like Psalm 127:3–5: "Sons are a heritage from the LORD, children a reward from him. Like arrows in the hands of a warrior are sons born in one's youth. Blessed is the man whose quiver is full of them. They will not be put to shame when they contend with their enemies in the gate."

These verses tell us that children are a gift handed over to us by God for our supervision on a temporary basis. If the word *stewardship* means anything, it certainly applies to parenting. Children are also a reward. God's greatest gifts are people, not possessions.

The psalm adds an interesting simile in which the psalmist wrote that children are "like arrows in the hands of a warrior." We don't know the answer to the question, "How many arrows did warriors of that day carry in their quivers?" Even if we could figure that out, Charles Swindoll likes to remind parents that not everybody has the same size quiver. Let's emphasize to our parents the importance of focusing not on the quiver, but rather on who shoots the arrows.

Who Will Be Responsible for the Baby?

Early in this century no one would even consider a question like this. Even during the post–World War II period, economic growth in the United States made it possible for many one-income families to live comfortably. Not so today. With an ever-increasing percentage of mothers in the work force, many Christian parents find it necessary or at least convenient to place the new baby in day care as soon as possible so mom can get back to her job.

Your church's position on this issue needs to be heard. You may want to suggest that parents should explore other options first. Dramatic personality changes occur during the first few years of childhood, and the child's environment inserts a significant ingredient. Parenting with grace means doing all we can to make home a place in which children will learn and grow while feeling secure and loved.

This does not necessarily mean that mom has to stay at home. Working a job at home, job sharing, flextime, and different shifts can make it possible for dad to take a larger role here. Despite their lack of preparation in some areas, Joel and Amy did think this one through. Those extra years they waited before conceiving Jeremy were given to building enough of a financial base so that Amy could stay home for at least two years.

How Can Parents Share Responsibilities?

Let's take a closer look at Amy, Joel, and Jeremy to see how the situation can be changed to develop a healthy and happy atmosphere. Because Amy will be with the baby more hours than Joel, she has a greater responsibility to be sure Jeremy is fed, bathed, changed, well, and happy. She will handle routine checkups and other medical care for Jeremy.

But Joel has an important role too. He can encourage and support Amy by keeping Jeremy occupied for a while when he gets home from work, perhaps while she's preparing dinner. And he can bring in dinner from a nearby takeout one or two evenings a week. He can also arrange periodically for a baby-sitter so he and Amy can get out alone for a while. In response to this suggestion, Joel said, "Why should I have to do that? She could do that herself." Yes, she could. But it would be a wonderfully loving act for Joel to do it, and Amy will respond to that kind of love.

How Are Children Different?

Nearly a year has passed, and Joel and Amy have begun to feel more comfortable about their roles as parents. Once they resolved their initial tension and imposed some order on Jeremy's sleeping habits, they found him to be a great joy and decided they could handle another one. So, twenty months after Jeremy's birth, a new baby arrived— another boy, whom they named Nathan. They took him home, assured that their abilities, painfully learned by mistakes with Jeremy, would ensure a smooth transition with this second son.

Within weeks, however, they discovered that each child has his own distinct personality and must be handled individually. Little Nathan is far more demanding, rarely content, and doesn't care to be held often. His parents love him deeply, but the differences in personality and needs from those of his older brother make them wonder all over again about their parenting skills.

One thing that did help was a sermon their pastor preached on the individual and different ways Jesus treated the Twelve— His spiritual children. It gave Amy a new confidence to deal with the two boys differently when necessary.

Some basic guidelines apply to every child. Just because the second may be strong-willed and difficult to handle, parents dare not give in to avoid conflict. On the other hand, if one of the children is shy and sensitive, they don't withhold necessary discipline just because of a retiring personality. Parental approaches to respect, discipline, punishment, and nurture may be different from child to child, but they must be set in place.

How Do Parents Create a Spiritual Atmosphere?

Surely we can agree on a foundational parenting principle: *A proper family atmosphere provides the key to effective Christian nurture in the home.* As we help parents see this, we might focus on three basic steps to achieving a spiritual atmosphere: *instruction, modeling,* and *experience.* We've seen them before in this book.

The most commonly talked about and yet in reality the least important is *instruction.* Certainly we must help parents instruct their children. They must explain the difference between right and wrong. They must spell out the consequences of improper behavior: why children should not touch a hot stove or a burning log; why they must not run out into the street or approach a strange dog; who has the right to touch them in private places and who does not. However, instruction works best outside of formal situations when it vitally links with the other two basics necessary for building a spiritual atmosphere.

The middle item in our triad is *modeling;* the importance of parental example can never be overemphasized when churches teach the discipleship process. Children learn through imitation, and in that sense every parent becomes a model—good or bad—whether we like it or not. Through modeling, a child learns good manners, honesty in financial ventures, and kindness and patience in the interpersonal realm.

But the most important aspect of discipleship is *experience.* Every time something happens in the home (pricked fingers, injured pets, special holidays, deaths, births, and so on), a teachable moment appears. Wise, godly parents will immediately use that event or experience as an opportunity to communicate biblical values. That's discipleship.

The day our son's pet dog accidentally strangled herself brought sadness for the entire family. Oh, yes, we all loved that dog, but, more important, we loved our son, and he was hurting. He blamed himself for putting her on a choker chain before we went to church.

After giving Jeff some time to grieve in private, we talked of our loving God who had given us Spooky to enjoy for a time. We talked of the fact that God controls all life and death. God used those tender, teachable moments to bring our family closer as we shared that sad experience. Every parent in your congregation can develop discipleship skills based on instruction, modeling, and experience.

How Do Parents Develop Christian Attitudes?

Educators call this the affective dimension of learning. Parents constantly communicate their attitudes toward each other, toward the Bible, toward God, toward prayer, toward church, and toward neighbors. Attitudes form the atmosphere in which children learn about people and how they should think about those people. Everything parents say or imply about Scripture contributes to their children's attraction or aversion to biblical truth.

Parenthood stirs up both enormous responsibility and great joy. It requires the best attention we can offer to make sure the homes into which our church members bring children are ready for them spiritually, emotionally, physically, economically, socially, and in every other way. Remember the progression: first *godly people*, then *godly partners*, then *godly parents*.

Amy and Joel are students. No, they're not enrolled in any formal educational institution, but every day God teaches them more about applying His truth to all three areas of their lives. They realize the impact of the world and its potential to disintegrate the Christian family, and they intend to win their spiritual battles as people, partners, and parents. And every day they thank the Lord for a church that helped them prepare to be parents.

20

❧ ⟡ ❧

Teaching Children Responsibility

A*ccording to* U. S. Senator Daniel Moynihan, we may be the first generation of Americans whose children are worse off than their parents. Beyond the obvious problems of divorce, adultery, wife and child abuse, drug and alcohol abuse, and widespread immorality, there exists the subtle but genuine influence of a society that encourages accountability to no one.

In such an alien climate one wonders how churches can best help parents teach children responsibility. Jerry McCant say this about children and the church:

> Christian education in the church must become realistic enough to deal with the actual problems of this world. Idealism must be replaced by realism. Hard questions cannot be avoided and answers must be sought. That one has peace with God may not mean that he/she has peace with a marriage partner. That one is saved by grace does not guarantee that he/she will be a good parent or marriage partner. Communication skills, an understanding of the needs of the opposite sex, and child-rearing techniques do not come as a matter of grace. The church must not assume that all is well in the home of a couple actively engaged in church activities. A place to confess, counsel, and learn must be provided so that we can help some to avoid the tragedies of the divorce courts and beyond. That would be in the best interests of the children of the church.[1]

The following paragraphs include both a premise and a pattern. The premise suggests that *home training must be aimed primarily toward deferred and eternal goals.* Parents do not teach their children responsibility just to "make it through" the first eighteen years of the child's life, but to produce godly adult leadership for new families, and, more broadly, for the body of Christ.

The pattern may be regarded by some as a bit more unusual. It suggests that one way to communicate the significance of this important process is to observe the behavior of the displaced children of the Bible. Parents need every possible resource to carry out their responsibilities effectively. By focusing on displaced people, we see how children behave after being removed from the influence of their homes.

Perhaps I've been influenced in this study by the fact that both my wife and my daughter teach kindergarten. Their stories remind me how a child's behavior at school mirrors his or her home environment and have led me to wonder whether we can find such domestic loops in Scripture. This chapter attempts to demonstrate that we can, and that the lessons we learn there present not only interesting but useful historical models and scriptural teaching we can offer parents. Perhaps we can also see how family teaching can be developed from Bible passages that do not overtly focus on parental issues.

TEACH THEM TO LIVE BY BIBLICAL STANDARDS

Nebuchadnezzar was ruling as king in Babylon and the Hebrew captives Shadrach, Meshach, and Abednego had grown to young adulthood. The idolatrous king made a huge gold image of himself and required all his officials to bow before it. Such behavior would obviously violate the captives' devotion to one God. They refused, even under threat of death: "O Nebuchadnezzar, we do not need to defend ourselves before you in this matter. If we are thrown into the blazing furnace, the God we serve is able to save us from it, and he will rescue us from your hand, O king. But even if He does not, we want you to know, O king, that we will not serve your gods or worship the image of gold you have set up"(Dan. 3:16–18).

Notice that this passage describes the behavior of young adults, not children. But where did these men get their faith? Their response to the pagan king apparently resulted from their early home life before their captivity, which had stabilized their commitment to worship the one true God for a lifetime. Their behavior demonstrates total faith in God's power and God's choice, leaving the fate of their lives totally in His hands.

What component of family training might be at work here? Doubtless several could be named, but among them must appear one we noted in the previous chapter, namely, instruction. These young men had been taken from their homes long before this incident, but during their childhood they had been well taught the things of God. When young people from your church go off to college, particularly if they attend a secular school, they may enter an environment similar to the one found in Babylon. Some teachers will encourage them to worship at the altar of relativism and intellectual achievement. Will they stand firm?

We would all hope to be able to answer an enthusiastic yes to that question. But please take careful note of this caution: Part of good parenting is releasing children to full adulthood, and that releasing process carries no guarantees. We want parents to help their children benefit from their wisdom and avoid some of the mistakes they may have made. Skill development, however, takes place only on an individual level. Babies learning to walk fall down frequently. Children learning to ride a two-wheeler run into mailboxes. Young people learning to play a musical instrument hit a lot of sour notes. And young adults exercising their newly won freedoms often take wrong paths.

As we teach people how to parent with grace, we help them learn that forgiveness stands central to that concept.

- They must learn to accept God's forgiveness for all their own short-comings.

- They must learn to forgive themselves for their own foolishness and wrong actions.

- They must learn to forgive their children when they fail to live up to expectations, when they refuse to follow advice and come back with agonized souls. Forgiveness is essential even during periods of extended rebellion when they may flagrantly violate every standard their parents hold dear.

Were these three Hebrew young men tempted to give in and worship that statue? Probably. People in the Bible are not plastic saints. Their internal agonies must have overwhelmed them at times. Reread what they said to the king—they knew their mighty God could save them from the fire, but they dared not say He would save them. Being thrown into a furnace is a nasty way to die. But they did not give in, and their example gives us great hope for Christian children and young people today.

TEACH THEM TO PRAY

Some fifty years after the incident of the fiery furnace we find another demonstration of kidnapped faith in action. Darius the Mede had ascended the throne to reign over the Babylonian segment of the vast Medo-Persian Empire. Darius now ruled over three administrators and 127 satraps or lesser administrators.

The hero of the story is the hero of the book. Daniel had come to Babylon as a teenager in 605 B.C.; now he presided as a senior official in an alien land. Though he was now more than eighty years old, his behavior still reflected those lessons of godliness learned in his Jewish homeland during early years.

The temptation sounds familiar: A godly man required by his government to transfer his allegiance from the Lord God to an earthly king and to demonstrate it in public. The penalty for refusal had switched to the lion's den, since the Persians worshiped fire and would not use it for execution. How did Daniel respond? "Now when Daniel learned that the decree had been published, he went home to his upstairs room where the windows opened toward Jerusalem. Three times a day he got down on his knees and prayed, giving thanks to his God, just as he had done before. Then these men went as a group and found Daniel praying and asking God for help" (Dan. 6:10–11).

God's prophet displayed courage in the face of danger and death, his fixed habit of prayer as natural as life itself. In genuine godliness, he mixed gratitude with his petition. Only minimal speculation is required to recognize that, although Daniel's behavior was certainly fixed over many years of adulthood, this pattern of *worship* had been initiated before his captivity and can probably be attributed to childhood training.

Perhaps Daniel's story seems so far removed from possible happening today that we see no connection. But let's not forget that believers in the former Soviet Union often spent years in prison camps under repressive regimes. Believers in China under Chairman Mao faced brutal murders and persecution, and many other thousands of persecuted Christians suffer around the world today. While at present North American Christians do not face such dire possibilities, a young person standing up for his or her beliefs in an unbelieving environment may face rejection from peers, a process that can be desperately painful to children and teens. The habit of worship will help sustain them during these difficult times.

No Christian parents would deny the importance of their children learning to pray. All of us long for the kind of vivid courage (in ourselves as well as our children) that drove Daniel to his knees with daily regularity. But how do we help parents pull it off? We can teach them to do the following:

- Avoid memorized prayers as early as possible. "Now I lay me down to sleep" is tender, but prayer is not word repetition, it's talking to God. How silly to picture a child speaking to mom and dad only in memorized rhyming poems!

- Let their children pray as frequently as the adults. Don't dominate mealtime or bedtime prayers—ask the youngest to "lead" the family in prayer. God will hear and decipher those cute mumblings everyone at the table finds so funny.

- Help their children pray specifically. Not just "God bless the missionaries" but a direct request or word of thanks related to childhood experiences. Then follow up with discussions of how God answers— or perhaps why it seems He has not.

- Insist on respect for prayer. When anyone prays, the whole family respects the prayer and joins in as much as possible.

TEACH THEM FAITH IN GOD'S POWER

Ben-Hadad II ruled Syria (Aram) but his successful and courageous military commander, Naaman, suffered from leprosy. Had he lived in Israel he would have been isolated; not so in Aram.

In his household served a young Hebrew slave girl, taken from her home in Israel. Learning of her master's leprosy she uttered the only two sentences history has recorded from her lips: "If only my master would see the prophet who is in Samaria! He would cure him of his leprosy" (2 Kings 5:3).

The child's witness reflected a life of deepest faith. Only recently snatched from her mother's arms, the little girl demonstrated concern for others and a clear-cut knowledge of God's power. More importantly, she displayed a living faith in that power. Her spiritual maturity reached far beyond her years. Her family training reflects the importance of experience in the rearing of children.

Children in your church need to hear their parents pray in humble faith and then see God answer in powerful ways. They need to develop confidence in a living God who cares deeply about personal matters.

One young man we know has struggled for years with severe asthma. Twice he found himself in intensive care units in hospitals, only inches from dying. Many people came around that family and prayed for him. He did pull through and has since outgrown most of his health problems, but that experience left him with deep gratitude to God.

Encourage your families to take advantage of the hard times that force them to look to God as opportunities to build the experience of faith in their children. When finances get difficult, they pray together as a family. When someone falls ill, together they place that person before the throne of grace. When personal hurts overwhelm them or a member of the family, they express their collective grief to God. Teach adults to give Him the opportunity to provide the experience of living faith.

Then, just maybe, children will carry that faith into the public arena—like Naaman's slave girl. Just maybe, even when parents are not around, the faith they worked to develop will influence, even govern, their lives.

TEACH THEM TO AVOID SIN

Another vignette takes us back to Egypt almost two thousand years before Christ. Again the captive is a slave. Young Joseph, having had a tough life back in Canaan, now lived in Egypt. When faced with the lustful maneuvering of Potiphar's wife, he replied, "How then could I do such a wicked thing and sin against God? . . . He left his cloak in her hand and ran out of the house" (Gen. 39: 9, 12).

Particularly interesting in this story is Joseph's behavior, which cannot be attributed to brilliant parenting. One could even argue that Joseph "turned out all right" despite the questionable lifestyle and parental bungling of his father, Jacob. But remember Jacob's devotion to Rachel, Joseph's mother. Surely memories of true marital love penetrated Joseph's heart. Nonetheless, this story, among other things, serves to give failure-prone parents hope that even inadequate parenting (which we all do to some degree) is still undergirded by God's grace in their children's lives.

The incident described in Genesis 39 offers some very useful lessons, demonstrating a highly developed sense of responsibility. Joseph must have made a predetermined decision how to respond in times of temptation. He faced no need to search within himself, attempting to decide the appropriate behavior for the moment.

Like most teenagers in North America today, Joseph regularly encountered difficult decisions. He chose purity—a selection motivated by his accountability to God. We're seeing a movement today among young people to affirm the value of their sexual purity and keep themselves free from sexual involvement until marriage. Modern teens who make that decision demonstrate the same value system Joseph did: Make the decision during the time of clear thinking, not at the moment of overwhelming temptation.

How can modern parents develop this kind of spiritual determination in their children and young people? Certainly one important component is the educational tool of modeling. We cannot guarantee that parents who practice marital fidelity will raise children who honor that value, nor can we claim that promiscuous parents always create promiscuous children.

The point is that children have a much better crack at integrity, purity, and biblical morality when they not only hear about those virtues but also see them practiced in the lives of their parents.

TEACH THEM TO SERVE GOD COURAGEOUSLY

Our final story places us in Persian history about 480 B.C. Xerxes (also known as Ahasurerus) ruled over 127 provinces stretching from India to the upper region of the Nile known as Cush. Details of Esther's rise to the queenship are well known. From extrabiblical sources we learn that the Persian king Xerxes was notorious for his drinking parties and wild behavior.

Esther displayed obedience to a cousin (who was more like her father) and a willingness to seize an opportunity offered by a sovereign God. In a moment of personal danger and ethnic crisis, Esther responded to the faithful training of her earlier days at the feet of Mordecai as he prodded, "If you remain silent at this time, relief and deliverance for the Jews will arise from another place, but you and your father's family will perish. And who knows but that you have come to royal position for such a time as this?" (Esth. 4:14).

By saying this, Mordecai reminded Esther that she was different from the Persians around her. She was a Jewess from God's own chosen people. For her, responsibility consisted of taking advantage of God's grace to her in order to benefit the lives of others. We should remind parents of Jesus' warning: "From everyone who has been given much, much will be demanded; and from the one who has been entrusted with much, much more will be asked" (Luke 12:48).

Like many Christian young people today, Esther had to learn how and when to speak up for God. The ultimate answer to peer pressure is not parental pressure or church pressure—it is the internal power of the Holy Spirit working in the hearts of God's children.

Meaningless anecdotes of the past? From the past, indeed, but hardly meaningless. Instead they give us hope that early and consistent training will equip children to serve God and choose His ways in time of challenge and temptation.

I recall a story about new grandparents receiving a call from their son whose wife had just given birth to their first baby. On the phone the young man complained, "But, Mom—he didn't come with any instructions!" Of course he did. God's Word abounds with instructions detailing how to teach children and young people responsibility. Our task focuses on helping parents to find and follow them.

But what about those parents behind the scenes of our scenarios? Jacob we know, and Esther's cousin Mordecai represents the father-figure in her story. But the rest are anonymous. They live on in the reflection of their parenting demonstrated in the lives of their children. Parenting is not superstar duty. It carries no TV interviews and few front-page stories in the local newspaper. But the sometimes dreary, sometimes delightful task may result—by God's grace—in producing new Daniels for the twenty-first century.

21

❧ ❧

Parenting with Grace

C*had and Cindy* had struggled with Lance until the last drop of energy was drained from both of them. More than an hour earlier the plane had pushed back from the gate only to get caught in the tangled web of outbound schedules, sitting on the tarmac as passengers fumed over the delay. Clearly the most restless passenger was three-year-old Lance, slightly more than disenchanted that this first flight should be "grounded" even before it left the earth.

Cindy had already exhausted the supply of toys she brought on board. Coloring books, reading books, crayons, squeeze animals, stuffed animals, and candy wrappers littered her seat area so it looked like a nursery dumpster. If only they could take off, Lance would probably fall asleep. But cramped as he was into the tiny space, Lance's restlessness led to frustration and then anger, all quite uncontrollable by his desperate parents. At the height of the hubbub Chad was heard to say, "This is the last time we take this kid anywhere until he is twenty." He probably won't keep that vow, though muttered in sincerity and witnessed by at least a dozen passengers.

Sound familiar? You may need to substitute a restaurant or church for the airplane scenario, but the picture of frustrated parents doing their best to control equally frustrated children reflects a familiar scene in contemporary life, almost a necessary piece of late twentieth-century

217

Americana. Tragically, we also see it among Christians who, because they read the Bible, should know better and do better.

Unfortunately many Christians take the same view of parenting that the Galatians held about Christian living in general. Those early believers understood God's grace is essential for salvation; we agree that God gives us children by His grace. The Galatians strangely assumed, however, that they had to work their way to spiritual maturity; we behave as though God expects us to raise those children on our own. Both notions prove erroneous and dangerous. *This chapter proclaims that the single most important ingredient in godly living and godly parenting is an active dependence on the grace of God. This book calls on churches to provide the essential training and support so their adults can parent with grace.*

SAVING GRACE

Recognizing Reality

Let's get back to Lance for just a moment. (By the way, the names are fictitious but the incident happened precisely as I described it. I was seated directly across the aisle, scarcely three or four feet from the combat zone). Christian parents must be aware of sin in themselves and constantly conscious that their children enter the world already possessing a sin nature. That's tough to believe, looking over the crib rail at a charming new baby. But a few months will make it evident to the most doting parents!

Reflection of Rebellion

As soon as words are formed, parents look for "Dada" and "Mama"; and they know that there with those precious sounds will be "No," a word parents never have to teach a baby. Pouting, disobedience, and even temper tantrums arrive, showing that even the most optimistic of parents have trouble.

But that should surprise only those who have no access to God's Word and centuries of Christian teaching. Scarcely four hundred years after the birth of Christ, Augustine wrote, "We are capable of every sin that we have seen others commit unless God's grace restrains us." How many sins do children see others commit? And who are those sinning "others"? For one thing, children watch their parents. Count on it; Chad hollered at Cindy long before he hollered at Lance. Cindy expressed open and verbal disgust with Chad long before she felt bitter guilt over the failures she saw evidenced in Lance.

Reaching for Relief

To activate God's grace in family life, church leaders can start by helping parents list problem areas. If the children are old enough, they can discuss some solutions to the problems and then pray together regularly for God's grace to help them carry out those solutions.

For example, if television viewing is a problem, parents and kids can agree on some reasonable guidelines that govern what programs and how much time family members watch. Then they must trust God for the discipline and obedience necessary to be consistent in enforcing the guidelines.

Television was a major battle at our house. The novelty of TV was at its peak when Jeff and Julie were young children. We had to focus on *moderation, control,* and a *monitored viewing plan* to keep the potbellied glass idol in its place.

Of course, we teach parents how to apply everything we've learned about parenting—it's the most crucial task to which God will ever call us. But even after the books, the videos, the sermons, the Sunday-school classes, and the special seminars, only grace can tip the scales in their favor. God wants them to look up and say, "Lord, I depend on you for my salvation and I depend on you for the daily tasks I face as a parent. I just can't handle them myself."

SERVING GRACE

G. K. Chesterton once wrote, "You say grace before meals. All right. But I say grace before the play and the opera. Before the concert and pantomime. Grace before I open a book, before sketching, painting, swimming, walking. And grace before I dip my pen in ink." Interesting use of a pliable word. Chesterton's words surely refer to his grateful attitude for what theologians call "common grace," a magnificent gift of the Creator essential to any human being to walk earth's surface at anytime. Common grace provides rain and sunshine, fruit trees, milk cows, hospitals, and amazing cures for diseases. Those things are not the fruit of human hands. In the ultimate sense, all truth, beauty, and goodness come from the only One who can give common grace.

But Chesterton's words could also be taken in the sense of "special grace." God's special grace provided by Jesus Christ on the cross offers resurrection power for salvation and the curbing of the sin nature; but it also allows us to serve effectively in a number of strategic ministries—such as parenting. Paul wrote to believers at Rome, "For by the grace given me I say to every one of you: Do not think of yourself more highly than you ought, but rather think of yourself with sober judgment, in accordance with the measure of faith God has given you. . . .We have different gifts, according to the grace given us" (Rom. 12:3, 6).

Accurate Attitudes

How do pastors, elders, and Sunday school teachers carry out effective ministries for Christ in the church? By grace. How do missionaries, evangelists, and teachers in Christian schools serve effectively? By grace. Paul made it plain that serving grace results from meekness on the part of the recipient.

North Americans tend to suffer from an exalted sense of self-importance. The New Testament warns against that, primarily because it detracts or even destroys our dependence on the grace of God. In Romans 12:3 the apostle Paul wrote that we ought not think of ourselves more highly than is realistic. This emphasis demands that we never overestimate our abilities in any kind of ministry—including parenting.

Changing Challenges

As with most things, overconfidence comes with successful experience. Our two children posed very different challenges when they were small. Our son, Jeff, born three years before his sister, Julie, presented very few problems. His laid-back nature, coupled with the flurry of parenting initiatives we employed, created a fairly easy three years. Of course, there were minor skirmishes, but in general we were winning the war.

Then God dropped a bomb in the form of a beautiful, vivacious, stubborn, and challenging baby daughter. While I watched Lance wriggle and struggle in the airplane, my thoughts flew back to Julie's early years. Our second child brought a message from the Lord: "You thought you could do it yourselves; you can't—depend on Me." For the record, both children are now parents actively and effectively serving the Lord.

Spiritual Service

A study of the words *serve* and *service* in the Scriptures helps expand our definition of parenting. Here's just one example: "Be devoted to one another in brotherly love. Honor one another above yourselves. Never be lacking in zeal, but keep your spiritual fervor, serving the Lord" (Rom. 12:10–11). As we show kindness in the family and demonstrate consideration for each another, we serve the Lord.

Two ideas float to the surface here. First, parenting provides as much opportunity for service as the most demanding pastorate or the cultural challenges of a pioneer mission field. Until Christians acknowledge that and live accordingly, an appeal to God's grace will not likely occur. Second, when parents recognize that service in the family forms part of the warfare against the powers of darkness, they may more willingly and frequently throw themselves on God's grace, which alone can help win the battle for their children.

SUFFERING GRACE

Parental suffering? Not a common word combination in our day. Chad and Cindy were "suffering" frustration, embarrassment, and emotional stress on board flight 524, but that's not the way we commonly use the word. Sometimes—even among Christians—parenting contains genuine agony and heartbreaking grief that seems to fog out His love. Infants die. Small children are kidnapped. Teenagers turn to drugs. Bright, healthy

Christ-honoring kids are run over by drunk drivers. Husbands leave wives, and wives abandon their families. Like it or not, suffering touches the lives of God's beloved children. In the first century Peter wrote, "Clothe yourselves with humility toward one another, because, 'God opposes the proud but gives grace to the humble.' Humble yourselves, therefore, under God's mighty hand, that he may lift you up in due time. Cast all your anxiety on him because he cares for you. Be self-controlled and alert. Your enemy the devil prowls around like a roaring lion looking for someone to devour. Resist him, standing firm in the faith, because you know that your brothers throughout the world are undergoing the same kind of sufferings" (1 Pet. 5:5–9).

While Peter was not talking about the frequent heartbreak of parenting, the principle remains the same. Times of suffering drive us rather quickly to God. God calls us to humility (5:5–6), dependence (5:7), alertness (5:8), mutuality in suffering (5:9), and relief (5:10–11).

Mutual Struggles

Sadly, we tend to gravitate only to that last component (relief), ignoring the obvious fact that the first four lead to the fifth. How do parents spell relief? Not by working harder at parenting, though many probably need to do that. Certainly not by pretending the problems do not exist, though many hope thereby to free themselves of parental difficulties. We spell relief G-R-A-C-E.

When one member of the family suffers, all feel the pain. Even simple experiences like poor report cards hurt. The death of a child can devastate even close families. Their wider family, the church, must help with hurts and fears, talk about them, cry together, and pray for God's grace to be magnified in times of greatest need. God will glorify Christ through families when testing brings their members closer together.

Note your congregation next Sunday morning. In one way or another we are all walking commercials for God's grace. There sits a man who recently lost his wife or a woman her husband. That couple over there must daily nurture a brain-damaged child. On the other side three, four, or five divorcées struggle to pull together the threads of their lives. Two teenagers seated near the back face a drunken father four or five nights a week. How do these people do it? What keeps them going? Listen to Peter: "And the God of all grace, who called you to his eternal glory in Christ, after you have suffered a little while, will himself restore you and make you strong, firm and steadfast. To him be the power for ever and ever. Amen" (1 Peter 5:10–11).

Often after our daughter's early temper tantrums (she was "cured" before kindergarten), one of us would sit with her on the edge of her bed. Amid tepid tears and sobbing sentences, we would explain yet one more time how the current spanking merely expressed our love and devotion to her and God. Sometimes the sobs turned into smiles as we prayed and assured her of forgiveness, promising never to mention the incident to her again. In our frail human ways we attempted to reflect God's restoration and to demonstrate parenting by grace. That's what your congregation can offer. Not just emergency counseling after the major problems erupt, but solid family-life education which prepares people to parent by grace.

PART 4

Programming for Adult Ministries

22

Learning from Each Other

W*hen Randy thinks* of teaching, he thinks of what he does for students rather than how he helps them learn for themselves. Yet, as the early chapters of this book remind us, the bulk of research in education indicates that student experience—the participatory approach to learning—works best with adults. In the long run it produces the most satisfactory and lasting results.

But up to this point, we have focused almost exclusively on aiding the learning environment and utilizing teaching methods that engage adults in the learning process; we have said very little about how the students in an adult class relate to one another. Nor has Randy thought about that, even though he has been teaching adult Bible classes for a parachurch organization over the past two decades.

The creation of a good learning environment is not primarily an intellectual activity. Though extremely important in the learning process, the intellect is a factor that affects both teacher and student. But in adult education it is not the *primary* factor. Nor is a good learning environment primarily physical. Randy works hard at making his classroom look attractive with appropriate lighting and space, and all that adds significantly to his teaching. Nevertheless he dare not make it the central issue in the learning environment.

Sometimes Randy is tempted to think that the learning environment depends essentially on equipment. He uses an overhead projector consistently and shows video clips as discussion starters at least once a month. The students appreciate that, and it probably enhances their learning. But equipment is not the primary ingredient in learning environment.

The most important component is *attitude.* Randy has seen it all too often, despite his best efforts. Students with mediocre intellect, in an ill-equipped classroom, with less than desirable physical surroundings, can somehow demonstrate a tremendous capacity to learn. *In motivation, the student's attitude makes the difference; in terms of learning environment, the teacher's attitude sets the tone.*

Randy understands from experience and from what reading he has done in adult education that the uniqueness of each individual student is not just a biological phenomenon. He has a fairly good grasp of theology and understands that everyone he teaches was created in God's image. He knows that even though sin has defaced the image, redemption can restore it. Randy has worked hard on improving his attitude toward students as a group, each student individually, and each student's attitude toward him. However, he has neglected what most teachers of adults, both professional and lay, have also forgotten, primarily because books and articles on adult education have not emphasized it: *Learning takes place best in a cooperative rather than a competitive environment.*

The major hindrance to establishing cooperative education patterns in our adult ministry programs lies in the fact that North American education itself remains highly competitive. Students vie with one another for grades, for placement in advanced classes, for admission slots in highly ranked colleges, for awards, and for the general approval of teachers, family, and friends. We talk about cooperation, but we practice competition from kindergarten through doctoral studies. Perhaps as long as grades and grade-point averages dominate the system, there may be little hope for change in formal education. But adult education, particularly in the church, has every opportunity to turn this deficiency around.

There is no need and no value in structuring learning experiences for adults in ways that pit them against one another in any kind of competition. Note the words of Harold Westing, who has specialized in adult Sunday school classes for decades. "Fellowship is the major purpose of the adult Sunday school. However, few classes take steps to see that intimacy and personal caring actually happen. A certain amount of that will occur naturally, but dynamic classes need to be proactive in seeing that it does happen. . . . As class members share common experiences, those experiences tend to create a community of memories, and then those memories tend to build a sense of commitment to the community. Again, class members ought to have some say in the events which build that community of memories, and these events ought to happen often enough to expedite that sense of belonging."[1]

Good advice. But Westing is still addressing class environment. We must move on to teaching strategy if we want to help Randy and others like him.

DIFFERENCES IN COOPERATIVE LEARNING

Before we look at how cooperative learning differs from competitive learning, we might want to start with a definition: Cooperative learning (sometimes called "synergogy") is a set of learner-centered teaching strategies that apply the principles of andragogy to peer group situations. Let's not assume here that cooperative-learning procedures do not work well with other groups, because they do. In fact, in modern education one would be likely to find a group of kindergarten students working together to assist each other in completing group work at a learning center. In the church, unencumbered by the trappings of formal education, we should be able to make this work very well. How does it differ from what we already know? In at least four rather specific ways.

Cooperative Learning Centers in Learning Designs

In the early chapters of this book I emphasized how much pedagogy focuses on authority figures and how andragogy needs to move away from that impediment. Cooperative learning replaces those authority figures with a specific learning design, a preplanned format of the manner in which students will learn interdependence. Specifics will be mentioned later in this chapter.

Cooperative Learning Enables Learners to Become Proactive

Too much education, both formal and informal, is reactive. Teachers tell students what to do and how to do it, then students attempt to react in ways that will best please the teacher. They know this will earn them the best grades and sadly, that is too often the ultimate goal. As long as learning is dominated by an authority figure (such as a controlling teacher), learners usually do not become proactive unless their teacher designs some program to move them into that mode.

In cooperative learning, however, students take responsibility for their own learning and the learning of their peers. At this point we can see how synergogy moves one step beyond andragogy. In andragogy students take responsibility for their own learning; in synergogy they also take responsibility for the learning of their peers. Can you think of any teacher in history who sent his students out in small groups to help each other achieve learning and ministry objectives? Doubtless there are several, but we could well start with Jesus and His disciples.

Cooperative Learning Requires Teamwork

In my book, *Team Leadership in Christian Ministry,* I attempted to show how biblical leadership can best take place in a team approach.[2] Certainly one could argue that the same applies to biblical learning. When we practice cooperative learning correctly, the educational gain resulting from team effort exceeds the gain by individual learning. In one sense, this is almost the major axiom of the system. As I read about synergogy, I wondered why I did not put the pieces together much earlier.

As a college and seminary student I clearly recall learning some of the most difficult information in informal study groups we designed completely apart from structured classes. Before a major theology exam, for example, we would gather at the home of one of our group members, get out the Pepsi and popcorn, and work through the material until we had "taught each other" what we collectively believed we needed to know in preparation for the exam. Having come through very traditional educational systems, however, I never really made the application from my own peer group learning experiences to restructuring my classes in a cooperative mode until recent years.

I recall those study sessions with great joy, though the trauma of the moment permitted very little joy at the time. Three or four of us would divide the material into sections. For the final exam of a fifteen-week semester, I might have the responsibility for five weeks of material which needed to be combed through, synthesized, and focused for that exam. My job was to come to the group with questions I thought the professor might ask and help the other team members master that section of the material.

Sometimes we would smoke out differences in our notes and had to come to a collective agreement on what the prof had really said about some issue. What points did he emphasize? How much time did he give to a particular section? Who had asterisks or underlining in their notes at this point? Whatever else happened those evenings (and they sometimes turned to great hilarity and fun), one thing seems clear—we were completely interdependent, focused on how we could each do better work because we had prepared together. The single student cramming for an exam in a lonely library carrel presents a different picture, and a very different approach to learning on the part of his teacher.

At first glance we look at all this and say, "Of course. Anybody can figure that out. Cooperation is always better than competition." Yes, it makes sense when we really grasp a picture like this. But watch a teenager who sits in a high-school class next to another teenager. He's thinking about "number one," and in many situations cheating may be the answer to achieving the competitive goals the system requires. *Cooperative learning emphasizes the achievement of the group, not the individual.*

Cooperative Learning Emphasizes Colleague Affiliations

I look back on my own extensive student years and remember how often I felt isolated in the lonely role of learner. Comparing that with those seminary study groups, I wonder why I didn't always seek "colleague affiliations"; the motivational value seems so obvious. When Randy's students try to learn on their own, they must be self-motivated. In adult education, self-motivation is much better than external motivation. But the motivation that comes from team effort exceeds even individual self-motivation. The camaraderie and encouragement of one another in the study groups, some of the stimulating discussions and even disagreements about a certain issue, provided outstanding learning experiences. Competitive learning tends to encourage memorization, a rote system of ingesting the information. Cooperative learning with colleague affiliations, however, promotes friendship and interdependence, which carries far beyond the boundaries of the study group or the class session in which it was experienced.

PRINCIPLES OF COOPERATIVE LEARNING

The teacher's facilitating role centers in helping students learn rather than conveying information. When we take the next step to cooperative learning, facilitation means designing the learning system. Let's get back to Randy. He's already committed to participation and a high level of student involvement. What's the next step in creating learning teams in his Bible class? The answer is the design of learning instruments, documents specifically created to help students function interdependently. That leads us to the first principle.

Cooperative Learning Offers Meaningful Direction

This chapter does not offer facilitation as a free-rein approach to instruction. There may be times in adult learning situations in which teachers decide to throw students completely on their own resources. But that does not necessarily throw them on each other's resources, which is the focus here. The learning designs described above may be any set of documents that makes peer support possible. Actually, we can differentiate between "learning design" and "learning instrument." The design gives direction by providing a format that suggests a framework of orderly steps to acquire knowledge, attitudes, and skills. The instrument is the actual paperwork or software enabling students to implement the design.

Cooperative Learning Requires Effective Learning Tools

Let's take a specific example from Randy's class. He will be teaching the first chapter of John's Gospel in a new class beginning the first Tuesday evening of next month. We note that the beginning date is at least three weeks away; the creation of effective learning instruments cannot be done over coffee on the morning of the class. But we assume something else—that Randy's students will study carefully in advance. Early in the class Randy divides the entire group into segments of three or four and provides a quiz on the chapter. After students have worked independently on the quiz, they form their groups and Randy distributes an answer sheet. Please understand that the quiz represents only one illustration of a learning instrument.

LEARNING QUIZ ON JOHN 1

1. Which of the following does verse 1 not tell us about the Word?
   - a. He was God's Son
   - b. He was in the beginning
   - c. He was with God
   - d. He was God

2. What or Who does John tell us was "the Light of men"?
   - a. The Word
   - b. The Life
   - c. The Christ
   - d. The Father

3. Which of the following correctly identifies the purpose of John the Baptist?
   - a. To witness
   - b. To testify
   - c. To lead people to faith
   - d. All of the above

4. What word does John use to describe what we have seen about the One and Only who came from the Father?
   - a. Flesh
   - b. Grace
   - c. Glory
   - d. Truth

5. What have we all received from the fullness of His grace?
   - a. Eternal life
   - b. One blessing after another
   - c. Grace and truth
   - d. Access to the Father

6. According to John, who has made the Father known?
   - a. The Light
   - b. The Word
   - c. The One and Only
   - d. The Son

7. What segment of the Jerusalem population sent messengers to ask John the Baptist who he was?
   a. The Jews
   b. The priests
   c. The Levites
   d. The Pharisees

8. When John replied to the messengers who questioned him, what Old Testament prophet did he quote?
   a. Elijah
   b. Isaiah
   c. Jeremiah
   d. Amos

9. All the events in John 1:1–28 took place in which town?
   a. Bethany
   b. Bethabara
   c. Bethlehem
   d. Bethsaida

10. According to his own testimony, why did John come "baptizing with water"?
    a. For the repentance of sinners
    b. For the rebuking of sin
    c. For the revelation of the Lamb
    d. For the restoration of Israel

11. During his two days of questioning, John referred to Jesus in three of the following four ways. Which term did he *not* use?
    a. The Son of God
    b. The Lamb of God
    c. One who comes after me
    d. The Christ

12. Who were the first two disciples Jesus talked to?
    a. Peter and John
    b. Andrew and Peter
    c. Andrew and Philip
    d. Philip and Nathanael

13. Philip, Andrew, and Peter all came from which town?
    a. Bethany
    b. Bethabra
    c. Bethlehem
    d. Bethsaida

14. About which of the first disciples did Jesus say, "Here is a true Israelite, in whom there is nothing false?"
    a. Peter
    b. Philip
    c. Nathanael
    d. Andrew

15. Which of the early disciples said to Jesus, "Rabbi, you are the Son of God; you are the King of Israel"?
    a. Peter
    b. Philip
    c. Nathanael
    d. Andrew

COOPERATIVE LEARNING QUIZ ANSWER SHEET

1.	a	(v. 1)
2.	b	(v. 4)
3.	d	(v. 7)
4.	c	(v. 14)
5.	b	(v. 16)
6.	c	(v. 18)
7.	a	(v. 19)
8.	b	(v. 23)
9.	a	(v. 28)
10.	c	(v. 31)
11.	d	(vv. 20–34)
12.	b	(vv. 35–45)
13.	d	(v. 44)
14.	c	(v. 47)
15.	c	(v. 49)

The third document Randy needs is an interpretation of scores and how the group can arrive at them. Obviously from the moment the quiz ends, everything becomes teamwork; it makes no difference any longer who answered questions correctly. Now we find out how group members can help each other arrive at better answers than each has brought to the group. We can never forget that cooperative learning depends on teamwork and denies competition. An old philosophical cliché comes into play as the group begins its work—the whole is greater than the sum of its parts. When people pool their information on a subject they have studied, the end result is usually better than any one of them could do individually, or better than the average of all of them before they discussed it as a group.

LIMITATIONS TO COOPERATIVE LEARNING

What difficulties can Randy expect to encounter when he puts this system into operation? Who will complain? Why would anybody oppose the kind of affiliations arising from such a joint effort?

Educational Attitudes

Many professional educators simply do not like learner-centered models; they prefer to put the teacher in the limelight all the time. But the approach being suggested here focuses on the learner and particularly the collective association of learners. Randy may have some professional educators in his Bible class. Or class members may have been affected with the "big jug/little mug" approach to the learning process, expecting Randy to pour out all the information they need as they passively drink it in. Cooperative learning actually pulls the teacher out of the process after the distribution of the learning instruments. To be sure, designing the strategy and creating the instruments form the major step in the system, so one could hardly argue that the teacher is unimportant. During the actual process, however, general supervision alone is required.

Student Attitudes

Cooperative learning provides very few individual extrinsic rewards. The system produces no "most valuable player," no superstars, no valedictorians, not even individual grades. Everything centers on what the group did together. Without grades, plaques, trophies, stars, happy faces, or individual recognition of some kind, students may feel they have surrendered too much autonomy to the group. But such feelings can hardly be attributed to biblical understanding or to the Holy Spirit's work in our lives. Our own egos push us to competitive education, aided too often by the system itself. Because, as stated already, cooperative learning emphasizes what the team achieved, it leaves little room for recognition of individuals. It's a team sport, not a chess game or a duel.

Difficulty of Design

Teachers committed to the traditional process of competitive education may not do well in creating learning instruments and implementing learning designs of this type. They have been viewed as the custodians of information who provide it in an orderly fashion for students to receive. Seminary faculty, for example, tend to be high on knowledge of content; few students doubt the expertise their teachers bring to their classes in the subject areas of their specialties. However, they tend to be consistently low on testing and evaluation because only the occasional faculty member has any formal instruction in creating a test of any kind. Furthermore, the tests they have seen as students emphasized competitive design.

None of these hurdles is insurmountable. Randy can deal with the attitude issues, and he can learn to make effective learning instruments; but it will take time, and not all experimental attempts will be successful. First, he must explain to his class precisely what he intends to achieve and why.

APPROACHES TO COOPERATIVE LEARNING DESIGN

There are many ways to implement cooperative learning, from the informal seminary study group I mentioned earlier in the chapter to a highly structured classroom setting which employs very formal learning instruments. Of the following, I prefer the first, but, with practice and patience, Randy can probably use any of them effectively.

Team Effectiveness Design

We have already hinted at this pattern for Randy's class in the Gospel of John. To implement the design he needs to take five steps:

First, assess knowledge before you hear team discussion. In the case of John 1 they should study the chapter in advance of their class meeting. We then find out what each individual student knows before any group work takes place.

Second, prepare a test. This does not have to be a sophisticated instrument; the four-alternative multiple-choice quiz provided on John 1 exemplifies a simple approach. Randy could use true or false tests, but they would give him only half the opportunity of a four-alternative multiple-choice quiz to really get at what his students know.

Third, agree on the best answers and appropriate team adjustment. As the team members bring their answers to the group and go over the answer sheet Randy has provided, they must discuss where they differ and why. Each team member fills out the following sheet to compare his own answers with team answers. *Team agreement does not lead to the change of individual scores which are listed in a separate column.* When this is completed every student has two answers to each question, his own and the group's. Obviously these answers may be the same or different.

A sample scoring sheet comparing group and individual choices is outlined below.

COOPERATIVE LEARNING GROUPS SCORING SHEET

	YOUR CHOICE				GROUP CHOICE
1.	a	b	c	d	_____
2.	a	b	c	d	_____
3.	a	b	c	d	_____
4.	a	b	c	d	_____
5.	a	b	c	d	_____
6.	a	b	c	d	_____
7.	a	b	c	d	_____
8.	a	b	c	d	_____
9.	a	b	c	d	_____
10.	a	b	c	d	_____
11.	a	b	c	d	_____
12.	a	b	c	d	_____
13.	a	b	c	d	_____
14.	a	b	c	d	_____
15.	a	b	c	d	_____

YOUR SCORE_____   GROUP SCORE_____

% HIGHER/LOWER_____

Fourth, the group then discusses the best answers. They evaluate individual versus team effort. How did individual answers on a given question relate to the team answers? Better or worse? The ultimate goal is to ascertain how much learning came about because the group provided peer support for each member.

Fifth, the team evaluates the process. At this point there is no longer a focus on answers, but rather how the process, design, and instruments worked. We'll come back to interpreting scores in just a moment, but let's take a quick look at some other designs.

Team-Member Teaching Design

This really describes my seminary Pepsi-and-popcorn group. Each member of the team masters a certain portion of the content and teaches it to the others. Then the team evaluates the knowledge and comprehension of the group on all areas of the material. In every case team members try to help each individual do his or her best. This particular design lends itself very handily to adult groups in which a variety of expertise is already present because of the experience of the group members. Someone particularly effective at personal evangelism could help the group understand witnessing better. A class member particularly effective in leading home Bible classes might help her group grasp how that can best be done.

Performance-Judging Design

In this pattern the team designs effectiveness criteria for a certain task. Let's say that after they finish their study in the Gospel of John, Randy's class decides to lay the groundwork for opening a new class on the other side of the city. Rather than Randy or some other professional leaders in the organization initiating the class, it will be a collective project of the existing group. They must first decide what they want to see in that new class, and then how each member of the present class can work toward achieving those goals and meeting the criteria.

Clarifying-Attitudes Design

Essentially this pattern centers in affective learning. Group members assess their attitudes through some kind of instrument (considerably more difficult to design than a Bible quiz), and then assemble to identify and discuss positions on an attitude scale. In other words, they try to help each other think differently about some controversial subject. One can see this lending itself very nicely to a class in doctrine, Christian behavior, or a variety of social issues.

EVALUATING THE PROCESS

The fifth step in the Team Effectiveness Design model needs further amplification because it will help any class determine whether the design and the instruments are working properly. As the team discusses gain or loss, they will want to follow several principles to guide their interpretation of team and individual scores.

1. A substantial loss in which the team score falls well below the average individual score suggests that discussion was not fruitful; the process somehow prevented the team from using its group resources more fully. If the team score is near or equal to the lowest individual score, the team may conclude that the most uninformed person was the most influential in the discussion.

2. A small gain or loss suggests that discussion was of no substantial help, but neither was it of any harm in arriving at good answers. However, even in this situation, the process may be worthwhile though the product does not suggest improvement.

3. A substantial gain in the team score (though still not as high as the highest individual score) may indicate that discussion was helpful but some resources in the group remained untapped. The fault does not always rest with the instruments; it could be the way the group utilized the knowledge available to it.

4. A team score that exceeds the highest individual score is considered a positive measure of cooperative learning, indicating that

members combined their partial knowledge to reach a more effective team understanding.

In all this, Randy's class will discuss learning efficiency and the quality of their interaction. In other words, they will evaluate process as well as product. Sometimes the recognition of the highest team score is so obvious people see immediately that none of them (or few of them) could have achieved alone what the group achieved together.

Often group members will dispute the answers in the answer key provided by the teacher. No problem. Those discussions should be resolved in a nonauthoritarian way and not by anyone's insistence that the key be accepted at face value. Cooperative learning groups assume that the answers and rationale represent the best reasoning the designer could utilize on that particular instrument.[3]

One final suggestion for Randy and any other reader who wants to move from competitive to cooperative education: *It takes considerably more time.* You already know that about group teaching methods compared to lecturing, and many teachers will say they don't use groups for precisely that reason. However, since Randy is more interested in quality of learning than quantity of content, since he is committed to process as well as product, and since he wants people to learn how to work together in a genuine spirit of *koinōnia* ("fellowship"), cooperative learning may be his best option.

23

❧

Setting the Table

Jan is about to enter a new phase of her ministry at her local church. She has just been asked to serve on the church's adult ministries committee (AMC). As an English instructor at a nearby community college, Jan will bring some interesting insights to that strategic committee. She is thirty-four, never married, and has completed her doctoral residence work. Her entire life is wrapped up with adult education, though she has never had any formal training in that field.

Jan is well aware of the educational problems that face the nation and the church. At the community college where she teaches she deals with many students who struggle with basic reading skills, since over 30 percent of entering freshmen in American colleges read below the seventh-grade level and hundreds read below the fourth-grade level. Though her church has maintained a viable Christian education program for most age levels, Jan is aware of the general decline in Sunday school attendance across denominations, and she is also aware that almost 20 percent of people in America say they have had no religious instruction of any kind. If the AMC genuinely wants to improve adult ministries, and particularly adult education in their church, Jan stands ready to help all she can.

ADULT EDUCATION AND CONTINUING EDUCATION

Here is one place where Jan can help the AMC almost immediately. Like most people just beginning work in adult education, many committee members are confused about the terminology common to the field. Jan has frequently read that there are more adults involved in some kind of educational activity than all the children in all elementary schools combined. Most of it is informal, ranging from a Bible-study group at church to a photography class held one evening a month at Jan's campus. But several things differentiate between adult education and continuing education.

Academic Credit

Continuing education describes the ongoing training of professionals. An example is a Doctor of Ministry program for pastors. However, continuing education does not necessarily require academic credit, since Jan's pastor could attend seminars to earn continuing education units (CEUs) in lieu of academic credit. *Adult education*, by way of contrast, usually refers to "lay-level" classes, people taking courses for whatever informational purposes they wish, but not necessarily to increase competence in a profession. This leads us to a second defining quality.

Organized Instruction

Sometimes academic credit becomes the domain of the socioeconomically privileged. That happens not only because of the cost but also because of the kinds of jobs that enable or even require additional formal learning. Organized instruction certainly describes any program for academic credit, but it can be broadened to mean adult education as well as continuing education. The issue here centers in people who have the motivation and the opportunity to get involved in some kind of classwork. Jan's church has considered starting a Bible institute with some kind of academic credit planned for the future. Whether it ever advances to that level, adult education at the church can be viewed as formal instruction, and participation depends on the learners' interest and motivation.

In a recent faculty meeting Jan's dean introduced a piece of research developed by J. M. Keller and T. Kopp, which she thinks will help her committee structure adult programming at the church.[1] Researchers call it the ARCS model, an acronym built on the four components they found indispensable to adult learning: *attention, relevance, confidence,* and *satisfaction.* The committee does not need to see the technicalities of research to benefit from their prescriptions. Table 4 shows the handout Jan intends to take to her first AMC meeting.

TABLE 4—ESSENTIAL COMPONENTS IN ADULT LEARNING

A. To make instruction *interesting* or *attention-grabbing* to adult learners, it should be designed and delivered so that it:
    1. creates curiosity through the use of novelty, unpredictability, and personal elements
    2. increases curiosity through the use of paradoxes, inquiry, and analogies.

B. To make the instruction *relevant* to adult learners, it should be designed and delivered so that it:
    1. is immediately useful to the learner
    2. clearly demonstrates the benefits of learning
    3. addresses the expectations and goals of learners
    4. provides opportunities to try for high standards of excellence.

C. To promote *confidence* in adult learners, instruction should be designed and delivered so that it:
    1. maintains a relaxed low-risk atmosphere
    2. helps learners connect success to effort.

D. To make the instruction *satisfying* to adult learners, it should be designed and delivered so that it:
    1. confirms newly acquired knowledge and skills by having learners practice them in realistic situations

2. allows learners to share and discuss their projects and new skills
3. avoids threats, surveillance, and other negative influences

Each of these components was identified by Keller and Kopp as helpful for for promoting learning. These strategies should therefore help make instruction more motivationally appealing to adult learners of both genders and all ages.[2]

If the committee takes seriously the Keller and Kopp model, they will immediately see that their adult-ministries program should spread beyond any organized classroom. Self-directed learning includes reading, watching educational television and videotapes, participating in informational discussion groups, and numerous other approaches to increasing one's knowledge and skills. The church serves a wide cross section of adults, so they expect highly educated professionals (like Jan) as well as people who just finished high school to participate in the program.

Academic credit aside, how can the AMC design a program of adult ministry that makes the best use of organized instruction and informal learning to help its adults grow in knowledge and wisdom as well as in effective service for the Lord? That's what this book, and particularly this chapter, gives attention to.

GROWING AN ADULT-EDUCATION TREE

Roots

The biblical and theological foundations of adult education in any evangelical church form the root system of its educational programs. We saw this earlier in the educational cycle as well as in an overview of Titus 2. The AMC must understand adult needs viewed through the eyes of Scripture. Based on the mission of the church, objectives help guide the development of programs and keep them on target. Without solid roots sunk deep into biblical commitment and a genuine awareness of both prescribed and felt needs, the tree will not grow well.

DIAGRAM 12—GROWING AN ADULT-EDUCATION TREE

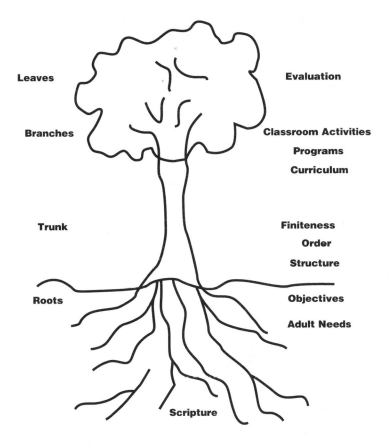

Leaves   Evaluation

Branches   Classroom Activities
      Programs
      Curriculum

Trunk   Finiteness
      Order
      Structure

Roots   Objectives
      Adult Needs

Scripture

Trunk

Every educational program needs some kind of structure. The above ground portion of the tree indicates visible parts of the curriculum (which we'll discuss in the next chapter), particularly the general *structure* and *order*. Within a serious climate for learning, several features arise, such as an emphasis on purpose. Adult education must be intentional, not accidental. The order or programming has to do with sequence and organization, the relationships of various program elements. How will things fit together? How do we keep from overlapping? How does one unit of study build on another? How will we keep a strong focus on age-group developmental tasks?

Then *finiteness* is important. This simply means that educational programs should have a beginning and an ending. Too many adult ministry experiences began at one time in the past to meet genuine needs, but have outlived their usefulness. An educational program is not a marriage—there should be some built-in protection against its obsolescence.

Branches

Curriculum describes the visible parts of the tree such as teaching aids and materials, but also the general scope and sequence of learning. Curriculum spreads across programs but, as we are using the term, it follows the actual structure of the program.

Perhaps a specific example will help. "Family cluster scheduling" as some call it, narrows the program to two or three days a week rather than scheduling activities across almost every night. A local church will not collapse if its programs are moved to other nights or days of the week and in different age-group ministries stacked side by side. Flexibility and adaptability are keys to developing family-oriented programming.

To develop programs that stem from objectives based on needs, church leaders need to see very specifically where the branches of adult ministry will spread out. Space is a factor, of course, and the AMC will have to balance its ministries alongside teen Bible studies, choir practice, a variety of children's ministries, and assorted outreach activities. Great difficulties lie ahead for the committee, but they have observed that too many congregations unduly stretch out activities and meetings which could, with a little creative thinking, be compacted and concentrated.

Leaves

The task before the AMC will not be completed when the program gets underway. At least once a year they need to evaluate the ministries they have set in motion to see how they can be enhanced, modified, or even eliminated. Their evaluation will be based on their objectives—objectives for the entire program and for each specific ministry program. They also need to develop an evaluation tool (see table 5) related to the general survey they used to structure the program in the first place. It contained ten items with opportunity to respond to each one on a scale of one to ten. Since they distributed and gathered it in the two Sunday morning services, they have nearly a 75 percent response, giving them a great basis for putting together a meaningful adult-education program.

TABLE 5—ADULT EVALUATION FORM

1. I would like the church to help me develop my gifts and abilities for God's service.

   1   2   3   4   5   6   7   8   9   10

2. I would like the church to help me with struggles at work.

   1   2   3   4   5   6   7   8   9   10

3. I would like an opportunity to study how to be a more effective parent with emphasis on self-control, discipline, patience, family relationships, and family time.

   1   2   3   4   5   6   7   8   9   10

4. I think the church should offer me more opportunities to study the Bible in-depth.

   1   2   3   4   5   6   7   8   9   10

5. On a scale of 1 to 10 I would rate my current Christian walk as follows:

   1   2   3   4   5   6   7   8   9   10

6. I think the church should offer classes or study groups dealing with

practical Christian ministry issues such as witnessing, relating to neighbors, and dealing with pagan culture.

| 1 | 2 | 3 | 4 | 5 | 6 | 7 | 8 | 9 | 10 |

7. In addition to Sunday morning worship the best time for me to participate in an adult learning group would be:

a.During the Sunday-school hour

| 1 | 2 | 3 | 4 | 5 | 6 | 7 | 8 | 9 | 10 |

b.   Sunday evening

| 1 | 2 | 3 | 4 | 5 | 6 | 7 | 8 | 9 | 10 |

c.   Weekday evening

| 1 | 2 | 3 | 4 | 5 | 6 | 7 | 8 | 9 | 10 |

8. I would be willing to host a study group or assist someone else in doing so.

| 1 | 2 | 3 | 4 | 5 | 6 | 7 | 8 | 9 | 10 |

9. I am willing and available to teach an adult study group.

| 1 | 2 | 3 | 4 | 5 | 6 | 7 | 8 | 9 | 10 |

10. I believe the current structure of adult education at our church is adequate and meets my needs as well.

| 1 | 2 | 3 | 4 | 5 | 6 | 7 | 8 | 9 | 10 |

This evaluation form may differ from what you would design, but it gets at some of the basic questions the AMC needs to deal with in its planning.

BASIC COMPONENTS OF ADULT MINISTRY PROGRAMMING

After the AMC met a couple of times, the issue of criteria for programming came up. No church can carry out every possible adult ministry, and no church should try. The size of the congregation is a significant factor, but it is not as important as objectives. Personnel (the number of people able and willing to serve) stands high on the list as well, but it is not as important as needs. Applying the criteria it selected, the AMC decided that its church would focus on five adult ministries. They expect to refine these after a year of observation and perhaps add others at that time. For now, they want to do a good job on these five.

Adult Sunday School

The committee is toying with names for this ministry, though the basic structure will be the same as in the past. Also the new program will contain more training for adult teachers. The church will start with traditional or age-group classes, but will include a series of rotating electives on both expositional and practical biblical themes.

Until they see better reasons to change, the AMC will continue with Sunday school as the flagship ministry for adults. In the words of Harold Westing, "Growing an effective adult Sunday School doesn't happen by accident—it takes godly, dynamic leadership. Adult departments can expand rapidly and greatly increase effectiveness if leaders give creative supervision and apply these principles and structures. God has gifted people for leadership just as he gifted others to teach. Both gifts must be applied to adult education. Spiritual nurture can happen in the adult Sunday School. It is worth all the time and effort our churches can give."[3]

Small Groups

Apart from the significant nurture she has gained from her pastor's teaching of the Bible, Jan has profited most at her church from the singles group. She began attending while in college and now serves as president of the group. In her view, formal small groups may well be the cornerstone of adult-education ministry. Since fellowship is so crucial in adult education, this means of providing a place to explore Scripture and develop relationships is essential.

The Sunday-evening service, though completely restructured and now informal compared with what it had been for years, continues to shrink in attendance. The elders have asked the AMC to recommend some system of small-group meetings to take the place of that service within the next year. The committee is also considering formulating a men's group and a women's group, probably built around breakfast or lunch meetings. Again objectives and needs stand central. They will have to work out exactly what they would like to see accomplished in each small group. Not every aspect of adult-ministry programming must center in Bible study; there are other needs to consider.

The church John attends has been conducting their Sunday evening program in geographically arranged "flock groups" for several years. The church is too large for fellowship and relationship-building on Sunday mornings, so they hope their evening groups can concentrate on those needs. Size seems to be the critical issue here, since small congregations have a relational dynamic all their own.

Fellowship Events

Speaking of "other needs," the need for fellowship looms large in almost any church. As we read the early chapters of Acts, we see how important it was for the early Christians to get together frequently. Stan Olsen says that "a good adult program will plan to offer a variety of activities that will allow: recreation, intergenerational interaction, cultural exposure, and family programs." He suggests that churches need at least "one fellowship activity for each 200 adults in the membership of the church. This means the church calendar will offer one additional fellowship event each time the membership increases by another 200 adults. All adult programs should have a minimum of two all-church fellowship events each year."[4]

Spiritual Mentoring

Some would use the word *discipling* here, but I see discipling going on quite regularly in adult Sunday-school classes and small groups. In fact, the New Testament concept of discipling consistently emphasizes small groups rather than what the modern church has come to identify as a one-on-one approach. In conjunction with the church's elder board, the AMC is trying to match up mature adults with younger adults for mentoring programs. They understand that this can happen only when mentors are both willing and competent to handle the mentoring process, and mentees really want to participate in the experience.

The church has some specific goals for the early days of this program—the enlisting and training of new leaders and teachers. The church has both elder and deacon boards, and sometimes the leadership seems spread quite thin. Furthermore, many of the younger men in the church don't have the strong Christian background that seemed more common thirty or forty years ago. A new elder-in-training program will focus on developing future prospects for that board.

Information Resources

That self-directed learning we talked about earlier requires a repository of information available to people who want it. Probably the most obvious resource is the church library. Since self-directed learning is still viewed as adult education, the elders have decided to put the church librarian under the supervision of the AMC so the library holdings and processes can complement other elements of the adult education program. Here's another area where Jan can help immediately. Her work as a college professor has shown repeatedly that the number of books is not the issue; *quality* and *accessibility* counts most. The AMC has to figure out how to make the library more user-friendly and more coordinated with adult needs and interests.

BIOGRAPHY OF A MINISTRY

When Luke wanted to illustrate the generosity of the early church, he first described the church's ministry of sharing and then used Barnabas as an example (Acts 4). Let's follow that pattern here for ministry programming. Taking the mentoring program described above as the example, we can follow it through various life cycles common to many church ministries. Laurent Daloz describes the kinds of people we want adult ministries to serve: "unlike traditional students, these folks are not tomorrow's leaders.

They are intimately enmeshed in the real world, here, now. They are literally our neighbors; they come to us out of the family or the workplace, and after classes, they return. What they are learning from us has immediate relevance and application in their families, their neighborhoods, and in the society. Moreover, many of them hold significant decision-making positions today in labor and industry, the professions, and the military. . . . With them, we don't have to wait. We can begin right now."[5] Daloz speaks out of the context of higher education, but the paragraph aptly describes what Jan's church wants to do with its mentoring program. Let's follow it through.

Idea

Most pastors think a lot about mentoring and most do it, formally or informally, much of the time. In this particular case Pastor Stevens, associate pastor for Christian education, came up with the idea of a specific leadership mentoring program simply because he found himself frequently trying to replace leaders and noticed repeatedly the shallowness of the leadership pool. His church needs ten to twenty new leaders a year—elders, deacons, Sunday-school teachers, small-group leaders, committee members—to handle newly established ministries or replace leaders who move on for a variety of reasons. After discussing his idea with the senior pastor, Stevens presented it to the AMC.

Objective

Every ministry, new or continuing, must know precisely what it is supposed to achieve. In this illustration it seems quite obvious—to produce spiritual, mature, competent, and willing leaders for the church's variety of ministries. Mentoring situations will vary; the preparation of an elder will look different from the preparation of a Sunday-school teacher, but the general objectives remain the same.

Feasibility

Any church can say it will produce twenty new leaders in the next calendar year, but some may find themselves trying to make bricks without

254

straw. Feasibility raises many important details. Do we have the resources? Can we afford to do this? Do we have people willing to take it on? Are they competent to see it through? How many of the present elders and deacons could actually mentor a potential leader for a full year with good results?

Staffing

Certainly we could include the issue of personnel under feasibility, but it is so important I want to mention it separately. Once we have the idea, the objectives, and the possibilities in place, we must ask who will do it. In the case of present teachers mentoring prospective teachers, for example, modeling can be the deciding factor in the effectiveness of the entire program. Brad Stych reminds us that "many adult educators tend to isolate methods from other aspects of the instructional process. This practice is particularly detrimental when objectives suggest that it would be more beneficial to use some methods than others. Thus, in order to increase learner proficiencies, some type of match must be made between methods and objectives."[6]

Schedule

One of the biggest questions voiced all over the country has to do with the best schedule for training leaders in the local church. Doing it through mentoring rather than formal classes alleviates the problem to some extent, since formal mentoring only requires a schedule coordination between the two parties involved. But the AMC does not want to leave anything to chance. When they announce their new mentoring program, they want to have the design well in line. Furthermore, scheduling is even more important for the other ministries under discussion.

Implementation

When will a new ministry begin? So far everything in this list can go on behind the scenes. But there comes a day when a class begins or a new fellowship group gets underway. The timing is important. Some programs suffer and die because they were launched at the wrong time—either too early or too late. But timing isn't the only issue in implementation. The way we initiate a new program will also affect its health.

Integration

The AMC will have to ask about every aspect of adult ministry, "How does it fit into the big picture?" Each learning experience stands in relationship to other learning experiences within a given group or class. And each group or class fits into the total framework of adult ministries. The AMC is sewing a quilt in which all the pieces need to be properly related to each other or the intended design may be askew. Jan and her friends have the responsibility to coordinate the overall picture of adult ministries—everything from individual mentoring to library supervision. Coordination and correlation must be built into the whole program or it will look like a set of fragmented offerings, a smorgasbord of unrelated items. Churches suffer from a lack of educational integration when program leaders do not know what other program leaders are doing and curriculum overlaps from one group to another.

Evaluation

As noted earlier, Jan and company are by no means finished when a new program has been launched. They follow it through all the years of its active life, making necessary adjustments along the way. They evaluate the quality of teaching in the Sunday school classes and the effectiveness of relationships in the mentoring program. They evaluate how well different age groups are served and whether genuine relationships come to life in small groups and fellowship events.

So much centers in the effectiveness of the AMC. It shouldn't be difficult to picture them hard at work in their monthly meetings, listening to reports and recommending changes. Some members of the committee may head adult-ministry groups just as Jan leads the singles. Others may be participants but not group leaders. But all the committee members are adults, and therefore they are dealing with issues they understand. Jan has found them a deeply committed group. As they get to know each other and work together more effectively, adult ministries at their church will take several major steps forward to the glory of God.

24

❦

Making the Shoe Fit

As *this chapter* is being prepared, Betty and I have been looking for several weeks—and the search continues. After fifteen years in one city we have relocated in retirement and face all the usual challenges such as new friends, new medical services, getting accustomed to a different house and community—and finding a new church.

For forty years we have joined churches in which we could serve, usually without any concern for whether the church met our needs. In almost every case God was gracious to grant both, and our church experiences have been a highlight for most of our adult lives. This time, however, we are making a conscious effort to find not only a church where we can serve by utilizing the gifts and experience God has given us, but also one that ministers to us. I would guess that most adults consider both of those questions; for those with children, the issues become even more complicated.

That's where programming and curriculum come together. As we noticed in the last chapter, curriculum is an important component in any adult-ministries program. Too many churches don't consider the details of adult curriculum, even though they may invest significant amounts of time and money in curriculum for children and teenagers. Such carelessness results in some inferior approaches. James Galvin and David Veerman put it plainly:

Unfortunately, teachers often design educational programs for adults by copying the wrong educational models. This can be a fatal mistake for adult education. These teachers may organize and run the program:

- Like educational programs for children (pedagogical model),
- Like an extension of a seminary (academic model),
- Like a place where knowledge is deposited in the heads of the learners (banking model),
- Like a debate or like a trial (adversarial model).

These improper models don't fit the "consumers"—the students. Each of these educational approaches may be very effective with a specific audience. But just because an approach works well in one classroom is no guarantee that it will work with adults generally. Effective curriculum design must begin with a careful analysis of the prospective students.[1]

Shoes that do not fit well tend to be uncomfortable; they can even cause pain. Walking in them too long could produce injury, sometimes permanent. Educational leaders in any congregation face a great challenge in adult ministries—making the shoe fit.

VALUE OF CURRICULUM

The traditional terms *program* and *curriculum* have both fallen on hard times in the field of Christian education. Somehow they seem like stilted constraints of the past, unadaptable to the more flexible learning systems of today. However, they are both good words; one need only understand them in contemporary context. *Curriculum* comes from a Latin term meaning "race course," implying some distance within given boundaries one must cover to finish a project. Every church-education program uses a curriculum: professionally printed or locally designed; planned or haphazard; integrated or chaotic. This chapter will talk about curriculum materials (study guides, books), but the big picture has to do with an organized pattern of learning carefully designed to achieve clear-cut goals. What can a good curriculum do for us?

Provide Balance and Coordination

Since most teachers of adults will be lay leaders, we cannot expect them to initiate standard curriculum principles for their classes. A well-designed curriculum can guide them into the kind of balance and coordination so necessary in meeting the needs of adults. We all know that some teachers in adult classes have pet themes or favorite portions of Scripture. The church might get on a "prophecy kick" and offer an overabundance of studies in eschatology, as important as those studies may be in balance. Or since many teachers find the Old Testament more difficult, some classes focus exclusively on the New Testament, perhaps for years. A good curriculum plan can help alleviate that common and troubling deficiency.

A good curriculum also helps reduce the constant tension between covering the content and teaching material. As Maryellen Weimer puts it, "It is possible to cover the content (which is to win the race) but not teach the material (which is to win the race, but not receive a prize). Faculty absolve themselves of this tension when they assume that the teacher's only task is to transfer information. They are the full vessels; it is their job to pour knowledge into the empty ones. If those vessels are too small, or improperly placed, or overflow, that is not the teacher's problem."[2]

This refers to college teaching, but the same tensions exist in the church, particularly in adult ministries. The relationships between adult classes and the application of God's Word to life in each class depend on sound curriculum structure.

Predetermine a Study Plan

Some larger churches with extensive resources find it effective to write their own curricula. Most of us, however, would do well to depend on a professionally designed curriculum because it provides an organized study plan. Obviously we want a curriculum that is both theologically solid and educationally sound. Materials for adult ministries should be written and edited by people familiar with the andragogical process and should strongly support basic evangelical theology and the doctrinal distinctives of your congregation or denomination.

Prepare Teacher Readiness

Ultimately the curriculum helps students, but along the way it should serve the important task of preparing teachers for classroom experiences. If we push the shoe analogy just a bit further, we might think of the curriculum publisher as the manufacturer (Bass, Rockport, Hush Puppies); the Adult Ministries Committee becomes the marketing chain (Sears, J. C. Penney, Shoes R Us); the teacher serves as the salesclerk with shoe-horn in hand, always pinching the toe to make sure the fit will work; and the student is the shopper. Good manufacturing and distribution help the clerk provide the right shoes for each customer.

Promote Staff Development

People who learn how to adapt and utilize well-designed curricula will increase their competence and enhance their leadership skills over the years. In one sense the teaching staff helps select the curriculum; in the long run, however, the curriculum forms the staff, and, to a great extent, determines their effectiveness. The scope, sequence, and content of any curriculum leave their imprint on those who use it. Surely we can assume that a beginning teacher handling a well-designed curriculum for a year will be a better teacher at the end of the year, assuming a respectable investment in personal study time and appropriate training.

KEY CURRICULAR QUESTIONS

So many issues jump to the front when we talk about curriculum in local churches. We could discuss types of curriculum, subjects to be covered, relationships between developmental tasks and classroom experiences— the options go on and on. But let's stick our heads into a meeting of any church's Adult Ministries Committee and glance at five questions they must answer to plan a well-designed curriculum for their adults.

Who Will Use It?

We begin with the student question. Shoes must fit people. People do not fit shoes. Precisely at points such as this we see the shortcomings of a denominational curriculum produced in some city where the publishing house is located and then sent across the country, the continent, or even around the world in hopes that everybody can wear size 9D. To borrow another metaphor, such a practice reminds us of the story about the ancient innkeeper who had only one bed. If a guest happened to be too short for the bed, he stretched his visitor; any guest too long for the bed had his legs chopped down to size.

Obviously the question of who will use the curriculum immediately raises the programming issue. The AMC will deal with the Sunday school curriculum. But that must be coordinated with the Bible study groups, men's meetings, women's meetings, and the relationship of the whole curriculum to pulpit preaching. Will our church minister to singles? Do we need curriculum for a college/career class? How will we serve our senior saints? In short, how many different shoe sizes, styles, and colors do we need, and how can we make them fit?

Who Will Teach It?

There's nothing wrong with assuming that using a good curriculum can improve a teacher's skills, as noted earlier. But we have to take a realistic view of the current talent pool. People who have professional skill in selling wing tips may not know a tennis shoe from a walking shoe. People who have given their lives to handling children's shoes may be at a loss as to how to help adults make a good selection. We don't choose a course of study and then wonder if we have people to run the race. The teacher question becomes part of the planning process.

What Should It Cover?

Some churches will decide to put this question first since the content question seems so obvious. Decisions about content take us right back to the coordination and balance problems we discussed earlier in the chapter. Without being dogmatic, let me say quite firmly that it is not a good idea to let adult teachers choose their own subject matter. They may make recommendations, but the AMC with its wider view must hold ultimate authority. May I also add that a teacher who refuses to teach unless he or she can deal with some favorite topic probably shouldn't be asked. The answer to the content question comes when we correctly balance our understanding of prescribed needs (what adults in different stages and experiences of life need to know) with felt needs (what the adults in our congregation want to know).

What Do We Hope to Achieve?

Whenever educational leaders get together to plan anything, the objectives question will surface almost immediately. In fact, professional educators will more than likely address the issue of goals before they determine content, though both will be major participants in the curricular wedding. Warren Benson puts it this way: "If we would be catalysts for educational change, we must function in more exact ways and leave less to chance. Be aware of both process and outcomes. Do not be consumed with content. Keep these in proper balance. Measurable objectives reflect a concern for students and their growth and accomplishments. I have found that the clearer my objectives, the more free I am to have the Holy Spirit change and nuance what I teach, what emphases I make, and adjust my prepared material to the time allotted. The Holy Spirit nudges me to sense what people need and how the Bible can speak to their situational contexts. This does not minimize the absolute necessity for thorough study and well-honed objectives."[3]

Let's keep in mind that objectives function on at least three levels: the entire program of adult ministries (which may well have its own mission statement); each individual ministry such as a Sunday-school class for middle adults; and each teaching/learning session.

How Will We Deliver It?

This is the program question. Since we have dealt with this in the last chapter, we touch on it here in passing. When we understand our students, adapt our teaching talent, determine our outcomes, and identify our basic content, we still have to figure out how best to arrange the shoes in the store so people can find what they need. College and seminary educators today commonly talk about "delivery systems," by which they mean that traditional resident classes can and perhaps should be augmented by modular units of study, video conferencing, weekend seminars, on-line courses, and other options.

Remember, adult learning takes place through interacting with and applying information, not by watching a teacher perform. Furthermore, in the hectic modern world we may discover that informal, geographically arranged Bible study groups may offer better learning experiences than some of the traditional patterns of the past. Once shoestores were downtown with most other businesses. Now your chances of finding one are much better in a shopping mall.

Consider the way many adult Sunday-school classes have been arranged for the past two or three decades. Adult classes were once strictly age-grouped, but the use of electives has been much more popular in recent years. One day I brought potential elective study materials to a seminary class to show students the wide availability. At least fifty different items covered the desk and the front of the classroom. They represented over a dozen publishers, and most were usable in a number of different situations, from Sunday-school classes to early-morning men's Bible studies.

Using electives in any curriculum calls up a major guideline so important as to be nearly axiomatic—*electives require a long-range plan.* If we start spinning off one topic after another, we can lose curriculum coordination rapidly. We end up depending strictly on popularity, teacher availability, and pet themes. Without a multiyear plan, adult electives become a minefield of disorganization. Table 6 on the following page shows one year of a three-year elective plan for four Sunday-school classes meeting concurrently, designed to serve between 100 and 150 adults.

HOW WILL WE EVALUATE?

Sooner or later we must get around to the measurement question. In the most narrow sense, evaluating curriculum comes down to the issue of

TABLE 6—SAMPLE ONE-YEAR ELECTIVE PATTERN

	CLASS A	CLASS B	CLASS C	CLASS D
Fall	Bible Survey I: Pentateuch and Historical Books	Friendship Evangelism	School Choices for Your Children	Pastor's Class for New Members
Winter	Bible Survey II: Poets and Prophets	Becoming Global Christians	Creative Family Worship	Pastor's Class for New Members
Spring	Bible Survey III: Gospels and Acts	Devotional Study of Psalms I	Controlling Television and the Computer	Pastor's Class for New Members
Summer	Bible Survey IV: Epistles and Revelation	Devotional Study of Psalms II	Winning the Discipline Game	Pastor's Class for New Members

whether the learning experiences it produced met the objectives we set. In the broader sense we evaluate the quality of instruction, the clarity of outcomes in student growth and knowledge, the satisfactory coverage of content, and the effectiveness of our delivery systems. Galvin and Veerman are helpful here again:

Five levels of learner outcomes help us determine the effectiveness of any educational program for adults. Failure at any of the levels shows the planner where additional refinement is needed in the course.

- If adults do not become involved, more attention needs to be given to their needs, interests, and concerns at the beginning of the course.

- If the learners do not explore the content, more attention needs to be given to the appropriateness of the content than how it is delivered.

- If learners fail to understand, then more time to discuss and think about the information is needed.

- If they fail to perform the skills adequately in class, then more practice time is required.

- If use of the skills deteriorates after a short time, then more attention to transfer of learning and overcoming barriers is needed in the class.

The primary purpose of evaluative information is to improve the class by making midcourse corrections along the way, or for improving the course for the next time it is taught. This feedback can also be useful in the continued development of the teacher and the students. Evaluation of the course itself can also be used as a summary learning exercise in some settings.[4]

MAKING NECESSARY ADJUSTMENTS

What does one do when the shoe does not fit? Sometimes adding a pair of Dr. Scholl's innersoles can help, or perhaps a strong "shoe tree" can stretch the leather a bit. Sometimes a pair of shoes gets so old they no longer offer any support at all and need to be thrown away.

A curriculum is like that. Sometimes we can tinker just a bit and improve learning experiences significantly. Other times we shake our heads and acknowledge something has outlived its usefulness and needs to be discarded. Within a given learning situation such as a classroom, however, teachers and leaders can apply corrective measures to adjust a curriculum that doesn't seem to be working. Any experienced educational leader can remember a teacher bringing in a curriculum guide and pointing out theological errors or statements that may conflict with the denomination's stated beliefs. Sometimes these situations can be turned into active learning. How can teachers actually adjust curriculum in a classroom setting?

Question Troublesome Misconceptions

This kind of thing happens in any educational setting at almost any age level. Indeed, recognizing deficiencies in textbooks or even lectures is a major part of educational integration. Rather than saying, "Please disregard the last paragraph on page 137 because the author obviously does not understand the uniqueness of our denomination," teachers should ask their students, "Did you find anything unusual in your reading for this week?" If we achieve nothing else with such a question, it opens discussion and leads to participational patterns, which we already know are effective in teaching adults.

Discuss the Bible Inductively

In Christian education, Scripture is our most important curriculum element. Therefore hermeneutics (the art and science of interpretation) becomes a part of every Bible teacher's task. Good teachers guide students in observing textual phenomena and responding with the three time-tested questions of inductive Bible study: What does it say? What does it mean? What do I do about it?

Too often we allow adult students to get by with the most cursory skimming of a passage, which then leads to misguided and even bizarre interpretations. I remember an old story by Louis Agassiz describing his first biology class. The professor put him in a corner of the lab, handed him a dead fish, and said, "Look at your fish." So he looked at his fish for a while and made some notes—it has scales, fins, a mouth, teeth, a tail. He took the fish back to the instructor and asked a number of questions about it. Then the professor again said, "Look at your fish." Throughout that day every time Agassiz or any other student approached the teacher with questions the only response they heard was, "Look at your fish."

Maybe we need to take that kind of approach with Bible study. How often in adult classes we hear people say, "Well, I think that . . . ," "My pastor used to say . . . ," "In my opinion Paul means. . . ." People who want to be meticulous about business decisions and prefer their surgeons to be scrupulous about medical procedures offer the most off-the-wall opinions about the Bible. Adult teachers should be trained to say repeatedly, "That's an interesting idea; where in the Scriptures is it supported?"

Offer Solid Biblical Evidence

How futile to counteract a student's erroneous opinion with a teacher opinion. In some subject-matter fields, that may be all we have to offer—

but not in Bible study. We challenge student misunderstandings with clear biblical evidence and ask them to respond. Jesus modeled this for us with His disciples and many others who crossed His path. Who can forget his words to "an expert in the law," when He said, "What is written in the Law? . . . How do you read it?" (Luke 10:25–26). Questioning student opinions formed a basic foundation of our Lord's interactive ministry.

Ask Applicatory Questions

When teachers explain biblical concepts in a way that makes sense from a student perspective, it allows adults to implement truth in their lives. Here again, just as in correcting biblical misunderstanding, the question approach is better than a declaration. Make no mistake about it; good applicational teaching takes time. People need time to think through how they should respond to God's Word. Teachers should encourage their adults to state how the truth applies to them. "What do you think God is leading us to do because we've studied this psalm?" "How can the Holy Spirit produce this kind of behavior in us?" "What is there in this passage that might impact the way we deal with non-Christians at work?"

My wife tells about an evangelistic Bible study she once taught for young women. The key to the group was that believers were always a minority and unbelievers a majority. The purpose of the group was Bible-study evangelism.

One day the ladies were reading a passage from Mark and commenting on the meaning when one of the newcomers, with no prompting, paused, looked up, and said to the group, "If this verse means what I think it means, I'm not a Christian." What a marvelous example of the Word and the Spirit accomplishing God's work. That's what we want in our adult-learning groups.

Explain How Behavior Follows Value

Knowledge leads to belief, belief to value, and value to behavior. In many churches teachers of adults have not yet understood that there is no direct line from knowledge to behavior. Nowhere does the Bible guarantee that if we tell people the truth often enough their lives will change.

Diagram thirteen illustrates the linking of knowledge and behavior.

DIAGRAM 13—FROM KNOWLEDGE TO BEHAVIOR

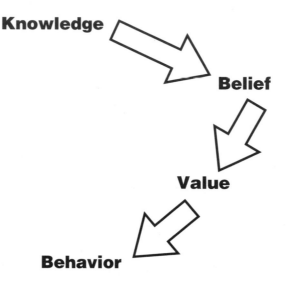

Knowledge

Belief

Value

Behavior

Maturing adult Christians understand that the Bible commands us to pray—that's *knowledge*. God doesn't need our prayers; we need to pray. The next step is to to develop belief that prayer is important. No, prayer doesn't change things, God changes things through prayer. When we know biblical truth about prayer and believe it, we should value praying. That means making time to pray privately, with the family and at church. Already we are describing *behavior* resulting from the three prior influences. That behavior reflects what we value; our values reflect what we believe; and our beliefs are based on knowledge.

Applying curriculum—that's what this section describes. Curriculum only makes sense when knowledge translates into belief, valuing, and behavior.

INTERGENERATIONAL CURRICULUM

Intergenerational learning found much greater popularity in a society in which extended families lived together and people in general were much less mobile. But many churches have experimented with cross-generational educational opportunities, and sometimes with significant success. "Intergenerational" simply describes a learning situation made up of people from various age groups meeting together for learning purposes.

Twenty years ago Margaret Swain talked about "family clusters," which she described as "a group of four or five complete family units which contract together periodically over an extended period of time for shared educational experiences related to their living and relationship within their families."[5] In her book Swain reminded readers that family-cluster learning works because families provide the most intensive framework for growth and change.

My own experiences with intergenerational learning have been largely positive, and two criteria of effectiveness stand out in my memory. First, intergenerational learning works better when it is strictly voluntary rather than coerced. Standing alongside several more traditional classes grouped by age or topic, an intergenerational class which brings together people at various stages in life can afford a very rich growth pattern in adult education.

Second, the most effective intergenerational groups of which I have been a part have been narrowly focused. Rather than just ranging across a series of topics that anyone in the group might introduce, the best intergenerational groups aim at a specific target, utilizing the experiences and abilities of group members to get there.

What do you want for your congregation as a result of adult-learning experiences of various kinds? What kinds of instructional shoes are you making available so that people can walk the walk of faith? Your primary list might be somewhat different from mine, but three things jump to an early lead as I think about congregations in which I have served.

The first is *evangelical theology*. As a result of studying Scripture, we want people to get a handle on biblical doctrine, theology that can guide their lives. Obviously we desire that outcome for all age levels, but maybe if we infect our adults with a hefty dose of theological accuracy they might just spread the virus to young people and children.

But theological accuracy is useless without *congregational unity*. I sometimes think that in any congregation a careful adherence to the first five verses of Philippians 2 could bring revival in weeks with no fanfare, no money, and no additional public meetings.

Third, another top three goal for adult curriculum is developing *global vision.* Affirming the exclusivity of the gospel, Daniel Clendenon wrote,

> The vast majority of people who have ever lived and are living today are not Christian. Does it make sense, therefore, to believe that God wants to save people only through Christ? Exact figures are hard to come by, but even rough estimates are disturbing. In a.d. 100, about a half percent of the world population was Christian, in a.d. 1000 about 19 percent and today—after 2000 years of missionary effort—only about 30 percent of the world identifies itself as Christian. What can we say about the eternal destiny of this vast horde who have never named the name of Christ? Taken together, these factors help to explain a new awareness of a very old challenge: the vast diversity of world religions polls competing claims and offer "gospels" other than that of Christ alone as Savior and Lord.[6]

Through preaching, teaching, study groups, fellowship activities and everything else that make up adult-ministries program and curriculum we want to make sure people grow in their relationship to Jesus Christ. One could argue that the cornerstone of adult curriculum is found in the familiar letter Paul wrote to the church at Ephesus:

> It was he who gave some to be apostles, some to be prophets, some to be evangelists, and some to be pastors and teachers, to prepare God's people for works of service, so that the body of Christ may be built up until we all reach unity in the faith and in the knowledge of the Son of God and become mature, attaining to the whole measure of the fullness of Christ. Then we will no longer be infants, tossed back and forth by the waves, and blown here and there by every wind of teaching and by the cunning and craftiness of men in their deceitful scheming. Instead, speaking the truth in love, we will in all things grow up into him who is the Head, that is, Christ. From him the whole body, joined and held together by every supporting ligament, grows and builds itself up in love, as each part does its work. (Eph. 4:11–16)

25

❦

Just Do It!

I*n his wonderful history* we call the Book of Acts, Luke colorfully describes the mission and ministry of the early church. These believers gave themselves to Bible study, prayer, fellowship, praise, and worship. Without special programs or slogans, "the Lord added to their number daily those were being saved" (Acts 2:47). We've seen in the chapters of this book that worship, fellowship, learning, and service allow God to work through His people in order to create a spiritual community. All this depends on the understanding and application of spiritual gifts and their role in the body of Christ (Rom. 12:6–8). The unity, diversity, and mutuality of the church abound when worshipers serve and servants worship—and to a great extent, learning makes both possible.

Church health begins neither with overt evangelism nor missionary sending—those both must follow. Biblical church health begins with a Christ-centered, Bible-centered congregation determined to be, in its personal, family, and corporate life, precisely what God wants of His people. And it makes no difference whether they number fifteen, fifteen hundred, or fifteen thousand. Though the gospel has always been transcultural, Christians have frequently been tempted to adapt so dramatically to their cultural surroundings that they often fade into the scenery of the world and can't even be seen. To be sure, this is most often done from sincere motives, a desire to contextualize the gospel or to be "relevant to the times." We are hooked on futurism, movements, groups, and slogans.

But the first-century church was different. Rather than programs and slogans, they were marked by unity and generosity. "All the believers were one in heart and mind. No one claimed that any of his possessions was his own, but they shared everything they had. With great power the apostles continued to testify to the resurrection of the Lord Jesus, and much grace was upon them all. There were no needy persons among them. For from time to time those who owned lands or houses sold them, brought the money from the sales and put it at the apostles' feet, and it was distributed to anyone as he had need" (Acts 4:32–35).

No wonder the world was interested! The believers spoke the Word of God boldly and proclaimed the name of Jesus and the resurrection—wherever they went. And their message carried meaning because people knew what kind of relationships they maintained when they were together. Ray Ortlund reminds us, "The Epistles command believers to unite together on the basis of their new family relationship in Christ. Over and over come the instructions: suffer together (1 Cor. 12:26), rejoice together (Rom. 12:15), carry each other's burdens (Gal. 6:2), restore each other (Gal. 6:1), pray for each other (Rom. 15:30), encourage each other (Rom. 1:12), forgive each other (Eph. 4:32), confess to each other (James 5:16), be truthful with each other (Eph. 4:25), spur each other to good deeds (Heb. 10:24), and give to each other (Phil. 4:14–15)."[1]

Most Bible students agree that Ephesians identifies biblical goals for the church and describes how they can be achieved. In that letter Paul did not deal with error or heresy but instead he wrote to expand the spiritual horizons of his readers particularly in relationship to the body of Christ. Obviously Ephesus was a healthy church. Where in the Book of Ephesians do we find programs and statistics? Where did Paul talk about growth or plateauing? What about buildings and fund drives—both marks of a "healthy church" at the turn of the millennium?

Of course we find none of that. Instead, the apostle described humble people making spiritual progress with God and each other, and offered a formula that could change a church of any size from sickness to health in a matter of weeks. "Be completely humble and gentle; be patient, bearing with one another in love. Make every effort to keep the unity of the Spirit through the bond of peace. There is one body and one Spirit—just as you were called to one hope when you were called—one Lord, one faith, one baptism; one God and Father of all, who is over all and through all and in all" (Eph. 4:2–6).

But some may say, "That kind of ideal may have marked the churches of the New Testament. But after two thousand years of spiritual warfare, the enemies of the soul seem more darkly arrayed against the people of God."

It may seem that way, but modern secularism affords neither a lesser nor a greater threat to biblical truth than Roman paganism; indeed, the similarities are striking. Furthermore, we're not talking about some kind of victim-oriented survival here; we're talking about *health*. In this last chapter we want to come to a synopsis of adult ministries and how they work in healthy churches of the twenty-first century.

DESIGNING A MINISTRY CONTEXT

What adjectives best describe the kind of community we should develop in individual groups and throughout the entire congregation to make effective adult ministries possible?

Caring Environment

A caring community provides an environment desperately needed in a society of loneliness and alienation. Throughout the first half or even two-thirds of the twentieth century, Christian adults found this kind of sanctuary at home and at church. With the breakup of the family, however, and the increasing institutionalization of the church, it becomes essential again to work at creating the kind of community described in Acts.

To win the lost to Christ, believers first need to be nurtured and trained. Until Christians gathered in a local congregation are formed by the Word and the Spirit into a solid family, displaying mutuality and generosity, nothing else matters. What could be less effective in fulfilling the Great Commission than inviting unsaved people into a congregation scarred by complaining, bitterness, criticism, and hypocrisy?

Nurturing Context

When unity is established, believers can grow spiritually. They can expand their horizons of service and flex their ministry muscles. Adults need to minimize conflict between roles and goals. Earlier in their lives they faced conformity to expectations. Now most adults can be independent people without constant conflict with what someone else requires them to be. Goal-striving and role-playing run rampant in North American society. Part of adult education should minimize that competition in order to promote spiritual unity and personal growth. As Peter wrote, believers are to "grow in the grace and knowledge of our Lord and Savior Jesus Christ" (2 Pet. 3:18).

Need-Sensitive Content

Without abandoning the heritage of the past and traditions we want to perpetuate, our adult-education programs certainly do need to prepare people for what's happening now. We've talked a good bit about need assessment and need-meeting content, so further emphasis here may not be necessary. Christian educators need not struggle to find new or different methods for varying adult age groups. As we understand age-group characteristics, the distinction appears in content, not process.

Ministry Ownership

How often we use terminology like "Pastor Smith's church" or "Tom's adult class." Although very innocent, such language leads us away from the participation and involvement we work so hard to attain. We want everyone in the congregation to relate personally to ministries in which they are involved—"my church, my class, my service."

MODELING AN ADULT LEARNING PROGRAM

Throughout the book we've seen several models pertaining to adult education. Nearly every model should be *adapted and not adopted* for your own ministry to adults. Here we look at five essential elements that should characterize an effective adult-ministries program.

Biblical Content

Though we have emphasized process and implementation throughout this book, my intent was to provide a corrective balance, not in any way to minimize the importance of biblical content. Ed Hayes states it well: "The Bible is the primary source of our theological and educational commitments in Scripture. Evangelicals must test all opinions on faith and practice by their adherence to the inspired writings. To what source can we go to find renewal of thought and action—'to what source but the Holy Scriptures?' asks Lois LeBar. . . . Christian adult learning based on authoritative Scriptures, however, need not be a caricature of learning, a subtle brain washing, a matter of running an intelligible cookie cutter which stamps out the same stereotype on plastic minds."[2]

Spiritual Tone

Adult-ministry programs should never be something we have constructed on the basis of sound educational logic alone. The adult-ministries committee of any church needs to spend a good bit of time in prayer and to recognize that the Holy Spirit's role is hardly confined to the actual classroom session alone; He breathes life into the entire program. Too often we ask God to bless something we have designed—after we have designed it. An effective adult-ministries program begins with an appeal for the Holy Spirit's guidance in everything we do from needs-assessment to evaluation.

Obviously the role of the Holy Spirit in the teaching process looms large. As Roy Zuck puts it, "The strength of Paul's spiritual life stemmed from his dependence on the indwelling Holy Spirit. . . .The apostle wrote repeatedly about the Holy Spirit, urging believers to live by means of the Spirit (Gal. 5:16), and to be filled (i.e., controlled) by the Spirit (Eph. 5:18). The Holy Spirit's central role in the lives of believers is seen in His many ministries."[3]

Dynamic Application

Significant learning always involves change. It might be change brought about by the adding of information, but more likely it will include affective as well as cognitive results. We talked about these terms earlier in the book. Affective learning deals with attitudes and feelings. Serious adult education should produce changes in thinking about lifestyle and relationships. True, many of the things we teach in adult education cannot be measured immediately, perhaps not at all. Nevertheless life changes produced by the Holy Spirit—because we have designed programs to teach them and develop their spiritual lives—are no less important because they are reflected only in private or family contexts.

Practical Outreach

In the early verses of Acts 8, Luke wrote that the believers (probably Greek-speaking Christians known as Hellenists) were driven out of Jerusalem after the stoning of Stephen. Verse 4 offers one of the most poignant guidelines for New Testament evangelism found anywhere: "Those who had been scattered preached the word wherever they went." The efforts of these witnessing Christians found fruit in the development of the true mother church of the New Testament at Antioch (11:19–30). There, bolstered by the encouragement of Barnabas and developed by the teaching of Saul, the disciples first picked up the name "Christian," forming a distinctive identity. This vital congregation, founded by anonymous witnessing laypeople, sent out the first missionaries and served as a base for the missionary team for approximately two decades.

Somehow we need to reconnect teaching and witness in the church. So often educational programs center on transmitting information, while a different committee staffed by different people focuses on evangelism. The structure is immaterial, but the inseparable relationship between learning God's truth and sharing it with others cannot be denied.

Essential Flexibility

Church ministries for adults must respond to an ever-changing environment. If we take seriously the evaluation phase of the various models, adapting to that fluid need pattern will be much easier. If we refuse to make the shoe fit, however, and persist in our erroneous idea that "one size fits all," flexibility will be hard to find.

IMPLEMENTING INSTRUCTIONAL DESIGN

Models of adult education abound and some are quite complicated. In this book I've tried to select basic models that you can adapt to specific situations. Here I suggest three phases of designing an adult education program—objectives, instruction, and evaluation. You plan it, you do it, you assess it.

Determine Objectives

Yes, this is review, but few things could possibly be as important in any educational program as the clarity and specificity of objectives. I have taught the Gospel of John at both graduate and undergraduate levels as well as in local church classes. Since this is one book of the Bible Christians think they know well, I begin class with a fifty-question learning quiz. Hit cold, students usually do poorly, scoring in the teens and twenties. Obviously my point is to emphasize need, to be able to say, "You're in the right class; now let's decide what we want to learn." Measuring entry competencies is one way to link objectives and needs. When we know what students do not know about a given study, we will be better able to ascertain what they need to know.

Design Instruction

Finally we come to the question of methods which, for reasons noted earlier in this chapter, I have placed in a rather low position of importance. Since the adult teacher is primarily a facilitator, planning learning activities and organizing learning groups takes center stage. Designing instruction for adults requires providing adequate learner options and allocating time and space for learning to take place.

Choosing methods for an adult-learning group does not differ significantly from other levels except in the emphasis and effort to help those adults become independent learners. Actually the word *method* simply describes the process and technique used by a teacher in communicating truth to students. Because classes differ in interests, intellectual ability, and attention spans, teachers should use teaching methods appropriate for the group.

In adult education two-way communication among teacher and students seems most effective. It emphasizes involvement of both in a mutual quest for truth. Brad Stych, a specialist in adult education, talks about "the finer points of choosing instructional methods:

> Many factors shape the selection of instructional methods. These factors are both person-specific and situation-specific in nature. In practice, most instructors make some intuitive decisions concerning method selection. However, selection decisions are likely to be more comprehensive when the decision-making process is more intentional. It is unfortunate that many teachers of adults tend to choose and use only those methods with which they are comfortable. Fear and uncertainty do have a terrible impact upon instructional practice—one which can be diminished. For growth purposes, I recommend that timid instructors give themselves permission to experiment with new methods. Otherwise, they will have difficulty increasing their expertise over time.[4]

Develop Evaluation

When I was an assistant pastor, I taught a young-adult class in a fairly large downtown church. At the end of the first quarter I gave a written test over what we had studied. The reactions ranged from stunned disbelief to mild anger. The test was voluntary, and, in a class of about thirty, maybe three people handed back the paper, while the rest politely slid it into their Bibles until they could get home and throw it in the trash. Next quarter I did the same thing and the number of papers returned doubled or tripled. When I left that church, they selected another teacher—and asked him to provide them with tests at the end of each unit of study!

People *can* change. People can adapt to educational methods that will help us achieve our objectives. People can provide feedback to help us in the evaluation process.

Always remember that evaluation exists for the purpose of improvement—improving the teaching process, the class context, the overall educational program for adults. As long as people see evaluation as corrective and judgmental, they resist it. If we can convince them we are serious about improving our adult-ministries program, participation will increase.

FACILITATING ADULT LEARNING

I draw this book to an end by referring to two outstanding professional educators. First is Stephen Brookfield, whose book *Understanding and Facilitating Adult Learning* has become a classic since its publication in 1986. In describing adult learning, Brookfield chooses a series of words to help us understand how the process must look.[5]

Principles for the Process

The operative word here is *facilitating*, which describes how an adult ministries committee and teachers assist adults in achieving learning goals. To do that, Brookfield says, adult learning must be *compliant*, by which he means that participation in learning is voluntary. Adult learning is self-directed—no coercion allowed, no intimidation permitted. Also, Brookfield says, it should be *confirming*, a context that builds mutual respect among the participants with a strong focus on self-worth and constant affirmation. Adult learning is also to be *collaborative.* The facilitator and the learners have joined a cooperative venture aimed at a team approach to truth and its application in life.

Adult education should also be *conative*, since practice or application stands at the heart of effective facilitation. The cognitive and affective domains may precede the conative, but *learners should take away from any class or group a clear understanding of how what they have learned can be implemented.* Adult learning must also be contextual, fostering a spirit of reflection and introspection. Christian adults need to understand who they are and where God has placed them in the cultural climate of the twenty-first century. Then they are prepared to move on to the issue of what God expects them to do and how He wants them to live.

Adult education is also *continuous.* Adults should be concerned for lifelong learning. Facilitated education is proactive rather than reactive;

we don't give people a drink, we show them how to dig a well. We show learners how to study the Bible for themselves.

Procedures for the Program

A second educator is Michael Lawson, who researched twenty-three churches in preparation for his chapter in *The Christian Educator's Handbook on Adult Education*. After tabulating and interpreting his results, Lawson counsels, "Churches wishing to move toward a more thorough approach to adult education may wish to consider the following procedure." What follows offers readers Lawson's analysis of the research, tempered by his own nearly thirty years of experience in adult education. [6]

1. List each category of ministry available to the adults of your church, along with each specific offering.

2. Identify the single or dual focus of each ministry, for example, instruction/fellowship for Sunday school.

3. Decide exactly how each piece should fit into the whole adult education puzzle.

4. Lay out a dual agenda: one from leadership's perspective and one from the adult student's perspective. Decisions about content, fellowship, emotional support, spiritual ministry, and personal enrichment, among others, should be made here.

5. Acquire a resource inventory of adult curricular materials from various publishing houses to make available at all times. Purchasing these over time spreads out the cost.

6. Look at the actual teaching time for each year along with general attendance patterns for each program.

7. Lay out an evaluation device that will help adults keep track of everything they read, study, attend, or listen to.

8. Leave open windows in adult programs so the curriculum remains flexible as needs and interests change.

9. Consult adults often in the process to be sure the overall plan maintains a correct focus.

10. Educate the church about the cost of quality training for adults.

Current thinking tells us change in a church doesn't happen without every leader being "on the same page" philosophically. Maybe so. But I dare say healthy adult ministries will never arise merely from change or philosophical unity. The biblical commitments of each congregant, each leader, and each denominational official must first target God's priorities and then allow Him to produce in our churches what He wants—*from the inside out.*

Far from detracting from the fulfilling of the Great Commission, this approach, because it is biblical, enhances our individual collective mission: to know Jesus Christ, to understand God's Word, and to win others to Christ and build them up spiritually. Yes, God wants us to serve, teach, and train adults in His church by His power. Let's make sure the methods, movements, and manipulations of traditional education or modern cultural Christianity don't get in the way.

Endnotes

❧

CHAPTER 2—FROM PRESCHOOL TO GRAD SCHOOL

1. Malcolm S. Knowles, "Contributions of Malcolm Knowles," in *The Christian Educator's Handbook on Adult Education,* ed. Kenneth O. Gangel and James C. Wilhoit (Wheaton, Ill.: Victor, 1993; reprint, Grand Rapids: Baker, 1996), 96–98.
2. Ibid., 97.

CHAPTER 3—IS IT BIBLICAL?

1. This chapter is adapted from the author's earlier work, "Biblical Foundations for Adult Education," in *The Christian Educator's Handbook on Adult Education.*
2. Roy B. Zuck, *Teaching as Jesus Taught* (Grand Rapids: Baker, 1996), and *Teaching as Paul Taught* (Grand Rapids: Baker, 1998).
3. D. Edmond Hiebert, "Titus," in *The Expositor's Bible Commentary* (Grand Rapids: Zondervan, 1978), 11:437.
4. Ibid., 11:438.
5. Daniel J. Levinson, *The Seasons of a Man's Life* (New York: Ballantine, 1978), 40–68.
6. Lawrence O. Richards, "Developing a Family-Centered Educational Program," in *Adult Education in the Church,* ed. Roy B. Zuck and Gene A. Getz (Chicago: Moody, 1970), 372.

CHAPTER 4—HOW DO THEY LEARN?

1. Kenneth O. Gangel, *Leadership for Church Education* (Chicago: Moody, 1970), 45.

CHAPTER 5—WHO NEEDS WHAT—AND WHY?

1. Malcolm S. Knowles, *The Adult Learner: A Neglected Species* (Houston: Gulf, 1978), 288.
2. James C. Wilhoit, "Christian Adults and Spiritual Formation," in *The Christian Educator's Handbook on Adult Education*, 58.

CHAPTER 7—TEACHING WITH STYLE

1. David A. Kolb, *Experiential Learning* (Englewood Cliffs, N.J.: Prentice-Hall, 1984);Bernice McCarthy, *The 4 Mat System* (Barrington, Ill.: Excel, 1980); and Harvey F. Silver and Jocelyn Chu, *Teaching Styles and Strategies* (Moorestown, N. J.: Hanson Silver and Associates, 1986).
2. Roberta Hestenes, "Teaching So Adults Listen," *Leadership* (spring 1996): 102.

CHAPTER 8—THE MILLENNIALS ARE COMING!

1. Wendy Murray Zorba, "The Class of '00," *Christianity Today*, 3 February 1997, 20.
2. Dennis W. Hiebert, "Toward Adult Cross-Sex Friendship," *Journal of Psychology and Theology* 24 (1996): 281.

CHAPTER 9—BOOSTING THE BUSTERS

1. Laura Zinn et al., "Move Over, Boomers," *Business Week*, 14 December 1992, 77.
2. Kenneth L. Woodward, "A Grandparent's Role," *Newsweek*, spring/summer, 1997, 82.
3. Ibid.

CHAPTER 10—CAUGHT IN THE MIDDLE

1. Melinda Beck, "The New Middle Age," *Newsweek*, 7 December 1992, 52.

2. Jordan Bonfante et al., "The Generation That Forgot God," *Time*, 5 April 1993, 46.

3. Jim Conway, *Men in Midlife Crisis* (Colorado Springs: ChariotVictor, 1997), 158 (italics his).

4. Robert J. Samuelson, "Middle-Aged America," *Newsweek*, 27 July 1987, 45.

CHAPTER 11—THE BEST OF TIMES, THE WORST OF TIMES

1. Tom Morganthau, "The Face of the Future," *Newsweek*, 27 January 1997, 60.

2. Conway, *Men in Midlife Crisis*, 176.

3. Jim Conway and Sally Conway, *Women in Midlife Crisis* (Wheaton, Ill.: Tyndale, 1983), 178 (italics theirs).

4. Ibid., 182.

5. Melinda Deck, "The New Middle Age," *Newsweek*, 7 December 1992, 53.

6. Reuel Howe, *The Creative Years* (New York: Seabury, 1959), 198–208.

7. Wesley R. Willis, "Teaching Middle Adults," in *The Christian Educator's Handbook on Adult Education*, 218.

8. Conway, *Men in Midlife Crisis*, 248.

9. Catherine M. Stonehouse, "Learning from Gender Differences," in *The Christian Educator's Handbook on Adult Education*, 111.

10. Conway, *Men in Midlife Crisis*, 80–81.

11. Ibid., 81.

12. Stonehouse, "Learning from Gender Differences," 118.

CHAPTER 12—WISDOM AVAILABLE: 1-800-S-E-N-I-O-R-S

1. Melinda Beck, "Attention, Willard Scott," *Newsweek*, 4 May 1992, 75.

2. John Nesbitt, *Megatrends* (New York: Warner, 1982).

3. Bureau of the Census, *Sixty-Five Plus in America* (Washington, D.C.: U. S. Government Printing Office, 1992).
4. Morgenthau, "The Face of the Future," 58.
5. Martin Marty, "Cultural Antecedents to Aging" (source unknown).
6. J. B. Priestley, quoted in Tim Stafford, "How Does It Feel to Grow Old?" *Evangelical Beacon* (February 1991): 4.

CHAPTER 13—THE LAST FOR WHICH THE FIRST WAS MADE

1. David R. Enlow, *How to Grow Older without Getting Old* (Toccoa Falls, Ga.: TFC, 1994), 6.
2. Ibid., 6–7.
3. Kenneth O. Gangel, "Nurturing Grandparents in the Church," in *The Christian Educator's Handbook on Family Life Education,* ed. Kenneth A. Gangel and James C. Wilhoit (Grand Rapids: Baker, 1996), 225.

CHAPTER 14—SWINGING WITH THE SINGLES

1. Charles J. Hanley, "Have We Reached the Limit?" *Anderson (S.C.) Independent Mail,* 28 December 1997, 14A.
2. Hazel Ruth Bell, "Trends among American Singles," *Search Magazine* (summer 1992): 15.
3. Patricia A. Chapman, "Single Adults and Single Parents," in *The Christian Educator's Handbook on Adult Education,* 235.
4. Ibid.
5. Carol King, "Viewpoint," *Baptist Bulletin* (February 1994): 15.
6. Bell, "Trends among American Singles," 12.
7. Ibid., 12–15.

CHAPTER 15—FLYING SOLO IN THE FAMILY

1. "Assets of Youth Who Thrive in Single-Parent Families," *Source* (June 1993): 3.

2. Ann Li Puma, "Why Are We Afraid to Be Single?" *McCalls* (November 1984): 208.

CHAPTER 16—PARTNERING WITH PARENTS

1. Laura Shapiro, "Taking Care of Family Business," *Newsweek,* 12 May 1997, 62.
2. Charles M. Sell, "Family Ministry Is Church Ministry," *Family Matters,* 2d ed. (Grand Rapids: Zondervan, 1995), 1.
3. Ibid., 7.
4. Nancy Leffert, Peter Benson, and Jolene Rochlkcpartain, "Starting Out Right," *Source* 13 (February 1997): 6.
5. John H. Westerhoff, "The Church and the Family," *Religious Education* 78 (spring 1983): 260.
6. Ibid., 263.
7. Ibid., 264.
8. Sell, *Family Matters,* 7.

CHAPTER 17—DEVELOPING BIBLICAL HOMES

1. Thornton Wilder, *The Skin of Our Teeth,* in *Best Plays of 1942–46,* comp. Mantle Burns (New York: Dodd, Meade, 1943), 129.

CHAPTER 20—TEACHING CHILDREN RESPONSIBILITY

1. Jerry W. McCant, "The Best Interests of the Child," *Christian Education Journal* 6 (1985): 45.

CHAPTER 22—LEARNING FROM EACH OTHER

1. Harold J. Westing, "Adult Sunday School," in *The Christian Educator's Handbook on Adult Education,* 293.
2. Kenneth O. Gangel, *Team Leadership in Christian Ministry* (Chicago: Moody, 1997).

3. Jane S. Mouton and Robert R. Blake, *Synergogy* (San Francisco: Jossey-Bass, 1984), 33–35.

CHAPTER 23—SETTING THE TABLE

1. J. M. Keller and T. Kopp, "Applications of the ARCS Model in Courseware Design," *in Instructional Designs for Computer Courseware*, ed. D. H. Jonassen (New York: Lawrence Erlbaum, 1988).
2. Karen S. Viechnicki, Roy M. Bohlin, and William D. Milheim, "Instructional Motivation of Adult Learners," *Journal of Adult Training* 4 (1991): 7–8.
3. Westing, "Adult Sunday School," 298.
4. Stanley S. Olsen, "Programming Adult Education in the Local Church," in *The Christian Educator's Handbook on Adult Education,* 307–8.
5. Laurent A. Parks Daloz, "Slouching toward Bethlehem," *Journal of Adult Training* 3 (1991): 25.
6. Brad E. Stych, "The Finer Points of Choosing Instructional Methods," *Journal of Adult Training* (spring 1996): 19–20.

CHAPTER 24—MAKING THE SHOE FIT

1. James C. Galvin and David R. Veerman, "Curriculum for Adult Education," in *The Christian Educator's Handbook on Adult Education,* 178–79.
2. Maryellen Weimer, "Teaching Tensions—Confronting Opposing Forces in Today's Classrooms," *Journal of Adult Training* 3 (1990): 22.
3. Warren S. Benson, "Setting and Achieving Objectives for Adult Learning," in *The Christian Educator's Handbook on Adult Education,* 173.
4. Galvin and Veerman, "Curriculum for Adult Education," 185–86.
5. Margaret M. Swain, *Family Enrichment with Family Clusters* (Valley Forge, Pa.: Judson, 1979).
6. Daniel B. Clendenon, "The Only Way," *Christianity Today,* 12 January 1998, 34–40.

CHAPTER 25—JUST DO IT!

1. Ray Ortlund, "Priorities for the Local Church," *in Vital Ministry Issues,* ed. Roy B. Zuck (Grand Rapids: Baker, 1994), 91.

2. Edward L. Hayes, "Theological Foundations for Adult Education," in *The Christian Educator's Handbook on Adult Education,* 36–37.

3. Zuck, *Teaching as Paul Taught* , 65–66.

4. Stych, "The Finer Points of Choosing Instructional Methods," 22.

5. Brookfield, *Understanding and Facilitating Adult Learning,* 36–37.

6. Michael S. Lawson, "Illustrations of Effective Education with Adults," in *The Christian Educator's Handbook on Adult Education,* 352.

Bibliography

Atkinson, Harley, ed. *Handbook of Young Adult Religious Education.* Birmingham, Ala.: Religious Education Press, 1995.

Brookfield, Stephen D. *The Skillful Teacher.* San Francisco: Jossey-Bass Publishers, 1990.

Cherlin, Andrew J., and Frank F. Furtstenberg, Jr. *The New American Grandparent.* Cambridge, Mass: Harvard University Press, 1992.

Cross, K. Patricia. *Adults as Learners.* San Francisco: Jossey-Bass Publishers, 1981.

Edge, Findley B. *Teaching for Results.* Rev. ed. Nashville: Broadman and Holman Publishers, 1995.

Fagerstrom, Douglas L., ed. *Baker Handbook of Single Adult Ministry.* Grand Rapids: Baker Book House, 1997.

Foltz, Nancy T. *Handbook of Adult Religious Education.* Birmingham, Ala.: Religious Education Press, 1986.

————. *Religious Education in the Small Membership Church.* Birmingham, Ala.: Religious Education Press, 1990.

Fowler, J. W. *Becoming Adult, Becoming Christian: Adult Development and Christian Faith.* San Francisco: Harper & Row, 1984.

Gangel, Kenneth O., and Betty Gangel. *Your Family.* Gresham, Oreg.: Vision House, 1995.

Gangel, Kenneth O., and James C. Wilhoit., eds. *The Christian Educator's Handbook on Adult Education.* Wheaton, Ill.: Victor Books, 1993; reprint, Grand Rapids: Baker Books, 1993.

————. eds. *The Christian Educator's Handbook on Family Life Education.* Grand Rapids: Baker Books, 1996.

Gorman, Julie A. *Community That Is Christian: A Handbook on Small Groups.* Wheaton, Ill.: Victor Books, 1993.

Hull, John M. *What Prevents Christian Adults from Learning?* Philadelphia: Trinity Press International, 1991.

Kesler, Jay. *Grandparenting.* Ann Arbor, Mich.: Servant Publications, 1993.

Knowles, Malcolm. *The Adult Learner: A Neglected Species.* Houston: Gulf Publishing Co., 1973.

Lawson, Michael S., and Robert J. Choun, Jr. *Directing Christian Education.* Chicago: Moody Press, 1992.

LeBar, Lois E. *Education That Is Christian.* Rev. ed. Wheaton, Ill.: Victor Books, 1995.

McBride, Neal F. *How to Build a Small Groups Ministry.* Colorado Springs: NavPress, 1995.

Mouton, Jane Srygley, and Robert R. Blake. *Synergogy.* San Francisco: Jossey-Bass Publishers, 1984.

Parks, Sharon. *The Critical Years.* San Francisco: Harper & Row, 1986.

Peters, John M., et. al. *Adult Education.* San Francisco: Jossey-Bass Publishers, 1991.

Reed, Bobbie, ed. *Baker's Handbook of Single Parent Ministry.* Grand Rapids: Baker Books, 1998.

Sell, Charles M. *Family Matters*. 2d ed. Grand Rapids: Zondervan Publishing House, 1995.

———. *Transitions through Adult Life*. Grand Rapids: Zondervan Publishing House, 1991.

Stubblefield, Jerry, ed. *A Church Ministering to Adults*. Nashville: Broadman Press, 1986.

White, James W. *Intergenerational Religious Education*. Birmingham, Ala.: Religious Education Press, 1988.

Wickett, R. E. Y. *Models of Adult Religious Education Practice*. Birmingham, Ala.: Religious Education Press, 1991.

Wilbert, Warren N. *Strategies for Teaching Christian Adults*. Grand Rapids: Baker Book House, 1984.

Williams, Dennis, and Kenneth O. Gangel. *Volunteers for Today's Church*. Grand Rapids: Baker Book House, 1993.

Wlodkowski, Raymond J. *Enhancing Adult Motivation to Learn*. San Francisco: Jossey-Bass Publishers, 1985.

Zuck, Roy B. *Precious in His Sight: Childhood and Children in the Bible*. Grand Rapids: Baker Book House, 1996.

———. *Spirit-Filled Teaching: The Power of the Holy Spirit in Your Ministry*. Swindoll Leadership Library. Nashville: Word Publishing, 1998.

———. *Teaching as Jesus Taught*. Grand Rapids: Baker Book House, 1995.

———. *Teaching as Paul Taught*. Grand Rapids: Baker Book House, 1998.

Scripture Index

Subject Index

⚜